Praise for

Grocery Story

A great read! Full of energy and eyes-wide-open hope.
In an era of extreme economic concentration, Jon Steinman
awakens us to elements of an arising democratic economy, hidden
in plain sight. *Grocery Story* is, above all, an empowering
tale we need now more than ever.
— Frances Moore Lappé, author,
Diet for a Small Planet and *Daring Democracy*

Wake up folks! Co-ops are cool. They bring power
back to conscious citizenship. Co-ops are democracy at
work in an age calling out for common sense.
— Joel Solomon, co-author, *The Clean Money Revolution*

Steinman skillfully blends the history of food retailing
with contemporary examples to explain how cooperative food
stores consistently have served as a principled alternative and
moderating influence on corporate consolidation of
food retailing in North America.
— John Ikerd, Professor Emeritus of Agricultural Economics,
University of Missouri-Columbia

An important consideration of the impact that can happen when
going to the grocery store becomes an activity and not a chore, and
when a grocery cart can ultimately become a vehicle for social change.
— Melissa Cohen, General Manager, Isla Vista Food Co-op

On par with many of the other food books that have
inspired me — *Diet for a Dead Planet, Food Politics, Slow Money, Stolen
Harvest, Fast Food Nation, Omnivore's Dilemma, In Defense of Food.*
— Ari Derfel, General Manager, Kootenay Co-op, past Executive Director,
Slow Money, and cofounder, Gather Restaurant

Explores how capitalism distorts the food system from farm to plate. A pleasure to read and is crammed with valuable information, stories, and analysis. If you eat, you should give this book a read.

— Tom Webb, author, *From Corporate Globalization to Global Co-operation* and president, Global Co-operation

An impressive synthesis of critical analysis of systemic societal ills and a very practical "how-to" manual on how to address them. This is literally the best thing I've read about cooperatives, monopolization / oligopolization, and the industrial food system in ages.

— Christopher DeAngelis, Food Co-op Manager (formerly Apple Street Market Cooperative, Mariposa Food Co-op)

Presents a clear and engaging historical perspective on the evolution of our food co-ops and illustrates the many benefits that they offer their owners and customers by sharing the stories of co-ops today. *Grocery Story* should be required reading for anyone helping to organize a new food co-op and everyone who cares at all about their food.

— Stuart Reid, Executive Director, Food Co-op Initiative / Past General Manager, Just Food Co-op and Seward Co-op

Steinman shows us we can confront the power of food retailers and create an inclusive, health promoting, and sustainable food system.

— Rod MacRae, Associate Professor, York University

It's worth studying the history of how and why food co-ops formed as a model to ensure continuing access and authenticity in an alternative local and organic food supply.

— Mark Kastel, Cornucopia Institute

Not just a "must-read" for advocates and participants of the local food movement, it is a "must-implement" to pave the way toward a sustainable and just food system for us all.

— Rob Greenfield, author, *Dude Making a Difference*

GROCERY STORY

THE PROMISE OF FOOD CO-OPS
IN THE AGE OF GROCERY GIANTS

JON STEINMAN

DISCARD

new society
PUBLISHERS

For the next seven generations

Cover design: Jon Steinman/Diane McIntosh.

Cover photo: ©Shutterstock 183247076

All interior photographs © Jon Steinman 2019, unless otherwise noted.

Interior background image © MJ Jessen

Printed in Canada. First printing May, 2019.

This book is intended to be educational and informative. It is not intended to serve as a guide. The author and publisher disclaim all responsibility for any liability, loss or risk that may be associated with the application of any of the contents of this book.

Inquiries regarding requests to reprint all or part of *Grocery Story* should be addressed to New Society Publishers at the address below. To order directly from the publishers, please call toll-free (North America) 1-800-567-6772, or order online at www.newsociety.com

Any other inquiries can be directed by mail to:

New Society Publishers

P.O. Box 189, Gabriola Island, BC V0R 1X0, Canada

(250) 247-9737

LIBRARY AND ARCHIVES CANADA CATALOGUING IN PUBLICATION

Title: Grocery story : the promise of food co-ops in the age of grocery giants / Jon Steinman.

Names: Steinman, Jon, 1980- author.

Description: Includes bibliographical references and index.

Identifiers: Canadiana (print) 2019006871X | Canadiana (ebook) 20190068736 | ISBN 9780865719071

(softcover) | ISBN 9781550927009 (PDF) | ISBN 9781771422963 (EPUB)

Subjects: LCSH: Food cooperatives—Canada. | LCSH: Food supply— Canada. | LCSH: Grocery trade—Canada.

| LCSH: Food industry and trade—Canada. | LCSH: Food—Social aspects—Canada.

Classification: LCC HD3448 .S74 2019 | DDC 334.0971—dc23

Funded by the Government of Canada | Financé par le gouvernement du Canada

Canada

New Society Publishers' mission is to publish books that contribute in fundamental ways to building an ecologically sustainable and just society, and to do so with the least possible impact on the environment, in a manner that models this vision.

MIX
Paper from responsible sources
FSC
www.fsc.org   FSC® C016245

Certified
B Corporation

new society
PUBLISHERS

Contents

"Food System" Defined

FOOD SYSTEM: *The processes and infrastructure involved in feeding a population: growing, harvesting, processing, packaging, transporting, marketing, consumption and disposal of food. It also includes the inputs needed and outputs generated at each of these steps. A food system operates within and is influenced by social, political, economic and environmental contexts. It also requires human resources that provide labor, research and education.*

Preface

THE RISE TO PROMINENCE over the past century of the modern supermarket has bestowed humanity with almost miraculous riches. Food is transported to and from every continent — some of it crossing oceans in airplanes. Food production technologies have driven down the cost to produce food to levels previously unimaginable — enabling the middle class of today to eat like royalty of centuries past. The shelf life of fresh produce, breads, and packaged foods defies basic concepts of food degradation.

By these standards, we live in a golden age of food.

We truly do.

Without question, I could have written a book about the marvels and wonders of the modern grocery store and the food system it has spawned. Readers would be gifted with page upon page of awe and imagination — like a journey through Willy Wonka's chocolate factory. It would be a fascinating book — a testament to human potential.

This is NOT that book.

This is a book about what we've lost along the way — the casualties. It's a book about the people and politics that fought ferociously to defend from the chain grocers a way of life, to protect culture, principles and values, and to preserve the conviviality of human relations on Main Street. It's also about the successes of a wonderful alternative — of the people, communities, and their cooperatively owned grocery stores who are today reminding us of what makes us human — about the kindness, empathy and celebration that can be found in the seemingly insignificant supermarket. This is a book about hope.

As I began my research for this book in 2017, I plotted out the stages of the "great revealing" — the slow, suspenseful pulling away of the grocery store wool from over the eyes of eaters. There were so many secrets to tell — moments where I could visualize readers shouting

"WHAT!," or "THAT CAN'T BE." Then... the news broke. December 19, 2017... Canada's largest grocer, Loblaw Companies Ltd, announces publicly that they've been cheating their customers for the past fourteen years ... and ... they didn't act alone. Four other retailers are said to have colluded on the nationwide price-fixing of bread.

All of my strategizing came to an abrupt halt. "Is this it?" I asked myself. "Does this mean I can nix most of the book's early chapters — the 'great revealing' — and go straight into the good stuff — the good-food revolution? Has the supermarket swindle finally come to an end? Is this the overhaul of the grocery giants?" No more would eaters be comfortable patronizing criminal grocers, I thought. No way. For a moment after the news broke, I couldn't quite contain myself. I was giddy. Then I caught the *other* headline news of the day: "Trump unveils America First security strategy." Reality came rushing back with the force of a brick wall and a firm slap upside the head. "Right... if the most egregious acts of human behavior could not only be carried out by a sitting U.S. President, but could also be normalized by a considerable percentage of the population, then bread collusion among a handful of Canadian grocery giants couldn't possibly change the retail food landscape. Sure enough, it hasn't ... at least not yet ... and it probably never will. The investigation could take years. Meanwhile, it's business as usual in the aisles of our supermarkets. The grocery giants have grown into unshakeable institutions ... temples of consumerism ... marching on no matter the heinous abuses.

One analyst calculated that as a result of the price-fixing scheme, a family purchasing two loaves of bread per week was shelling out an extra $104 per year above the normal price of bread. Loblaw apologized by offering its customers $25 gift cards. It was a great PR move — the company most certainly profited off of the droves of people who would have never entered a Loblaw store had it not been for the gift card. In the twelve weeks ending June 16, 2018, Loblaw posted over half a billion dollars in operating income from its retail operations. The company is doing just fine.

The book would proceed on its originally imagined course.

As you've certainly gathered by now, *Grocery Story* is about an already-implemented alternative to the grocery giants — the consumer-owned food cooperative. Unexpectedly, as my research commenced, I became aware that the need for food co-ops had begun to expand. No longer were they solely the venue for those with an inclination toward natural and organic foods. A new category of consumer was taking a long and hard look at the food co-op model — people without easy access to any grocery store whatsoever. If you've opened this book with the belief that food co-ops are only for hippies or the food "elite," you're wrong. Flat out. The food co-op model is proving to be an appropriate response for every person of every color, race, income, and creed.

If you're also opening this book with any level of assurance that the smaller independent grocer in your neighborhood is your saving grace — your grocery giant alternative — don't get too comfy. The future of that grocer hangs on the decisions of a single individual, group, or family. They may very well be community-oriented folk, but what about the people they may one day sell their business to — what about the next generation who may inherit the business … if any? Of 280 independent Minnesota grocery stores surveyed in 2016, 63 percent were not planning on owning their store in ten year's time and few had developed succession plans.[1] In late 2017, Choices Markets — a small independent chain in British Columbia with eleven locations and a website slogan "Local Organic Grocery Store" — was sold to one of Western Canada's largest chains, owned by one of Canada's wealthiest individuals. The acquisition echoed that of many other smaller regional chains in the United States and Canada that have disappeared into the bellies of giants.

Rather than look outside of ourselves for the leader, the most solid security to be found in the future of our grocery stores is entirely in our hands.

Note from the Author:
Big Food

B EFORE WE SET OUT ON THIS GROCERY STORY, it feels important to offer an invitation to you, the reader.

Throughout this book, particularly the first few chapters, you will read about the actions and tactics of "big food." You will read about trade associations, multinational corporations, and some of the people behind them. You will learn of decisions that were made with what appears to be complete disregard for human rights, local economic well-being, and human health. You might find that upon learning of the actions of these companies, groups, and people, your inner rage will become highly activated. You might hear an inner voice shouting "those bastards" or "how could they!" You might find yourself drifting into the injustice itself, imagining or even devising ways to correct the matter or punish those responsible. This is OK. You're not alone. I know this voice, those reactions. It's the voice that originally compelled me to investigate food. Today, however, I don't hear it nearly as much. I have instead tempered that voice and have adjusted the way I receive the steady stream of surprise and shock that materializes during the journey deep into the rabbit hole of "big food." For the duration of this book, I'd like to invite you to do that too — to temper the anger and receive this information from a different place, a more measured, compassionate, and empathetic place. As one friend tells his students, "Hope comes from having the courage to look calmly at problems and imagine a better world."

Over the course of my food investigations, I've come to learn that identifying big food as the "perpetrators" and small food and eaters as "victims" does less to stimulate change than I had initially thought. The perpetrator–victim story only serves to preserve a deeply separated food system. It establishes an "us" and a "them," and from there arises the exhausting and often ineffectual work of assessing right from wrong, worthy from worthless.

As I have worked to temper the reactive voice, I have also watched this perpetrator-victim story lose its relevance and begin to fall away. As it has, an opening has appeared. From this more measured, compassionate, and empathetic place, I have found a deeper well of capacity to take the time to *understand* the so-called perpetrators and how they have woven themselves into existence.

At a certain point, you might find, as I did, that the "perpetrator" is no longer a perpetrator, but merely the product of all that came before it. In economic and social sciences, this is called path dependence — how the set of decisions for any given circumstance is limited by the decisions made in the past, even though past circumstances may no longer be relevant.

How does this apply to the big food corporation? To the food system? How much of our food system, for example, is dependent or built upon past circumstances that are no longer relevant? What were those decisions, those circumstances?

Grocery Story will ask those questions and follow those paths.

As the paths and decisions that have been made over time are laid out, new perspectives can unfold. From this vantage, the people and the corporations they work for are no longer perpetrators, but merely the by-product of an unexamined system — unexamined paths. Rather than be seen as perpetrators, they can be seen as perpetuators.

From this vantage, it might also become possible to find the perpetrator/perpetuator in each of us. In what ways are we a participant? Then, the separation falls away. No more is there a need for a perpetrator nor victim. We become both and neither at the same time.

I for one am no longer convinced that the human beings who are behind big food are the heartless, money-hungry monsters they are often made out to be. That only preserves separation. Behind big food are people who also care about their health, their families, their communities, and the planet. This book is for them too.

The big food corporation is not a person — it is an amalgamation of ideas, an inherited language that, when left unexamined and unchecked, becomes dizzyingly complex to comprehend.

For me, reimagining our food system means becoming aware of when and how we react to the challenges — to the actions of big food.

It's about first retracing our path *prior* to charting a course of action. It's about asking whether or not we've given ourselves sufficient time to consider that the health of a tree or plant is almost entirely in the care and attention we bring to its roots.

With this in mind, I invite you to read about big food and the grocery giants, and in each moment, instead of reacting, to simply file away each layer that has been peeled away.

The goal of "deconstructing" big food and the grocery giants is not to lay blame or point fingers but to see the emperor without his clothes and, in his nakedness, to see that the emperor is us.

Introduction

I'M HERE IN MY HOMETOWN of Nelson, British Columbia, 7:30 am, December 7, 2016, outdoors, 14°F (−10°C), cold! A group of about forty of us are gathered, all anticipating the arrival of Nelson's mayor, invited to cut the red ribbon extended across the entrance to Nelson's newest grocery store. The ribbon is cut, the crowd scurries indoors, shopping carts in tow, and for the hours that follow, I witness people in my community weeping for joy.

Weeping!

Yes!

Over a grocery store?

Yes.

How is that?

Why is that?

Weeping?

Those emotions expressed on that December morning are the same ones that, for me, inspired this book. They're the same sentiments I had experienced only days earlier when I walked through the automatic sliding doors of said grocery store's *previous* location for the very *last* time. As I approached those doors on that December evening — the same ones people had passed through for more than twenty-five years — I reminded myself that "this was it" — this was the final time I would walk into this building to shop for food. Even as I write this, those very waves of emotion that enveloped me in that moment are resurfacing — feelings not so different from those that might arise upon saying a final goodbye to a dear friend — feelings of deep, never-be-fore-examined gratitude, an appreciation never fully acknowledged nor embraced.

All this for just a grocery store?

Indeed.

1

As this flood of emotion swelled in my community over the course of that week as the store's former location closed and its new one opened, the imperative to write this book sunk deeper.

What is it that a grocery store represents to elicit the heartfelt reactions I witnessed that frigid December morning?

It's high time that this question be asked and this story be told. For the sake of all of us eaters, *someone* has to write a book about the importance of grocery stores!

Book after book, story after story are being written, published, read, and digested on all things "local food." If any one of us is in want of getting hyped, tooled, or infoed up on anything "local food," there is a perpetual harvest of food media flowing in all directions. Home butchering, cheese-making, aquaponics, urban farming — all the inspiration is there for a transition to more informed and engaged eating. This is good. This is more than good. This is great! I too have participated in this spreading of nutrients into the foodosphere through my radio and television series, but there is one gaping hole in the sum of analytical and inspirational tales of "good food." THE GROCERY STORE, the supermarket, the epicenter of our food-gathering ritual.

Every facet of our food supply is driven by the influence of grocery stores. From the pricing of items at a farmers' market to the proximity and accessibility of slaughterhouses to livestock producers or the curriculum of grade 7 cooking classes, very little escapes the influence of big grocery — the "grocery giants." The systems, the culture, the perspectives forming the whole of our food experience — all can be traced to historic and modern-day grocery retailing.

With so much emphasis of late being placed on "fixing" the food system of its ills (specifically its adverse effects on health, wellness, food access, waste, environment, culture, and economies), how has the grocery sector evaded attention? It's as if, in our efforts to re-imagine our food system(s), we have been treating the *symptoms* of the illness without a proper diagnosis. In turn, we have directed our attention and resources to treating the symptoms and have missed attending to the condition itself.

What is the condition? I call it "food system dysfunction," and at the heart of this dysfunction is the grocery retail sector. By directing the treatment of the illness towards the grocery stores operating within our communities, I'm confident we will overcome the affliction. The good news is that a remedy is not only within reach but is already being successfully administered with convincing results.

Perhaps I should describe my experiences to date that inspire such strong convictions.

My "Experiences" To Date

The experiences I've had of engaging physically, mentally, emotionally, and spiritually in the act of eating since I began my studies in food in 1998 at the University of Guelph in Ontario have been unique. From that point forward, I marinated in all things "local food" — my mind, my actions, my belly. I hosted a weekly radio show in my hometown of Nelson, British Columbia, that investigated the food supply. The show had quite a large base of listeners, and in short order, I became known in the small community of Nelson for this focus, this commitment. I became "the guy" who, if spotted near the supermarket checkout, would stir up your inner conscience about the food you were about to purchase. Quietly, strategically, the unloading of the shopping cart onto the conveyor would become an exercise in making absolutely certain that any of the products that you might *not* be so proud of purchasing were well hidden, underneath the most prideful of foods. "Oh God, I hope Jon doesn't see what I'm buying!"

Truth is, I never judged — but the perception was certainly there. I could feel it. Jon Steinman — the "Responsible-Food Police"! I can think of worse things to be perceived as.

The recipe for my marinade was extensive. Fifty to sixty hours a week on all things genetically engineered food, corporate concentration/consolidation/centralization of the food supply, urban agriculture, animal welfare, food marketing, farm workers' rights, farmed salmon, biofuels, farm income, fossil fuels, factory farming, climate change, permaculture, organics, food policy, food security, seed-saving, soil.

Ten years.

Marinating.

Now what?

Breathe.

Reflect.

What's next?

What does a fully marinated food systems radical do with all this information, all these experiences?

What were the common threads? The gaps? The missed opportunities? The untold stories of success?

Where did it all lead?

What was it all pointing to?

For me? It was here.

Grocery Stores.

Grocery Story.

Why?

Let me explain.

Deconstructing Dinner

In 2006, I began producing and hosting a weekly one-hour radio show and podcast called *Deconstructing Dinner*. Like this book, the idea for *Deconstructing Dinner* emerged out of an unmistakable lack of media dedicated to examining food systems through the perspectives of food-makers and eaters seeking good food — each of whom viewed the "system" through a unique lens. These were people whose perspectives and voices were being more and more marginalized — in tandem with the growing separation between land and mouth, producer and consumer.

At the time, there was a palpable groundswell of activity in communities across North America, some more than others, urging local governments, businesses, and organizations to look more closely at the challenges and opportunities of "local food." There was *not*, however, any one media source that made this their modus operandi. *Deconstructing Dinner* did.

Five years and 193 episodes later, and with fifty U.S. and Canadian radio stations rebroadcasting the weekly show, I gained a perspective on the food system that few journalists would have had at the time.

By 2012, *Deconstructing Dinner* had evolved into a television and web series. We filmed across the United States and Canada and produced six hours of content that would later be broadcast on Canadian television, American streaming-video-on-demand, and via the series' website. We visited the largest garlic producer in the U.S., the largest tomato processing facility in the world, and one of North America's largest growers/distributors of field tomatoes. We would meet a pollen detective — hired to investigate illegally imported or mislabeled honey.

Throughout these years, I was invited by nonprofits, governments, colleges, and universities to share my reflections, perspectives, and experiences with fellow (or soon-to-be) food systems reclamationists.

This was an important time to be immersed in the role of "witness," "observer," and "recorder." It was an important time because it was the beginning, the formative years, of what many would now consider the modern "local" or "good food" movement — a movement that would become tremendously successful in birthing fundamental and lasting change in all sectors of social and economic life. Its influence today has, in my view, touched all sectors of "big food" and passed through the consciousness of most eaters in one form or another. In our lifetime, good food has never been so in demand as it is today — the hunger for reunion between land and mouth so audible.

Perhaps it was inevitable that, by delving deep into the subject, I would not just assume the role of observer, reporter, muckraker, editorialist, but would further find myself drawn towards *actively* participating in food system reclamation with my own hands, within my own kitchen, my own backyard, and throughout my regional food community.

First up, in what would later become a seemingly inescapable volunteer commitment to all things "community development," I stepped forward in 2006 to be elected to the board of directors of my local cooperative grocery store. By 2008, I joined the steering committee of the first community supported agriculture (CSA) project in Canada for grains. I would found a grassroots group that would successfully lobby municipalities in British Columbia's West Kootenay region to pass resolutions opposing the cultivation of genetically engineered plants and trees within their municipal borders. In 2012, I would go on to found a flour mill co-op for Nelson residents and would also join a collective of families who would later develop an $8.5-million, twenty-four-home co-housing community of seventy people with food as its focus. I now call that home.

It was *at* my home, in the early days of food system sleuthing, that the contents of my refrigerator and pantry transformed post haste (the transformation being informed by whatever the topic on my radio show was in any given week). Anyone dependent on the familiarity of food brands (or even so much as packaging resembling such foods) would have opened my refrigerator or pantry, given them both a scan, and another, and another, and soon after, announced that there was "no food in the house."

In fact, my kitchen was bursting with food, just not food adorned with any recognizable labels, nor in packaging of familiar shapes and materials.

- In the freezer? Pink bricks of different sizes, each stamped with a mysterious acronym. These were butcher-wrapped meats — beef, pork, even alpaca — the acronyms indicating the particular cut, all sourced from unlicensed producer-processors — illegal in the eyes of food inspection authorities. You didn't hear it here.

- In the fridge? Unlabeled jars of orange sauce, shredded soggy vegetables, pasty pancake batter-like ooze, and a red sauce that could have been one of a half dozen different condiments (these were apricot jam, sauerkraut, sourdough starter, ketchup — prepared and canned at home, with love). Next to them, a one-gallon glass jar of what "must be milk"? Indeed it was — raw milk sold illegally to a collective I convened of eight families, each of us required once every eight weeks to devote a few hours in the day to retrieve our scandalous eight gallons of illegal milk from a nearby farm. Next to that, a plastic jug of illegal unpasteurized apple juice — delivered weekly to my front door. Like I say, you didn't hear it here.

- In the door of the fridge? Various sizes of squeeze bottles containing liquids of different consistencies (these were tamari, sesame oil, maple syrup, and apple-cider vinegar — all purchased in bulk and dispensed into reusable, *un*-labeled containers).

- In the refrigerator drawers? Bags of what *appeared* to be vegetables. They were familiar *looking*, but not quite family — argh! They resembled beets, potatoes, and salad greens. They were the long-lost cousins of the common mono-varieties of vegetables found at major supermarkets: chiogas, purple Russians, yau choy, tatsoi, all sourced from a farm with a CSA program just outside of the city, black soil still clinging to their skins — dirty.

- In the pantry? Twenty-pound brown paper bags of grains, also with secret codes: SWW, HRW, RF (they were bulk whole-grain wheats — Soft White Winter, Hard Red Winter and Red Fife — sourced from a grain CSA program in a nearby valley, and definitely not in a form to bake bread with; flour milling after all is only offered once a week down the street at David's house).

The picture is painted. What had I become?

Exhausted!

Absolutely exhausted.

Turned out, that as I sought greater self-sufficiency and deeper connections to my food sources, visited weekly farmers' markets, coordinated underground food-buying groups, became my own processor of raw ingredients, put in my volunteer hours at the vegetable CSA, u-picked my berries, and harvested urban tree fruits — and in turn relied less and less on grocery stores — my life had become ALL about food.

I may have been exhausted, but it felt good. There was a feeling of achievement, of reward.

It felt good to live a lifestyle like that of many people around the world who devote each day and most moments to gathering and preparing their sustenance. It felt good to connect with the ways of my ancestors — our ancestors. It felt like required life curriculum to learn about how to adapt my relationship to food to fit my paltry activist income. It felt important to experience the social, economic, and cultural relationships which form around food. It felt absolutely necessary to have at least a sense of what the reunion between land and mouth could feel like (particularly for an urban eater like myself). It felt good to walk the talk. And oh had I talked... A LOT.

Around 2014, I began surveying my surroundings — surveying the experiences I had had and of those around me. Is this way of life that I and others had been dreaming into existence, all that I (that we) had hoped it to be? Could the path this dream was taking continue to unfold in the same direction? Or was it at a crossroads?

The observational notes from my surveying looked something like this:

- At venues such as farmers' markets, the demand for many local foods seems to be getting met. Supply appears to be adequate, with farmers often returning home with unsold product. Overall, demand for local food seems to be growing but is plateauing (the USDA would later confirm this plateauing in a 2015 report to Congress[2]).

- Many farmers at the markets are thrilled to be connecting with their customers face to face, but there are many more who would clearly prefer to have stayed home at the farm. The options to reach their customers are limited. The markets are the only available options. The financial return for some is healthy — for others, an insult to the time invested.

- Am left with the distinct impression that the self-sufficiency craze (household food preservation, backyard gardening, CSA box programs, etc.) is *not* sweeping the nation. There is a dedicated demographic in it for the long haul, many young initiates, but the value of Kraft and Smuckers stock remains steady.

- My own personal engagement to food is maxed out. Simply no more time to devote unless sanity is thrown into the pot. Key staples are being met, but still many foods I'm left reliant on the supermarket for — particularly through the winter.

- My personal experience appears to be echoing the movement. Fun. Rewarding. Tiring. Struggle — still. Despite progress — a struggle — a relentless push forward under the tremendous weight of the status quo — the weight of "cheap food" — the weight of "convenience."

- "Food security" conversations among the already-converted seem mired in controversy. Butting of heads up against walls is commonplace. Conversations and decisions often seem to begin from a place of disempowerment, victimhood, and scarcity. The energy of "struggle" — present in the formative years (and likely a resonance from similar struggles of decades past) hasn't been shaken. Not yet. Big food watches. Big food smiles. Big food marches on.

- The political and legislative approach to systemic change is like swimming through half-dried glue. Kudos to those champions who have patiently waded in the sticky substance. There must, however, be a better, more efficient way.

- As predicted, the co-opting of the local- and good-food movement by the food system's dominant players begins. It was only a matter of time before the grocery giants would begin to demand a piece of the pie (even if it was the perceptual pie — the *perception* of "local," of "farm-fresh"). Perceptions appear to have high monetary value in a culture of separation.

These were just some of my observations, but it was through a particular direct experience that my questions of "what next" were answered, and I saw what direction I (and we) would most benefit from taking at that crossroads.

The Kootenay Grain CSA

Canada's first CSA program for grain was formed in 2007. The CSA model relies on a commitment from eaters to compensate a farmer at the beginning of the season rather than after the harvest. With many CSA programs, the eaters thereby assume some of the risks of farming rather than leaving farmers at the mercy of uncertain markets and erratic weather. Popular among diversified organic vegetable farms, the model is a highly evolved and cooperative approach to producing and purchasing food. CSAs invite eaters to *invest* in their food and the people producing it rather than perpetuating a model that keeps food producers separated from eaters. It really does fly in the face of the dominant model — one that depends on farmers receiving the smallest piece of the pie, and on separation and on manufactured perceptions.

In only its second year, the initiative secured the support of 450 shareholders and another twelve businesses (bakeries, restaurants, grocery stores) who purchased another 150 shares between them. Shares consisted of different varieties of wheats, oats, lentils, and dried peas. At $125/share, the CSA was helping keep $75,000 in the local economy and supporting three farm families. At $1.25 a pound, it was understood that these three farms were receiving more for their grain than any other grain farmers in the country. Grassroots weekly milling services opened up in the two main communities being served by the CSA, and bulk purchases of hand-cranked oat rollers were coordinated through the program. Breakfast never tasted so good. Baking and sourdough classes were offered by CSA members, and it appeared as if a local grain revolution was afoot. Its popularity was enhanced by the commitment of the Kootenay Lake Sailing Association to transport the grains from the Creston Valley to the city of Nelson along one of British Columbia's largest lakes. In one year, a total of eleven boats filled their hulls with organically grown grains, delivering them to enthusiastic shareholders waiting at Nelson's municipal pier. This project was nothing short of incredible. It offered a glimpse of what was and remains possible.

But then...

...year three told a different story.

Whereas many of us were predicting that, at the CSA's current rate of growth, we would see the entire region eating local grains in only a few more years, the level of interest in the CSA instead began to decline. I began to hear from more and more members that their reason for *not* investing in year three and four was that they were still sitting on the grains received in year one and two. In almost all cases, it wasn't about members having too much grain or any lack of interest to use it, but was instead a matter of lifestyle — particularly their lack of time to use those grains and begin replacing store-bought products with homemade. Looking back, this comes as no surprise. Purchasing a hundred pounds of whole grains is easy — using them, on the other hand, another thing altogether!

Using whole, un-milled grains at home is a substantial departure from the convenience of grocery store grain products — breads, crackers, pastas, pizza, cookies, cereal. Even those who enjoy baking and preparing food from scratch can find convenience in ready-to-use store-bought flour.

Those extra steps required by shareholders to drop their grain off at a location to be milled on a designated date and to then expand the use of that flour at home were a strong enough departure from the daily routine.[i]

The message seemed clear. While it turned out that the interest in the *idea* of the grain CSA was significant and the desire to support a local grain economy strong, the capacity among eaters for the required lifestyle shift was simply not there for this direct-to-consumer grain CSA model to thrive.[ii]

Working Within Our Capacities Rather Than Against Them

This experience with the grain CSA summed up my observations shared earlier. It made it clear that the idealism of the local food movement was plateauing for a reason. Beyond the dedicated food reclamationists, the rest of us (the royal "us") was/is simply not ready for the full-scale, population-wide transition necessary for a more hands-on and engaged

---

i   Alternative approaches were considered such as providing members with flour instead of whole grains, but this wasn't financially feasible. In order to maintain the affordability of shares and the price required for the farmers to produce organic grains on a small scale, it was believed necessary to distribute these grains *un*-milled. In other words, the CSA was reliant on shareholders to subsidize the farmers with their personal time and energy. I would later learn of a third (and surprisingly significant) factor that led to a decline in shareholder numbers. Many shareholders simply couldn't pull it together to write a check and drop it in the mail. Seems simple enough of a task but was yet another departure from the convenience of one-stop, bank-card shopping.

ii   Despite the declines, the grain CSA does continue today and is sustained by a small and dedicated group of farmers and eaters.

food system — one that relies on an increased investment of time by eaters. I have observed this among many local food initiatives of all types, sizes, and locations.

None of this should come as a surprise.

No matter what our individual engagement with the source of our food looks like, when it comes to considering adjustments to our routine (even if they do bring us into greater alignment with our values), I'm sure we can all relate to the delicate nature of this "readiness" — of this capacity to change.

Our engagement with food doesn't, after all, operate in isolation from North America's nine-to-five work culture and its average incomes. Our relationship to food and the time we have available for it also can't avoid being restrained by the cost of living, the design of our cities and the demands of raising a family. All of this too has a direct influence on our ability to step outside of the convenience that is the grocery store. The need for convenience is summed up in the news that came out in 2015 — restaurant sales in the United States had overtaken grocery sales for the first time in history. Communicating this hunger for convenience even more strongly has been the explosion of meal-delivery services in every urban center across the country.

There is a fast-moving convenience train hurtling down the tracks, ,and I've come to believe that the future of strong local-food economies depends on two modes of action: 1) Getting the hell off the train and designing a whole new "transportation" paradigm (the direct-sales approach, the meet-your-farmer, grow-your-own approach), and 2) Becoming a fully committed "we're-all-in-this-together" passenger. I think we need both. This book is about the second mode of action — using it to better prepare ourselves for the first. It's about plotting out our transition rather than the transition being a reaction to all that we believe to be wrong. It's about meeting the system where it's at, meeting people where they're at, and in doing so, having a far greater impact.

As I've come to see it, the "wall" being "hit up against" that seems to accompany many local food initiatives is *this* wall — the constraints of a society that are simply too complex and ingrained to be changed in short order, a society that is racing towards a culture of convenience as quickly as an emoji can be used to describe the events of the day. Stepping outside of this culture in any magnitude more than just supplementation will not be possible or interesting anytime soon to more than a dedicated contingent.

There is, thank goodness, a way for all of us eaters and lovers of good food to work within and outside of the "system" at the *same* time — the grocery store. Placing the bulk of our attention on the grocery store as the tool for systemic and cultural change is inviting *all* eaters to become passengers on the same train.

The numbers speak for themselves.

Since 1990, the share of total at-home food expenditures directed to farmers and processors through the direct-to-market model (farmers' markets, farm stands, CSAs) remained steady at 5.9 percent; the share of at-home food expenditures directed to retailers, 91.6 percent[iii].[3] There is little question where to assign our local and good food aspirations. It's time we place our food movement "eggs" into the grocery store basket. It's time for a supermarket shakedown.

---

iii   This figure represents all retail formats including supermarkets, warehouse clubs, supercenters, convenience stores and specialty food stores.

Rise of the Grocery Giants

"I would rather have thieves and gangsters than chain stores in Louisiana."

— Louisiana Governor Huey Long, 1934[4]

A&P — The First of the Giants

NO BUSINESS CAPTURES THE RISE of the mega-retailer better than the Great Atlantic & Pacific Tea Company (A&P), and no grocery retailer has been confronted with such hatred and condemnation as A&P. The fight was brought to the food retailer from all fronts — from mom-and-pop food shops and Main Street businesses, from farmers and food processors, from manufacturers and wholesalers, from consumers' rights groups and trade unions, from all levels of government, and even from a handful of U.S. presidents.

Founded in New York City as Gilman & Company in 1859, A&P grew to 150 stores by 1880. In its heyday of 1929, the company had come to manage 16,000 grocery stores with combined sales of $1 billion (equivalent to $14.8 billion in 2019). At the time, A&P was supported by its own factories — 70 of them — and 100 warehouses spread across the United States. In his painstakingly well-researched history of the company (effectively a history of grocery retailing in America), author Marc Levinson writes that the company was "the country's largest coffee importer, the largest wholesale produce dealer and butter buyer, the second-largest baker," and its sales were more than twice that of any other retailer.[5] Levinson's book is essential reading.

Of the too-many-to-count battles that A&P was entangled in over its 150-year history, its feud with the Cream of Wheat Company stands out. The debate was one of many that would continue for decades on what defines "competition" in the American economy.

For much of the early twentieth century, manufacturers of the most popular brands of packaged foods enjoyed ample power in the marketplace. Their base of customers was diverse — no one single retailer wielded any significant power over the food manufacturers or wholesalers supplying them with food. The grocery store landscape was dotted with many independents, regional chains, and a handful of fledgling national chains. By 1912, however, A&P had grown to 480 stores and was launching an all new format: the A&P Economy Store, the first ever "discount" food store. By 1915, half of A&P's 1,600 stores were of this discount format. In its aggressive rolling out of locations, A&P priced products at amounts never before seen in the food world. Case in point, A&P marked up Cream of Wheat (CoW) breakfast cereal by only one cent! They would purchase CoW at a wholesale price of eleven cents a piece and place it on the shelf for only twelve cents. How could A&P possibly profit from this? They didn't. This was the beginning of big food flexing its muscle at its competition. These were the early days of a company growing to such a large scale that it could justify any losses as a marketing expense (of sorts) — a powerful ploy to draw customers into its stores and gain their long-term, maybe even lifelong loyalty.

A&P's pricing, however, was not in accordance with an earlier agreement between the two companies. The agreement had made it clear that *any* retailers selling the cereal were required to retail it for no less than fourteen cents. A manufacturer specifying a minimum retail price was not an uncommon practice at the time — in fact, the practice continues in various forms to this day as a way to ensure retailers do not compete too fiercely on price. Thus A&P's rock-bottom price of twelve cents contravened the agreement and infuriated CoW. But why would CoW care what A&P priced their cereal at — after all, wouldn't those low prices only increase consumer interest in their cereal? Simple. Food manufacturers valued competition in the marketplace and wanted to maintain their power to negotiate with retailers. In those early days — before the dominance of national and global retailers today — CoW understood what the erosion of competition in the marketplace might do to their own business as a manufacturer. Retailers, after all, were the gateway to the marketplace on which manufacturers relied.

The equation looks like this:

- A&P sells Cream of Wheat at twelve cents (two cents less than competitors). Consumers flock to A&P.
- Smaller independent retailers can't possibly sell the cereal at such a low price and stop purchasing Cream of Wheat.
- Cream of Wheat loses its diverse base of customers (made up primarily of independents) and is left to negotiate with an increasingly powerful grocery giant.

In response to A&P's pricing, CoW turned off the tap, refusing to sell its cereal to the company. A&P filed a lawsuit, claiming CoW was price-fixing and was in contravention of the Clayton Antitrust Act of 1914. A&P lost. The U.S. District Court Judge presiding over the 1915 case concluded that no price-fixing had taken place and that A&P had been using its low prices to injure its competition, and once their competitors were down, would have raised its prices to pre-combat levels.[6]

> [The] defendant (CoW) and many retailers would be injured, and the microscopic benefit to a small portion of the public would last only until the plaintiff (A&P) was relieved from the competition of the 14 cent grocers, when it, too, would charge what the business would normally and naturally bear.[7]
>
> — Judge Charles Hough, 1915

This was one of the first cases against the practice of retail (or resale) price maintenance (RPM) and one of the first to challenge what is now known as "predatory pricing" — when a company prices a product in such a way to intentionally harm competition, perhaps pricing them out of the marketplace altogether.

This resistance to the rise of discount food retailing and predatory pricing held the capacity to alter the course of history. Would the food system evolve to become diverse and competitive, one that welcomed equal opportunity among merchants of all sizes, or would it head down the path of "cutthroat competition," leaving only a handful of companies dominating every link in the food chain?

Other Giants Emerge

With stores in thirty-nine of forty-eight states and two Canadian provinces, A&P would eventually grow to become the largest retailer in the world, collecting ten cents of every dollar spent on food in America. At one point, A&P "operated twice as many stores as the next seven chains combined." It put its discount pricing strategies into practice from its beginnings. "The Company [is] determined to undersell the whole tea trade," reads one 1863 advertisement that lauded its low prices and its commitment to undercutting the competition.[8]

It didn't take long for the company to begin exhibiting the traits of a ruthless corporation. A&P was found to be selling short weights of tea and adulterating both its tea and coffee with cheaper substitutes. By 1867, A&P was buying up advertising space in trade publications to print fake news articles and even went so far as to publish its own fake newspaper — *The Commercial Enterprise.*

In 1870, A&P became the first to market a branded tea. The tea was only available through the Great Atlantic & Pacific Tea Co. Before the introduction of brands, food manufacturers and retailers sold foods indistinguishable from one another and competed almost entirely on price. The introduction of brands opened the door to a food system that could now differentiate foods on quality and perceptions. In what also became the first known instance of a "private-label" food product, A&P added its own logo to baking powder in 1885.

In 1871, with the opening of a store in Chicago, A&P made its first move out of New York City. By 1875, the company had expanded its tea and coffee stores to sixteen cities, making it the first to have retail stores across much of the nation. By 1880, there were 150 A&P locations.

At the turn of the century, A&P was no longer the only chain grocer on the block. About fifty of them existed, and one of them was Kroger.

In 1883, at the age of 23, Bernard Kroger opened his first tea shop — the Great Western Tea Co. By 1902, the Kroger Grocery and Baking Co. had established forty grocery stores in cities throughout Ohio with combined sales of $1.75 million. By contrast, A&P was enjoying a healthy 2.5 percent profit margin on $5 million in sales and opening a new store every two weeks. Just like A&P, Kroger was innovating the grocery retail business by vertically integrating. Combining two or more stages of product development (vertical integration) wasn't entirely new in turn-of-the-century America, but Kroger's introduction of in-house bakeries was the first instance of it in the grocery retail business. The move enabled Kroger to dramatically lower the price of its bread from six to two-and-a-half cents a loaf. Other bakeries were enraged. Local newspapers dubbed it "The Bread War."[9] In a 1902 article, *The New York Times* warned of Kroger's pending arrival in NYC:

BIG PLANS FOR CHEAP BREAD

B.H. Kroger of Cincinnati May Establish Bakeries in Many Large Cities

Special to *The New York Times*

CINCINNATI, Nov. 11. — The advent of B.H. Kroger, who owns over forty retail and wholesale groceries here, into the bread-baking business, by establishing a plant, baking bread by electricity, and thereby inaugurating a bread war by underselling all bakers, now threatens gigantic opposition to the United States Biscuit Company, or the trust in all the big cities of the country. In addition to his local plant, Kroger is rapidly concluding negotiations for one in New York City, and if this proves the success that is expected, he stated today that he will establish other plants in Philadelphia, Pittsburgh, Baltimore, Washington, Chicago, and other big cities.

— *The New York Times,* November 12, 1902

As "The Bread War" waged on, Bernard Kroger received more than one death threat. "If you don't raise the price of bread at once, you will be killed or shot," signed "A. Citizen." Kroger was undeterred. Two years later, he bought up a chain of meat and deli operations along with a few local meat packinghouses and introduced the first in-store butchers.[10]

Consumers at the time were unfazed by the chain-store commotions. While the growing power of the chains might have been disconcerting to the independents, Levinson suggests that consumers likely cared less. Chains hadn't yet swept the nation, and many people hadn't yet set foot in one.

Self-Service

Prior to 1916, grocery stores were nothing like the stores of today. Items for sale were out of reach to shoppers. Store clerks would take orders and fill them from shelves and bulk bins located behind a counter. All changed on September 6, 1916, when, in Memphis, Tennessee, Piggly Wiggly — the first self-service grocery store — was born.[11] Kroger, who had already opened his first out-of-state store in St. Louis in 1912, followed suit and began a transition to the self-service format.[12] The concept became known as the "groceteria," after the already-familiar cafeteria concept of turnstiles and checkout counters. With customers now selecting their own products, brand recognition and packaging became more important than ever.

In Canada, self-service stores entered the scene a few years later. In 1919, Theodore Loblaw and J. Milton Cork opened their first Loblaw Groceteria at 2923 Dundas Street West in Toronto. Their slogan: "We Sell for Less." A second location opened within months at 528 College Street, and Loblaw would grow to become Canada's largest grocery store chain — a title it retains today.[13] In 1924, another Canadian giant materialized out of a meat delivery business — Sobeys — entering the grocery business in Stellarton, Nova Scotia, and eventually becoming Canada's second-largest chain.

The self-service model was revolutionary and enabled stores to lower their prices even further. Shoppers, who were spending a hefty one-third of their budget on food (compared to 7–9 percent today),[14] welcomed this innovation.

Chain store growth ramped up after the war. Between 1922 and 1925, A&P was opening seven new stores a day and had 13,000 of them by 1925. Kroger had grown to 3,749 stores by 1927.[15] To remain competitive, other chains began buying up smaller chains and consolidating them. It was in this wave of mergers and acquisitions that Safeway grew to prominence, becoming the largest grocery chain in the West. In 1929, A&P responded to Safeway's rise by opening 101 stores in Los Angeles in just one year,[16] and rumors later surfaced in the *Wall Street Journal* that Kroger and Safeway were considering a merger.[17] No merger ever took place, but the hunger for rapid growth and consolidation was evident. By 1932, Safeway had 3,411 stores,[18] and Bernard Kroger had sold controlling interest to Lehman Brothers, who then took the company into a period described as "galloping consumption."[19] In just sixteen months following the sale, Kroger acquired 1,828 stores,[20] many of them regional chains. In the 1920s, the largest American and Canadian chains had also gone international. Loblaw expanded into New York State and later into Chicago,[21] and by 1929, A&P, was operating 200 locations in Ontario and Quebec.[22] Safeway opened its first five Canadian stores in Manitoba.[23] The grocery giants had grown to a scale unlike anything the food world had ever seen.

Growth of A&P Stores —
1880–1929

1880	150
1912	480
1915	1,817
1920	4,588
1923	9,236
1925	13,000
1929	16,000

SOURCE: LEVINSON, *THE GREAT A&P AND THE STRUGGLE FOR SMALL BUSINESS IN AMERICA*[24]

A&P Supermarket in Durham, North Carolina, ca. 1940. SOURCE: COURTESY EVERETT COLLECTION

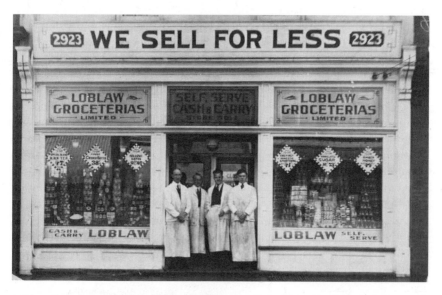

Loblaw Groceterias first location at 2923 Dundas Street West, Toronto, Ontario, ca. 1919. SOURCE: LOBLAW GROCETERIAS POSTCARD, CA. 1919

Regulating the Rise of Big Business

> The basic tenet of antitrust law's goals is to create a
> system whereby economic power in any given indus-
> try is spread out among numerous competitors. This, in
> turn, ensures that no single player leverages its size to
> the detriment of other, less powerful firms.[25]
>
> — Leo S. Carameli Jr., Attorney

In the handful of years commencing in 1912, a flurry of activity
would have lasting impacts on the decades to come and on competition
in America. A&P had launched its Economy Store discount format
and soon-to-be U.S. President Woodrow Wilson was actively cam-
paigning for president across the nation. He was outspoken on the rise
of "big business."

> Which do you want? Do you want to live in a town
> patronized by some great combination of capitalists
> who pick it out as a suitable place to plant their industry
> and draw you into their employment? Or do you want
> to see your sons and your brothers and your husbands
> build up business for themselves under the protection
> of laws which make it impossible for any giant, how-
> ever big, to crush them and put them out of business.[26]
>
> — Woodrow Wilson [at a campaign stop in Bradford,
> Ohio, on September 16, 1912]

Whereas previous presidents had fought the corporate trusts by
regulating them, Wilson vowed to break them up. He appealed to the
American public to support an economy built on innovation, *not* on the
power to control resources and manipulate prices on a whim. "If price
discrimination[iv] could be stopped," said Wilson, "then you have free
America, and I for my part am willing to see who has the best brains."

---

iv   Price discrimination is a pricing strategy that charges customers different prices
     for the same product or service. In pure price discrimination, the seller charges
     each customer (a consumer or another business) the maximum price he or she
     will pay.

Wilson was elected president in 1913. He attributed his victory, in part, to the work of lawyer Louis Brandeis.[27]

Brandeis has been called "a Robin Hood of the law" and among his many accomplishments helped form the American Fair-Trade League (AFTL).[28] The AFTL advocated for the liberalization of antitrust laws (fair competition laws) to promote inter-firm cooperation, rather than consolidation, and to foster market stability by eliminating "cutthroat competition" and "over-production."[29] What was being fought for was a defining of "competition" unlike that which sees soccer fans rioting after their team loses a game. This was a vision for "competition" that was friendly and in the spirit of innovating all aspects of life. It favored a reality in which two teams run out onto the field while the players and fans brim with anticipation of the skills that the athletes on *both* teams are about to exhibit. Winning would not be about creating a "loser" but about demonstrating the potential we have as individuals and communities to move beyond our perceived limitations and celebrate human potential. Imagine that! What a different reality could emerge, simply by choosing it. This was very much Wilson's vision — "I dare say we shall never return to the old order of individual competition, and that the organization of business upon a great scale of cooperation is, up to a certain point, itself normal and inevitable."[30] In this respect, Wilson was a visionary.

In working to manifest this vision, Brandeis argued vociferously against price discrimination. "In order that the public may be free buyers there must be removed from the mind of the potential purchaser the thought that probably at some other store he could get that same article for less money."[31] The idea of preventing low-priced anything seems preposterous today just as it did then. Who doesn't enjoy a good deal when they see one! But Brandeis and the AFTL were not positioning themselves and their interests for short-term gain; they were many steps ahead of the price-conscious consumer. Brandeis feared a future of disproportionately powerful retailers driving prices to rock bottom and leaving manufacturers little choice but to lower the quality of their products to remain viable. While some might call a "lowest cost" culture "fierce competition," others like Brandeis saw it as the *end* of competition.

> "We learned long ago that liberty could be preserved only by limiting in some way the freedom of action of individuals; that otherwise liberty would necessarily yield to absolutism; and in the same way we have learned that unless there be regulation of competition, its excesses will lead to the destruction of competition, and monopoly will take its place."[32]
>
> — Louis Brandeis, 1912

> "Shall we, under the guise of protecting competition, further foster monopoly by creating immunity for the price-cutters?"[33]
>
> — Louis Brandeis, 1913

Brandeis was Wilson's chief economic adviser from 1912 to 1916 and became an architect of an entirely new government agency to manage competition. This new agency would "steer a diverse economy away from destructive competition while maintaining product diversity, innovation, and productivity."[34] The Federal Trade Commission (FTC) would prevent unfair competition by conducting investigations, producing reports, and making legislative recommendations to Congress. Also passed in 1914 was another tool to preserve competition: the Clayton Antitrust Act.

The Federal Trade Commission Act, the Clayton Antitrust Act, and the earlier Sherman Antitrust Act are the three core federal antitrust laws remaining to this day.[35] The Clayton Act addressed shortcomings in the Sherman Act — most notably, by prohibiting "mergers and acquisitions where the effect may be substantially to lessen competition, or tend to create a monopoly."[36]

What developed here was a dramatically different view of "competition" than that which dominates economies and society today. This "new competition held that contracts were social, that effects of free market competition were ambiguous, and that economic organization and behavior could be steered by government and civil society to foster productive competition."[37] This new view of competition was not about eliminating restraints of trade but about distinguishing between productive and destructive restraints.[38] This left much open to debate; however, underneath the push to regulate competition more aggressively was something much greater. As Levinson writes on the work of the FTC in its early years, "No factual investigation could quell the growing concern about chain stores for the worry had less to do with price competition than with the survival of small town America. As the smaller, local competitors fell by the wayside, jobs vanished with them, destroying the social fabric and leaving communities bereft of capital and civic leadership."[39]

Expanding the War on Chain Grocers

> "Huge Corporations, Serving the Nation Through Country-Wide Chains, Are Displacing the Neighborhood Store"
>
> — *New York Times* headline, July 8, 1928

The 1930s began with the almost complete collapse of the American economy, out of which came a few important developments in the evolution of grocery stores. Looking back on this period, these developments communicate a very different vision for a society and food economy than what would instead evolve.

The number one belief at the time was that the Great Depression was caused by "excessive competition that was forcing down prices, decimating profits, and causing employers to lay off workers."[40] As later chapters will describe in more detail, this belief accurately summarizes the grocery retail landscape of today.

The Roosevelt administration was determined to halt deflation and prevent the continued erosion of prices. Introduced were post-Depression recovery mechanisms like the National Industrial Recovery Act (NIRA) and the Agricultural Adjustment Act (AAA) of 1933.

NIRA required grocery wholesalers and retailers to draw up codes that would outline a culture of "fair competition." Specifically, the codes would bring product costs and prices in alignment among competitors. The codes specifically applied to the chains, and thus a lifeline was extended to smaller independent grocers and wholesalers across the country.

The AAA introduced another important provision that prevented what is now known in the retail world as "loss leading" — the practice of a retailer willfully losing money on a particular item and subsidizing their losses with profits from other items. Loss leading is a key strategy employed by the grocery giants of today. In 1933, it was prohibited.

> "I do not think that any method of distribution has a right to take advantage of its strong position in the channels of distribution to sell the commodities that are processed from one set of materials at a loss, and to make up that loss on commodities that are produced by another set of producers."[41]
>
> — Hon. Charles J. Brand, Co-Administrator of the Agricultural Adjustment Act, addressing chain store executives on June 23, 1933

Main Street and rural America were being protected.

At the local level, a wave of resistance had also emerged to the chain store explosion. Independents and storekeepers had begun to organize themselves in protest. State governments also responded. By the late 1930s, twenty-nine states had implemented chain store taxes.

Examples of Chain Store Taxes:[42]

Minnesota:	$155/store for chains with more than 50 stores
Michigan:	$250/store for chains with more than 25 stores
Florida:	$400/store for chains above 15 stores (+ 5 percent tax on gross receipts)
Pennsylvania:	$500/store for chains with more than 500 stores
Louisiana:	$550 for each store above 500 stores *nationwide* (even if the chain only had one store in the state)

Louisiana's tax was the most onerous, acting effectively as a chain store ban. If A&P had had even a single store in the state, the tax would have consumed 50 percent of the company's 1934 profits. Louisiana's Governor, Huey Long, was one of the most ardent opponents to the chains, stating, "I would rather have thieves and gangsters than chain stores in Louisiana."[43] Ironically, Long was assassinated only a few years later.

Pennsylvania's aggressive tax was also effective, forcing A&P with its 2,000 stores in the state to shutter 80 locations.

Municipalities like Hamtramck, Michigan, and Fredericksburg, Virginia also introduced chain store taxes.[44]

The Chain Store Revolution (Number of Stores 1919–37)

Year	A&P	Kroger	Am. Stores	Safeway	F. National	C5
1919	4,224		1,175			4.2%
1920	4,600	799	1,243			5.6%
1921	5,200	947	1,274			6.3%
1922	7,300	1,224	1,375	118		7.1%
1923	9,300	1,641	1,474	193		8.0%
1924	11,400	1,973	1,629	263		9.3%
1925	14,000	2,599	1,792	330		11.5%
1926	14,800	3,100	1,982	673		13.6%
1927	15,600	3,564	2,122	840	1,681	16.9%
1928	15,100	4,307	2,548	1,191	1,717	20.4%
1929	15,400	5,575	2,644	2,340	2,002	24.5%
1930	15,700	5,165	2,728	2,675	2,549	27.6%
1931	15,670	4,884	2,806	3,264	2,548	29.3%
1932	15,427	4,737	2,977	3,411	2,546	28.8%

Am. Stores = American Stores / F. National = First National / C5 = National market concentration of top 5 companies

SOURCE: ELLICKSON, *THE EVOLUTION OF THE SUPERMARKET INDUSTRY FROM A&P TO WALMART*[45]

Enter the Supermarket

Automobile ownership became more accessible in the 1930s, and kitchen refrigerators began arriving in homes. These developments made the arrival of the supermarket format possible. They enabled consumers to easily travel to larger stores in the newly forming suburbs and purchase in greater volumes per visit.

With the arrival of supermarkets, the same economies of scale afforded to the chains could now be applied to a single store — high volumes, low prices. The first person to foresee what was likely an inevitable stage in the evolution of the food store was former Kroger employee Michael Cullen. In 1930, he opened King Cullen in Queens, New York — the first supermarket.[46]

At the time, a "supermarket" location was five to ten times larger than the average grocery store and ranged in size from ten to fifteen thousand square feet — the equivalent of a small supermarket by today's standards. Food prices dropped at the first supermarkets by an average of 13 percent, and in 1933 revenues at the most successful stores were the equivalent to a Walmart location today.[47] In Canada, the first supermarket was likely Steinberg's, which opened in Montreal in 1934.

After World War II, the supermarket format took off and grew in popularity for the subsequent three decades. Between 1935 and 1982, the number of supermarkets in America would grow from 386 to 26,640 (3.2 percent of the grocery market to 74.5 percent).[48] With this growth would come the most aggressive era of antitrust enforcement in U.S. history.

Supermarket Expansion 1935–82

Year	Supermarkets	Share of Overall Grocery Market (%)
1935	386	3.2
1939	772	10.0
1948	5,654	22.8
1954	14,214	41.3
1958	23,562	53.9
1963	31,484	59.9
1967	43,433	66.7
1972	64,960	69.6
1977	113,111	75.0
1982	175,655	74.5

SOURCE: ELLICKSON, THE EVOLUTION OF THE SUPERMARKET INDUSTRY FROM A&P TO WALMART[49]

Retailer Market Power

"We're all things to all men, all women .... Our market
share of U.K. retailing is 12.5% — that leaves 87.5% to
go after."[50]

— Sir Terry Leahy,
Chief Executive Officer, Tesco, 2004

IN OVER ONE HUNDRED YEARS following the birth of the modern
grocery store, the market power that has amassed into the hands of
an ever-shrinking number of food retailers is mind-boggling.

Commencing in the 1980s, a wave of buyouts, mergers, acquisitions,
and global expansions effectively colonized communities and foreign
countries with grocery giants — "retail conquistadors," as author
Joanna Blythman calls them.[51] Today, the top fifteen global supermarket companies account for more than 30 percent of world supermarket
sales.[52]

If we narrow our geographic focus, the concentration of power in
food retail widens.

In the United States, the five largest food retailers today account
for over 66 percent of national retail food sales. In Canada, almost 80
percent of retail food purchases end up in the hands of the five largest.
This is stunning to fathom.

While these numbers are already sufficient to communicate the
power of grocers in the marketplace, national concentration figures are
not an entirely accurate picture of the dominance retailers maintain at
the more regional and local levels.

In one example, in the entire south of Texas (San Antonio, Austin,
Corpus Christi), 60 percent of retail food purchases today are made at

Top 5 Grocers in U.S.
Share of Grocery Retail Sales 2016 (%)

Walmart	24.7
Kroger	15.2
Costco	11.1
Albertsons	9.2
Ahold-Delhaize	6.6
C5*	66.8

*Market concentration of top 5 firms
Source: Chain Store Guide 2018[53] /
USDA ERS Retail Trends, May 14, 2018[54]

Top 5 Canadian Grocers
Share of Grocery Retail Sales 2016 (%)

Loblaw	29.8
Sobeys	21.5
Metro	11.5
Costco	10.5
Walmart	7.2
C5*	80.5

Source: USDA FAS, Canada —
Retail Sector Overview 2018[55]

H-E-B stores. H-E-B and Walmart together command 87 percent of eaters' grocery dollars in that part of the state.[56]

Rural markets are the most concentrated of any, with usually one, maybe two grocers serving the area. In urban markets, market concentration can also be quite high. In the Denver, Colorado, metro area, five companies receive 82 percent of consumers' grocery dollars.[57] In Cincinnati, Ohio, just one company — Kroger — holds 60 percent of the market.[58] In Miami, Florida, Publix receives 46.3 percent of the grocery dollars, and the top three companies a whopping 75.2 percent.[59]

At the even more micro neighborhood level, residents often only have access to one store — particularly in lower-income neighborhoods where automobile ownership is less commonplace. Residents of these neighborhoods are genuinely at the mercy of a monopoly. But regardless of income level, in any place where eaters' access to a grocery store is restricted by distance or the time they have available to travel, the grocery giants acquire a unique tacit form of monopoly.

From this more localized perspective, we can get a more accurate picture of the power of the grocery giants and their impacts on local economies, food systems, and communities.

Locally, nationally and globally, this largely unrestrained concentration of power in the food system is going mostly unnoticed at the checkout counters of our neighborhood grocers. As Andrew Simms writes in his revealing book, *Tescopoly:* "Small, independent retailers are passing through a 'mass extinction event' at the hands of supermarkets — and in the process, an important part of the glue that holds communities together is being dissolved."[60]

Urban Market Concentration in Select Cities
Share of Grocery Retail Sales 2017 (%)

Miami, FL

Publix	46.3
Walmart	18.4
Southeastern Grocers	10.5
Whole Foods (Amazon)	3.6
ALDI	2.7
C3*	75.2
C5*	81.5

Houston, TX

H-E-B	28
Walmart	25
Kroger	23
C3*	76

Charlotte, NC

Walmart	26.2
Kroger	25.4
Ahold Delhaize	20.1
Southeastern Grocers	7.1
Publix	6.1
C3*	71.7
C5*	84.9

Nashville, TN

Kroger	40.2
Walmart	27.2
Publix	14.7
ALDI	2.3
Ahold Delhaize	1.9
C3*	82.1
C5*	86.3

* Market concentration of top 3 or 5 firms.

SOURCE: THE NIELSEN COMPANY — TDLINX, 2017[61] / JEFF GREEN PARTNERS, "GROCERY WARS INTENSIFY IN TEXAS," 2017[62]

Taming the Chains

How did we get here? The restraints of the early half of the twentieth century did little to quell the concentration of power seen today in retail food markets. It's hard to make a compelling case for successful restraint of market dominance when a single company like Kroger or H-E-B can today command 60 percent of an urban or regional market. But the spread of the chains following the Great Depression was not met without restraint at the highest levels of government.

After the Supreme Court declared the economic stimulus programs of the post-Depression era as unconstitutional, Congress passed two laws to replace them. The Robinson-Patman Anti-Price Discrimination Act of 1936 was the first. That's correct — an act discriminating against price discrimination! Take a moment and revel in knowing that, at one point in our history, there was an administration intent on ensuring that a small neighborhood grocery store would have access to the same products at the same prices that were afforded to the largest grocery chains in the country. The Robinson-Patman Act passed in the House with bipartisan support. This was a vision for an economy that placed *people* first. This bottom-up reconstruction of the American economy has been called "the second American revolution"[63] — a period of history largely forgotten.

The cosponsor of the bill, Congressman Wright Patman of Texas, was as anti-chain as they came, accusing the chains of "sapping the civic life of local communities with an absentee overlordship, draining off their earnings to [their] coffers, and reducing independent businessmen to employees or to idleness."[64]

The following year, the Miller-Tydings Act of 1937 was passed. It protected the practice of retail price-maintenance, thereby allowing foodmakers to set a minimum price that their products would be sold at in stores. Imagine that, before there was fair-trade coffee and fair-trade chocolate, there was domestic fair-trade everything in 1937 America!

As journalist Phillip Longman of the New America Foundation writes, "These laws [ensured] that large chains headquartered in distant cities didn't come to dominate the economies of local communities."[65]

President Franklin D. Roosevelt supported the managing of competition. In a 1938 message to Congress on curbing monopolies, FDR made an appeal to his colleagues to consider the limits that had been placed upon the American entrepreneurial spirit: "Men will dare to compete against men but not against giants."[66]

"If you believe with me in private initiative, you must acknowledge the right of well-managed small business to expect to make reasonable profits. You must admit that the destruction of this opportunity follows concentration of control of any given industry into a small number of dominating corporations."[67]

— U.S. President Franklin D. Roosevelt, 1938

The effects of Robinson-Patman and Miller-Tydings were felt immediately. Chain stores no longer had a price advantage over their smaller competitors, and their market share decreased correspondingly. A&P was likely hit the hardest. For the first time in its history, its profits were less than 2 percent of sales.[68]

The chains were impacted but undeterred. Enter Thurman Arnold, who headed up the Antitrust Division at the Department of Justice between 1938 and 1943. In 1940, Arnold authored *The Bottlenecks of Business*,[69] helping introduce one of the most effective analogies to describe the concentration of power in supply chains. No word describes the grip grocery giants have on the food system of today better than "bottleneck." More on that later.

Arnold ran a highly active series of investigations. Among the many charges he brought against A&P, the most serious was in 1942: "combination and conspiracy to restrain trade." It was one of three complaints filed against big food chains. Evidence had also surfaced that Kroger and Safeway had agreed to not compete with each other in certain markets, but the A&P case was the most extensively pursued. A&P was alleged to "dominate and control the production, prices and distribution of a substantial part of the foods produced, marketed, sold and consumed in the United States."[70] The case ended up in a Danville, Illinois, courtroom in 1946, and A&P was found guilty on all charges.

In one instance during the trial, a flagrant example of unrestrained power surfaced. A&P had requested that Ralston Purina (RP) manufacture a private label breakfast cereal for A&P's stores. With such a lucrative offer, RP invested one million dollars into a breakfast cereal facility. Then came the grocery muscle. Once the facility was up and running, A&P demanded RP lower its prices. If RP refused to comply, A&P threatened to commence manufacturing the cereal itself. Once again, this was a power that no other retailer could wield in the marketplace.[71]

When a circuit court of appeals in 1949 upheld the 1946 decision, the judges made a prophetic statement on the rise of grocery chain power in America:

> "The inevitable consequences of this whole business pattern is to create a chain reaction of ever-increasing selling volume and ever-increasing requirements and hence purchasing power for A&P, and for its competitors hardships not produced by competitive forces, and, conceivably, ultimate extinction."[72]

Despite the ruling, the chains and their supermarket format marched on. By 1948, the supermarket format had secured 23 percent of the U.S. market.[73] In Canada, Loblaw began a huge wave of expansion through acquisition of chains in Western and Eastern Canada, plus a major U.S. chain. Between 1946 and 1958, Loblaw opened 118 new stores (many of them supermarkets) and closed 45 older locations. In just ten years, the company's sales increased 431 percent compared to the national average of 185 percent. By 1958, Loblaw had 20 percent of the Ontario market — the largest market share of any chain grocer anywhere in North America.[74] Despite Canada being home to the oldest antitrust statute in the Western world (1889), antitrust enforcement was generally unambitious, often due to financial constraints and a disinterest in holding back the growth of big business. Before 1955, Canadian antitrust enforcement only tried thirty-five cases (less than one per year).[75]

In the United States, the anti-chain store movement had begun to decline, marked in 1949 by a failed attempt by President Harry Truman's Department of Justice to break up A&P's retail divisions, factories, and distribution operations into smaller companies.[76] Congress enacted an amendment to the FTC Act that effectively abolished "fair trade" laws.[77] Resale price maintenance was no longer in effect, and discount prices became commonplace once again. Chain store taxes were disappearing, and by 1958, eight companies sold over 26 percent of the food in America.[78]

While anti-chain store sentiments had faded, antitrust enforcement remained quite active. The merger laws of the 1960s have been described as "by far the most stringent in the world."[79] In what today is one of the most cited cases of the extremes that antitrust would go to protect competition and small business, in 1966 the Supreme Court blocked the merger of two supermarket chains in Los Angeles. Had they been allowed to merge, the chains would have controlled only 7.5 percent of the local market. Localized enforcement like this was never seen again.

From the end of WWII through the mid-80s, antitrust enforcement had tremendous effect on the food system. In the 1920s, the five largest processors of beef controlled almost 70 percent of the market; by 1975, their control had plummeted to 25 percent. In 1933, the four largest grocery retailers controlled 27 percent of the market; by 1982, their control was 17 percent.[80]

The Effects of Restraint on Retailer Market Concentration
Market Share (%) of National Grocery Retail (U.S.)

	1954	1958	1963	1967	1972	1977	1982
4 largest firms	20.9	21.7	20.0	19.0	17.5	17.4	17.8
8 largest firms	25.4	27.5	26.6	25.7	24.4	24.4	25.1
20 largest firms	29.9	34.1	34.0	34.0	34.8	34.5	35.6

SOURCE: MARION, *THE ORGANIZATION AND PERFORMANCE OF THE U.S. FOOD SYSTEM, 1986*[81]

The Giants Break Loose

In the world of U.S. grocery retail, everything changed in the early 1980s. The culture of taming the chains was about to come to an abrupt end. Public policy expert Phillip Longman describes the period as a time when "America forgot its own history."[82]

The new Reagan administration and its "laissez-faire" approach to government oversight decisively "eviscerated America's century-long tradition of antitrust enforcement."[83] In 1982, antitrust prosecutions came under new guidelines. In this new reality, considerations of social cost, regional equity, or local control were no longer relevant to decisions on mergers and acquisitions. In this new regime, antitrust enforcement became mostly a tool for combating the most egregious anti-competitive practices — namely, collusion or anything that would blatantly gouge consumers.[84]

"Reganomics" unleashed an initial wave of leveraged buyouts in the 1980s followed by another wave of mergers and acquisitions in the '90s. Whereas market concentration of the top four grocery chains was at 17 percent in 1982, by 1999 the top four were pulling in 28 percent of our food dollars.[85]

Walmart's entry into grocery in 1988 through its Supercenter format also accelerated market concentration in the United States[86] and influenced the transition from a regional grocery industry to a more nationalized one. Economist Paul Ellickson describes Walmart's arrival into food as the "largest change in market structure since the rise and fall of A&P."[87] Only fourteen years after entry, Walmart became the top grocer in the country. In that same time, twenty-nine chains filed for bankruptcy. Walmart is said to be responsible for twenty-five of them.[88]

Compared to the era of antitrust enforcement of the previous decades, the preservation of "competition" (that is "competition" as it had been understood over that earlier period) had suddenly come to an abrupt end. "The FTC is a gaunt and bloodied agency," said FTC Commissioner Andrew J. Strenio Jr. in 1988. "Since fiscal year 1980, there has been a drop of more than 40 percent in the work years allocated to antitrust enforcement. In the same period, merger filings skyrocketed to more than 320 percent of their 1980 level."[89]

The largest mergers to hit the grocery world took place in 1998. The first was between the largest and fifth-largest grocery chains in the country — Kroger's acquisition of Fred Meyer — forming a super-grocer almost twice the size of the next largest. Kroger came to operate supermarkets in 31 states. The other mega-merger was between the second- and fourth-largest firms — Albertsons and American Stores — with a combined 1,690 locations in 38 states.[90]

Major U.S. Mergers and Acquisitions of 1997–98

Acquiring and acquired retailer	Grocery stores acquired
Pacific Region:	
Safeway — Vons, 1997	325
Yucaipa — Fred Meyer, 1997	101
Yucaipa — Smiths Food & Drug, 1997	150
Yucaipa — Quality Foods Centers, 1997	203
Albertson's — Lucky (American Stores), 1998	448
Midwest Region:	
Albertson's — Jewel/Osco (American Stores), 1998	171
Northeast Region:	
Ahold — Stop & Shop, 1996	189
Ahold — Giant Food, Inc., 1998	176
Albertson's — Acme (American Stores), 1998	183
Food Lion — Hannaford, 1999	150
Southeast Region:	
Food Lion — Kash & Karry (Florida), 1997	100
Jitney Jungle — Delchamps, 1997	118
Inter-regional:	
Safeway — Dominicks, 1998	112
Kroger — Yucaipa/Fred Meyer, 1999	800
Safeway — Randalls, 1999	116

SOURCE: KAUFMAN, GROCERY RETAILERS DEMONSTRATE URGE TO MERGE, 2000[91]

The nationwide mega-merging of the late '90s concentrated markets even more intensely at the local level. In 1998, market concentration of the four largest chains was more than 90 percent in Buffalo-Niagara Falls, New York; 73 percent in Hartford, Connecticut; 68 percent in Cleveland-Akron, Ohio; and 66 percent in the Boston, Massachusetts, metro area.[92]

In the 2000s, the most influential factor in the concentrating of markets was the opening of new Supercenters by Walmart. With only 500 Supercenters in 1999, Walmart had amassed almost 3,000 of them by the end of 2011. Their national market share of grocery retail ballooned from 6.4 percent in 2001 to 30 percent in 2009. Walmart had left the other grocery giants in the dust.[93] This propelled another wave of mega-mergers among Walmart's most immediate competitors.

Today, with the advent of online grocery and smaller alternative format stores, yet another wave of mergers and acquisitions is expected.[94]

Notable Grocery Mergers and Acquisitions, U.S./Canada 2012–17

2012	BI-LO — Winn-Dixie
2013	Sobeys — Canada Safeway Ltd. (Canada)
2014	Albertsons — Supervalu
2014	Kroger — Harris Teeter
2014	Safeway — Albertsons
2015	Ahold — Delhaize
2015	Kroger — Roundy's
2017	Amazon — Whole Foods

The Accelerating of Supermarket Dominance

A few important historical developments aided in the accelerating of supermarket dominance: 1) Advancements in technology; 2) Commanding of authority over the supply chain; and 3) The entry of Walmart into grocery retail.

Through the introduction of computerized inventory management systems and retailer distribution systems, grocery giants were able to grow at a feverish pace. It was the grocery retail sector that introduced the Universal Product Code (UPC or barcode) in 1973, and this became the standard across most industries.[95] In the 1990s, as the price of computers came down, chain retailers adopted systems that revolutionized food retail like the integrating of inventory tracking across an entire company. Individual store locations would now communicate automatically with centralized distribution centers, and suppliers would be automatically notified when it became time for the next order. These innovations enabled individual stores to grow in size by an average of 1,000 square feet per year for three decades.[96] The average number of products available per store increased from 14,145 in 1980 to 21,949 in 1994[97] and over 30,000 by 2004.[98]

The accelerating of dominance was also aided through increasing power over suppliers. As the retail market concentrated into fewer and fewer hands, the number of markets for foodmakers to sell into decreased. As a result, grocery giants increased their power to dictate terms and conditions "upstream."

Another, often-overlooked influence on the rise to power of the chain retailers has been consumer naivety (or indifference). Today, the dominance of the chain stores operating in communities elicits little more than a murmur among eaters. Instead, dissent within the food system is often placed on the Monsantos, Coca-Colas, and McDonalds of the world — rarely do we see campaigns to expose Kroger, Sobeys, or Shop n' Save for their influence on food, people, and the planet. Compared to the chain store uprisings of the 1920s and '30s, North American eaters and regulators have been asleep at the plate.

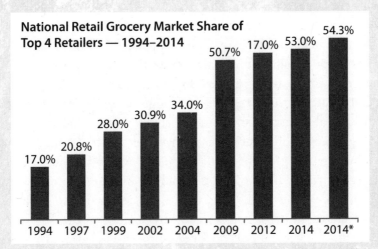

National Retail Grocery Market Share of Top 4 Retailers — 1994–2014

17.0% (1994), 20.8% (1997), 28.0% (1999), 30.9% (2002), 34.0% (2004), 50.7% (2009), 17.0% (2012), 53.0% (2014), 54.3% (2014*)

*Post Albertsons-Safeway merger. SOURCE: FOOD & WATER WATCH[99]

Regulating Market Power Today

The Reagan era put an end to enforcement of the Robinson-Patman Act despite the act having never been repealed. Antitrust cases involving grocery retailers have since been sparse.[100]

The most substantial case in recent memory was the approved acquisition of Safeway (U.S.) by Albertsons in 2015. The merger was the largest in the sector since the '90s. Prior to its approval by the FTC, it was clear that the merger as proposed would have left many local markets exceptionally concentrated, some of them becoming textbook monopolies. Baker City, Oregon (pop. 10,000), is a great example, with its two main grocery stores having been Albertsons and Safeway. This would have effectively left eaters in Baker City at the mercy of a monopoly. In the interest of protecting local markets like Baker City, the FTC ordered Albertsons to sell off 168 stores (7 percent of its total store count). A total of 146 of those locations, including Baker City's Albertsons, were sold to Haggen — a small Northwest chain of 18 stores. Then, in what would make for an excellent episode of an antitrust sitcom with a bit of corporate conspiracy thrown into the mix, only one year following the merger, Albertsons bought back 29 of those stores — including the Baker City location. The FTC did nothing to prevent the buyback.

It turned out Haggen's acquisition of the 146 stores was a disaster and they blamed Albertsons. On September 1, 2015, Haggen sued Albertsons for $1 billion. Haggen alleged that, following the acquisition, Albertons used its existing market dominance to engage in "coordinated and systematic efforts" to eliminate Haggen as a viable competitor in over 130 local grocery markets in five states.[101] The evidence presented by Haggen was telling, but the case never went to trial. Only one week following the filing of the suit, Haggen filed for Chapter 11 bankruptcy, and by March 2016, Haggen had become an Albertsons-owned chain of stores. This circus might be all that's needed to capture the modern era of antitrust enforcement. In practice, antitrust laws have become tools to keep prices low for consumers. The free rein granted to the oligopolies and oligopsonies of today has, as Barry Lynn suggests, become a "license to the powerful to fence off entire marketplaces ...

to pit supplier against supplier, community against community, and worker against worker for their own private gain."[102]

The Generational Effect and Self-Reinforcing Apathy

One of the most overlooked failures of the previous three decades of antitrust enforcement has been the inability of competition authorities to fully consider the multi-generational effects of highly concentrated grocery retail markets (the effects of which are expanded upon in the next two chapters).

The antitrust proponents of the first half of the twentieth century had understood how their efforts then would impact generations to come. So what could possibly have happened to the extraordinarily active resistance that had once reached the highest levels of our democratic institutions? This book will take us directly into the heart of where some of that resistance was channeled (thank goodness!), but the search for this lost defiance among our *dominant* culture and within our most influential institutions remains a highly relevant question. The Reagan era and its dismantling of mechanisms to protect people and communities might very well mark the beginning of one of the greatest dearths of resistance to one of the greatest removals of liberty in American history.

Thankfully, long before the attrition of community self-reliance, there were people who could foresee the impending societal crossroads that the industrial revolution was sowing. In his book *Democracy in America,* published in two volumes in 1835 and 1840, French diplomat Alexis de Tocqueville warned of the unrestrained powers that the emerging industrial revolution might one day yield.[103] He warned of the risks to the human spirit from the long-distance control of anything a community could otherwise manage on its own. Placing the power of our needs and desires into the hands of a centralized few would, Tocqueville believed, force people "to set their own will habitually and completely aside." In other words, should a small but increasingly powerful number of companies assume dominance over the economics of our lives, a self-reinforcing apathy among the population would install itself. Accompanying this centrally controlled consumerism would be "petty domestic interests" that would compel a narrow seeking of immediate pleasures to mask all that is missing from our lives. "I tremble, I confess," writes Tocqueville, "that [people] might eventually allow themselves to become so entranced by a contemptible love of present pleasures that their interest in their own future and the future of their offspring might disappear." Prophetic.

Who Owns Your Grocery Store?

Grocery Story has compiled a resource online of U.S. and Canadian grocery giants and the many banners they operate.

www.grocerystory.coop

Food Prices and the
People Who Grow Our Food

"The overwhelming consensus is that prices rise and in general supermarkets set prices less competitively, as concentration increases."[104]

— Richard Volpe, Economic Research Service,
United States Department of Agriculture

T HE PRICE WE PAY FOR GROCERIES might be one of the most persistent, anxiety-inducing deliberations that consumes (maybe even haunts) us. For some, current economic realities leave zero capacity to take the time to consider just *how* the price of food is determined or how our grocery bill impacts every other link in the food chain. Simply making sure food appears on our family's plates is all that we can realistically achieve, and to be sure, is an achievement to be well proud of. For those who *are* able to step beyond the food price "front lines," unpacking the complex world of food prices can aid us in the work of reshaping food systems and reimagining our grocery stores.

Not surprisingly, a direct correlation can be found between the concentration of power among the grocery giants and the prices we pay for food.[105] Similarly, as mergers among grocery retailers increase, prices paid to farmers decrease. This is significant. Most hidden from the aisles of our supermarkets is the effect our food system has on the people most responsible for feeding us. The evidence is beyond dispute — market power at all levels of the food system has dealt significant harm to the women, men, and families producing and harvesting our food.

The most extreme expression of this harm is the most difficult to speak of and yet the most important ...

... farmers are in crisis.

Incidents of farmer suicides receive little attention among consumers. Although it's been difficult to determine clear suicide rates among farmers as many incidents go unreported, it's well understood that suicides and underlying mental health challenges require urgent attention. Much of this is linked to the farm-income crisis of the previous thirty years.

While it would be inaccurate to place blame of farmer suicides on market power alone, the evidence we have available to us today draws a convincing line between the two. Without question, the cutthroat culture of grocery retailing and the upstream effects it has on the rest of the food system is pushing farmers to the brink.

The Farm Crisis of the 1980s

In her widely discussed *Guardian* article of December 2017, former Arizona vegetable farmer Debbie Weingarten writes of her own experience as a farmer that left her dealing with rising farm debt and depression before finally choosing to leave the profession in 2014. "We were growing food, but couldn't afford to buy it." [106] Her experience echoes that of many farmers over the previous decades.

The farm crisis of the 1980s was the worst to hit farmers since the Great Depression. A combination of increasing debt, soaring interest rates, a spike in oil prices, and the ensuing recession sent farm incomes and farmland value downward. It was out of this crisis that the Farm Aid organization was founded by Willie Nelson, John Mellencamp, and Neil Young. Farm Aid's annual concert to support farm families in crisis continues today, but the crisis remains. At its root is farm income.

Canada's National Farmers Union (NFU) has done excellent work tracking the over-thirty-year-old crisis. Between 1942 and 1982, realized net income (RNI) per farm remained steady between $10,000 and $20,000.[v] In 1985, RNI dropped to zero. With the exception of a mid-'90s rise, it remained near zero for the rest of the 1980s and 1990s. Then the crisis worsened. In 2000, RNI plummeted into the negative,

---

v   RNI is taxable income and does not include government subsidies. There was one exception to the steadiness between 1942 and 1982 of a three-year spike.

dropping as low as negative $20,000.[107] Farmers began subsidizing our food out-of-pocket or through debt. Despite modest increases since then, realized net income remains below zero. In the United States, it has declined 50 percent since 2013, with median farm income for 2018 projected to be negative $1,316.[108] How is this possible? How is it that, in their effort to feed us, the average farm family is losing money?

The most concise explanation for negative farm income can be found in commodity prices — the money farmers receive for the food they produce. Quite simply, the prices many farmers receive are below the cost it takes to produce the food.[109]

Following the release of a report on the farm income crisis published in 2005 by Canada's food and agriculture regulator, the NFU criticized the report for having "buried" among an extensive list of possible causes what the NFU believes is the "real" cause: "market power" — more precisely, a *lack* of market power among farmers and their "resultant inability to demand fair prices or to drive down costs."[110] That "power" has allowed the most dominant players in the food system to dictate terms and extract more and more out of the consumer food dollar, leaving less and less for farmers.

The "Farm Share" and "Marketing Share" of Our Food Dollars

An easily understood measure of farmer power in the marketplace is the "farm share" — the portion farmers receive of the food dollar that you and I each spend at restaurants, fast-food outlets, convenience stores, and the grocery checkout. It's the total cost to produce the food before it leaves the farm gate, as a percentage of the cost to the consumer. These figures have been calculated annually in the United States since 1946.

By comparing the farm share with the remaining share of the food dollar (the "marketing share"), we have a wonderful tool to help us understand how our food dollar is distributed throughout the food system.

> "Farm share": Portion of the food dollar ending up at
> the farm (the cost to produce the food, including what
> ends up in a farmer's pocket).

"Marketing share" (or "trade spend"): Every additional cost it takes to get food from farm to plate (includes "labor expenses for handling, sorting, cleaning, and packaging the product, transportation charges to move the product along at each stage, and fees for processing, storing, insuring, financing, and retailing the product"[vi]).[111]

So here's the most revealing of farm share figures.... For every dollar spent on food, the portion that ends up at the farm (the farm share) is at its lowest point in history: 14.8 cents.[112] In 1950, by comparison, farmers received considerably more of that dollar: 40 cents.[113]

The farm share and marketing share help us begin to understand where power in the food system resides — particularly the power to set prices. Without question, the plummeting farm share of the food dollar since 1950 has left farmers with less power to determine their future.

Farm Share of U.S. Food Expenditures Has Declined Since 1950

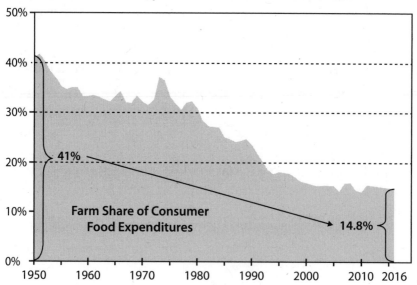

SOURCE: SCHNEPF, *FARM-TO-FOOD PRICE DYNAMICS, 2013*[114]; USDA ERS, *FOOD DOLLAR SERIES, 2016*[115]

---

vi   Retailing costs may include grocery store maintenance and utilities, refrigeration, labeling, shelf display, advertising, and promotional costs.

| Farm Share | Market |

| 14.8% | 85.2% |

Total Farm Share — 2016 (All Food Purchases^vii). Source: USDA ERS, Food Dollar Series, 2016[116]

Farmers' Share of Select Grocery Items — 2018^viii

	Retail ($)	Farmer ($)
Bacon (1lb)	4.99	0.74
Top Sirloin Steak (1lb)	8.99	2.01
Bread (2lb)	3.49	0.12
Carrots (5lb)	4.49	1.55
Cereal (18oz)	5.09	0.05
Tomatoes (1lb)	3.99	0.34
Potatoes (Russet, 5lb)	4.49	0.56

Source: National Farmers Union (U.S.), 2018[117]

---

vii   Includes both food purchased for consumption "*away* from the home" and for consumption "*at* home."

viii   Farm share figures differ between commodities. After leaving the farm, some foods require more processing and handling than others. A dozen eggs requires significantly *less* handling and processing than the wheat used in a loaf of bread. Accordingly, an average 53.7% of the price of eggs at the checkout ends up back at the farm compared to only 8.3% of the price of cereals and bakery products [Schnepf]. These differences are neither good nor bad — they're just the reality of a diversity of foods requiring different levels of processing.

Squeezing Food Dollars Through Bottlenecks

Whether you're a farmer, fisher, slaughterhouse operator, or cupcake maker, access to eaters in our communities has become concentrated into fewer hands — the grocery gatekeepers. As their share of the retail market has become more concentrated through growth, acquisitions, and mergers, so too has every other sector of the food economy concentrated into fewer hands. In the fertilizer sector, Agrium merged with Potash in 2018 to form Nutrien — a mega-producer/retailer of farm inputs. In the seed/chemical sector, Bayer's acquisition of Monsanto was approved in 2018 by the U.S. Justice Department. In the manufacturing sector, Kraft and Heinz merged in 2015 to form the fourth-largest food and beverage manufacturer in the world. These consolidations have been the inevitability of an unrestrained market. For every other sector of the food system to effectively negotiate with the grocery gatekeepers from a place of power and not servitude, the entire chain of events from farm/sea to retail has met that power with its own levels of concentration, thus transforming the entirety of the system into a series of bottlenecks that food must now pass through.

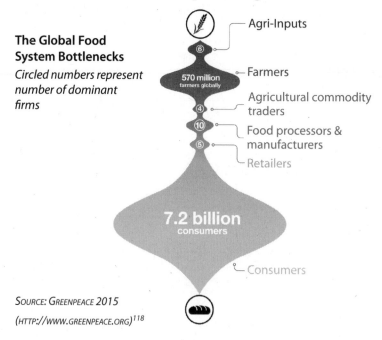

The Global Food System Bottlenecks

Circled numbers represent number of dominant firms

Agri-Inputs

⑥

570 million
farmers globally
Farmers

④ Agricultural commodity traders

⑩ Food processors & manufacturers

⑤ Retailers

7.2 billion
consumers

Consumers

Source: Greenpeace 2015
(http://www.greenpeace.org)[118]

At each bottleneck, the grip on the food dollar has become tighter and tighter over time, squeezing just a little more out whenever the opportunity arises. When viewed over a timespan of decades, these "squeezes" have become fully-fledged "drainings." The primary food producer — the farmer — has been drained most of all, receiving less and less of the consumer food dollar with each passing year.

One example of the lengths to which the system will go to extract wealth out of the food system and out of farmers' pockets is shown in a chart released by North America's largest retailer/distributor of urea (nitrogen) fertilizer, Agrium Inc., in their 2001 annual report. The chart demonstrates how, as the price of corn rose and fell between 1981 and 2001, the price of urea (on which farmers relied) followed it in perfect unison. In other words, at every point where farmers might have benefited from strong corn prices, the fertilizer giants were there to extract those gains. This pattern of extraction runs throughout the whole food system and would not be possible if traditional models of competitive agricultural markets had not been all but gutted.[119]

Nitrogen Prices Follow Grain Prices

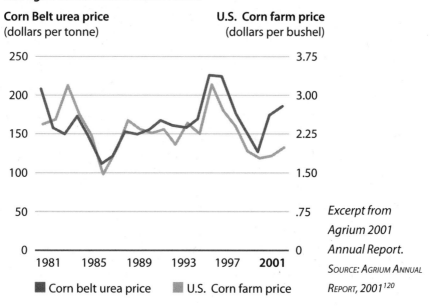

Excerpt from Agrium 2001 Annual Report.

Source: Agrium Annual Report, 2001[120]

Farm inputs like fertilizer are just one of the bottlenecks our food dollar passes through. Food manufacturing is another bottleneck receiving a hefty portion of the food dollar. In approximately one-third of grocery categories, at least 75 percent of the foods comprising that category are controlled by four or fewer companies. Kellogg, General Mills, PepsiCo, and Post Foods, for instance, manufacture 86 percent of all breakfast cereals found on supermarket shelves.[121] Breakfast cereal production has notoriously been a highly concentrated market, and not surprisingly, manufacturers have received their share of scrutiny for suspicious pricing. Between 1983 and 1994, while overall food prices rose by 45 percent, cereal prices skyrocketed by 90 percent.[122] This level of concentration is ubiquitous across many grocery categories. In baked beans, four companies control 91 percent of the market. Yogurt — three companies control 75.8 percent. Cream cheese — one company controls 60.9 percent of the market.[123] As consolidation throughout the food system has increased, so too has the ability of the system to extract wealth.

Consumer Demand for Convenience: A Contributor to Declining Farm Share

A declining farm share is not in and of itself a smoking gun for corporate greed. Eaters have played a role too. Rising consumer demand for convenience has played a substantial role in farm share declines. The more "value" is added to a commodity (e.g., frozen foods, precooked foods, ready-to-eat foods), the smaller the portion of the food dollar a farmer will receive.[ix] In fact most of the declines in farm share since

---

ix   In an ideal setting, so long as consumers are proportionally paying more for value-added foods, the prices farmers receive for their commodity should not necessarily change. But on average, that's not happening. Much of the analysis of these trends over time suggests that much of the cost of those innovations that add value for consumers have in effect been paid for at the producer level of the food chain in the form of substantially reduced margins. That's a clear sign of the power of the system to extract wealth *out* of the system and *out* of the farmer's portion of the food dollar.

the 1990s can be attributed to the rise in "away-from-home" eating as well as consumer demand for more processed and ready-to-eat foods. This is an important reminder for eaters — the more we eat out and the more processed and "convenient" are the foods we consume, the less power in the marketplace farmers have (not to mention the more we end up spending on food). Turns out, cooking at home and from scratch helps farmers retain greater power in the marketplace.

Farm Value vs. Retail Price

How about paying more for our food? Surely farmers would receive more income if food prices rose? Maybe so at a farmers' market but not necessarily at grocery stores, where a complex array of companies influence and handle the product from farm all the way into your kitchen — each wanting a greater piece of the pie. As checkout prices increase, farmers may not benefit correspondingly. The USDA maintains up-to-date data on the "farm-to-retail price spreads" of many foods. The charts below demonstrate how increases in food prices over time do not necessarily transmit into farm value.[x] Yes, some of that widening spread between retail prices and farm value can be attributed to rising costs of the marketing share (energy, transportation, packaging), but it's hard to believe that in an age of high technological advancements and greater efficiencies, such rapidly growing spreads are solely the result of increasing marketing costs. The breakdown of influences on price spreads is an ongoing debate. When former antitrust attorney for the U.S. Department of Justice Peter Carstensen was asked about price spreads in the beef sector, he refused to agree that "cost-increasing elements" are the sole cause of widening price spreads. "I'm very skeptical that unit costs have gone up as substantially as the spreads have gone up," Carstensen continued; "Most data suggests wages have gone down in [meat] packing plants — and many plants are increasingly mechanized in ways that are intended to lower costs, not increase costs." He

---

x   Farm value is the portion farmers keep for themselves *after* expenses.

believes the widening price spreads indicate a failure of the market-ing system to reflect back to the producer the revenue potential of the livestock.[124]

The late distinguished agricultural economist Wayne Purcell pointed the finger at the grocery giants: "Retailers ... are increasingly telling [meat] packers what to do.... Retailers mandate to packers how they want meat cut, packaged, labeled and bar-coded. They stipulate assur-ances on safety and, to top it off, they want packers to maintain and manage their inventory. If retailers are pulling $500–$600/head out of a $1,200/head retail value — as it appears they are — I wonder why it is that they need so much of the share? Of all the players along the beef supply chain, the retailers do the least to add value to the product."[125]

Retail price spreads offer us two windows into the role of grocery stores. They invite the question of how much of the spread can be attributed to market power, and they remind us of how the more dis-tant and complex a food system becomes, the more of our food dollar is invested into everything *but* farmers.

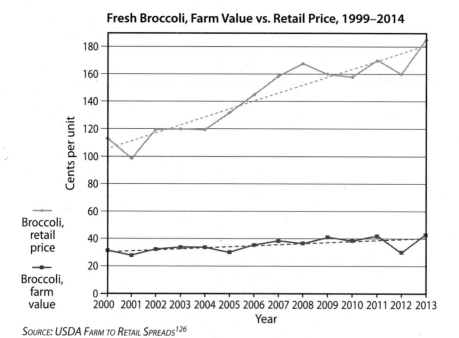

Fresh Broccoli, Farm Value vs. Retail Price, 1999–2014

Broccoli, retail price

Broccoli, farm value

Source: USDA Farm to Retail Spreads[126]

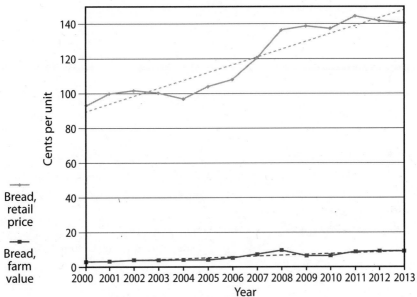

Bread, Farm Value vs. Retail Price, 1999–2014

SOURCE: USDA FARM TO RETAIL SPREADS

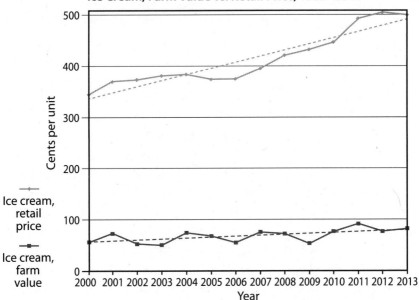

Ice Cream, Farm Value vs. Retail Price, 1999–2014

SOURCE: USDA FARM TO RETAIL SPREADS

Canada's NFU Describes the Farm Income Crisis Using a Loaf of Bread

"In 1975, from a [43¢] loaf of bread, the farmer received a nickel, and the millers, bakers, and grocers took 38¢. Today [for a $1.35 loaf], the farmer receives the same nickel and the millers, bakers, and grocers take $1.30. One might describe the Canadian farm income crisis thus: A customer puts $1.35 on a grocery store counter for a loaf of bread. Powerful food retailers, processors, and grain companies take $1.30, leaving the farmer just a nickel. Powerful energy, fertilizer, chemical, and machinery companies take 6 cents out of the farmer's pocket. Taxpayers return the penny."[127]

The National Farmers Union's Submission to
the Minister of Agriculture, 2005

Eaters Pay the Price for Concentrated Markets

So here we are, eating in a world where every time the price of food goes up, the largest agriculture and food corporations capture a little more of the food dollar while farmers are left in crisis. What about eaters?

From PricewaterhouseCoopers[128] to the FTC[129] to the USDA, the overwhelming consensus is that "supermarkets set prices less competitively, as concentration increases."[130] In concert, the consumer price for food rises.

At the more local level, high concentration among retailers enables competitors to *tacitly* coordinate pricing strategies. Put another way, they may never meet in a dark alley and plot their pricing strategies, but they do pay extremely close attention to one another's pricing, and with only a few others to watch out for, a form of indirect price-fixing emerges. In one study from 2011, two of Seattle's largest retailers were found to be matching each other's milk prices, leaving consumers to pay more for milk than in other parts of the country.[131] This is in line with general theories on oligopoly power, whereby in markets with only a few dominant firms, those companies are less likely to adopt aggressive strategies that might accelerate competition and jeopardize their chances of larger profits.

In one analysis of the localized impacts of market concentration, the grocery price index (GPI) was found to exhibit the largest increases in the most concentrated geographic markets between 2004 and 2011. The GPI increased three times more in "highly concentrated metro areas" than in "moderately concentrated" areas. The rising prices in the more concentrated areas outpaced overall inflation.[132]

Change in Grocery Price Index by Change in Number of Grocery Chains and Market Concentration Level, 2004-2011

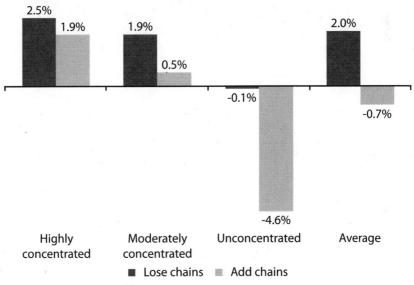

Source: Food & Water Watch[133]

But wait! What about those "low low" prices I always see? Doesn't a stronger supermarket sector with greater purchasing power lead to lower prices? Certainly in many cases it does. Deals may be so low, we make specific trips just for those products. When Walmart took over U.K. grocery giant Asda in 1999, Asda's banana prices dropped by 20 percent.[134] But once we're in the store for that great deal, bananas are likely not the only product ending up in our shopping cart. The grocery giants know this. While it's fun to *believe* that the low prices in the weekly flyer are the result of the grocer offering up some form of pseudo community service, the grocer is aware of such delusions among consumers. They may offer low prices on select items, but may very well increase retail prices overall, and, over time. They do. Those increases may be imperceptible in the short term, but in the long term they have the power to transform what we, at the consumer end of the spectrum, come to define as "normal."

What's happening in food echoes a general trend among goods and services in America. In a working paper from the National Bureau of Economic Research, the authors analyzed data on publicly traded American firms from 1950 to 2014. "From 1950 to 1980, average mark-ups — that is, what firms charge customers above their cost of production — were relatively low (and flat), at about 18 percent over cost. Since 1980, however, mark-ups have risen steadily, to 67 percent on average. That translates into growth in the consumer-price level relative to firms' costs of about 1 percent per year."[135]

Brazen Market Coordination

In some cases, market coordination is intentional, albeit secretive. In 2007, U.K. grocery heavyweights Asda and Sainsbury's admitted to fixing the price of dairy between 2002 and 2003. It was calculated that the scheme cost eaters the equivalent today of $438 million.[136] Despite a crime of such magnitude, Asda and Sainsbury's remained two of the largest grocers in the United Kingdom. Presumably, in 2018 (and with my own slight tongue-in-cheek), the two companies finally realized that colluding with one another was far too difficult and risky, and instead announced plans to merge into one single company.[xi] This might now be the most brazen example of tacit and legal "collusion" that the world has come to accept as normal — the merging of already-dominant firms.

---

xi   At the time of publication, the planned merger was being investigated by
        the U.K.'s Competition and Markets Authority.

Mergers Decrease Prices Paid to Farmers

In what is known as "perfect competition," there exists many buyers, many sellers, and many transactions taking place. The market price for any commodity is beyond the control or influence of any one buyer or seller. This diversity of participants and frequency of transactions creates what can best be described as a resilient economic "ecosystem." In this ecosystem, perfect competition thrives. Alternatively, when the number of participants decreases (i.e., fewer and fewer retailers), the number of transactions also decreases. The ecosystem loses diversity. It has been demonstrated that when the number of transactions in a food market decreases, so to do prices at the farm gate.[137]

Consider the menu at an upscale restaurant. Generally, each item on the menu is accompanied by a price; however, in some cases, there is one item on the menu with no price listed — the "Catch of the Day" — the fish dish. In place of the price; the menu reads "Market Price (check with your server)." This is one end of the food price spectrum where day-to-day consumer prices are completely dependent on what the market dictates. This is what perfect competition looks like from the perspective of the eater ... prices adjust relative to what the food producers (or fishers) require to sustain their business.

The general practice among retailers to avoid adjusting prices relative to general theories of supply and demand not only is indicative of oligopsony power, but is damaging to farmers, so much so it compelled California lettuce growers in 1992 to take out ads in major U.S. newspapers decrying retailers' high shelf prices despite the growers selling their product at historic lows.[138] Put another way, the lettuce growers were successfully producing a product at low cost, and by all logic, we eaters should benefit from that at the checkout. We don't. The grocer instead prefers to maintain a level price for as long as possible so as to not throw their shoppers off script. This practice completely upends general economic models. Experts warn of the consequences to even basic projections of the farm and food economy resulting from even modest departures from competitive pricing. "Predicting the market through traditional economic models no longer applies," says Richard Sexton. "Any analysis of the market based upon the traditional competitive model will lead anyone to severely biased conclusions."[139]

The uninitiated shopper would be left to wonder why the lettuce growers don't simply hold back their lettuce or refuse to sell it. It's an entirely logical question, and would be a wonderful option in a world of perfect competition. But that's not the world we live in. Power in the marketplace in most commodities, particularly in fresh fruit and vegetables, is heavily weighted toward the buyer — the grocery giants. Lettuce is the most perishable of all foods, leaving growers with little to no power to dictate terms to the mere handful of grocery gatekeepers available to buy their product.

When a former chief executive officer of the now-defunct Somerfield chain of stores in the United Kingdom was asked about the pending sale of Safeway (U.K.) to Morrisons in 2003, his insight into the power-over position of retailers was telling. "If [another supermarket chain] bought Safeway, terms for suppliers would be renegotiated down to the lowest price and a further volume discount demanded."[140]

This is exactly what happened in Canada when Sobeys acquired Safeway (Canada) in November 2013. In a letter addressed to its suppliers dated December 24, Sobeys informed suppliers that it would not accept price increases through 2014 and further demanded a 1 percent price reduction retroactive to November 3.[141]

The Most Extreme Expression of the Farm Income Crisis

One of the hardest hit groups of the farm income crisis are American dairy farmers. Studies have shown how when retail prices have risen, prices paid to producers have decreased. Often, the cost to produce milk is above the price farmers receive.

Suicide among dairy farmers is correspondingly high. On the morning of January 19, 2009, 59-year-old farmer Dean Pierson of Copake, New York, used a small-caliber rifle to kill each one of his cows before turning the gun on himself. In the note he left, one word described Pierson's turmoil: "overwhelmed."

At the time he killed himself, the price of milk had dropped to half of what it was the year prior. By comparison, in those first three months of 2009, the largest milk processor in the United States recorded earnings of $75.3 million — twice its earnings in the same period a year earlier.[142]

So why do farmers keep doing it? Why keep working at something that produces such hardship? In many cases, they don't, they pack up, treat their wounds, and either find alternative employment or retire. In describing those who stay the course and choose to suffer, some have identified a unique human quality among farmers that compels them to continue: "People engaged in farming have a strong urge to supply essentials for human life, such as food and materials for clothing, shelter, and fuel, and to hang on to their land and other resources needed to produce these goods at all costs." This is the Agrarian Imperative Theory put forward by Dr. Mike Rosmann, an Iowa psychologist on the front lines of the mental health crisis affecting farmers. When agricultural producers are unable to supply the necessities of food, as Rosmann explains, "they feel they are letting down those who depend on them — foremost their family and community — as well as consumers generally."[143] Rosmann is clear on one thing — the rate of farmer suicides rises and falls in accordance with their economic well-being.

At the Ontario Veterinary College at the University of Guelph in Ontario, a group of researchers studied responses to a national survey on stress filled out by 1,100 farmers. The survey found 45 percent of respondents had high stress. Another 58 percent were classified with varying levels of anxiety, and 35 percent with depression. The frequency with which farmers seek professional help is also low due to stigmas in agriculture associated with mental health. A total of 40 percent of respondents said they would be uneasy getting professional help "because of what people might think."[144] Another farmer commented, "We are not invincible, but we feel we must be." And another, "What makes me the most upset is that I have everything I dreamed of — love, family, and a farm — and all I feel is overwhelmed, out of control, and sad."[145]

Grocery Stores –
the Food System's Control Center

"With the exception of the recent price-fixing scheme of Canada's grocery giants, even in today's free-for-all marketplace buoyed by a highly receptive and responsive consumer, the grocery giants are generally not so naive to overtly, in broad daylight, gouge the food system upon which they rely — namely farmers, food processors, manufacturers, and eaters. Instead, there is a swindling of epic proportions that flies under the radar of even the most scrupulous of shoppers. Using cues from the once all-mighty A&P, the largest food retailers of today employ practices that in Wilson's and FDR's America would have left the big chains living their lives out in courtrooms (and possibly jail cells). In what has now grown into an often subtle, and sometimes overt, way of doing business, a sort of "tacit collusion" has become the new and accepted norm. This anti-competitive business as usual goes completely undetected because, for the most part, few of us are paying close enough attention ... until now."

G ROCERY STORES ARE LIVING MUSEUMS of the Earth's bounty and of the relationships humans have cultivated with each other, with plants and animals, and with the creatures of the sea. The "exhibits" of the grocery "museum" are nothing short of amazing — exotic foods like Nicaraguan bananas, Thai shrimp, or Chilean asparagus. But unlike a museum, the grocery store offers little information on the history of those foods, how they were curated or the journeys they took to get there.

To maintain such power locally, regionally, nationally, and globally, the grocery giants have had to successfully test the boundaries of the law, assess the responses (or lack thereof) of regulators and policy-makers and use those experiences to carefully position themselves on the fence of legality. While the grocery giants may present themselves as authorities on health and nutrition and purveyors of abundance and choice, behind the curtain is one of the greatest cons in the history of food. So pervasive and acculturated is the deception that many working the con don't even know they're working it.

Business as usual for the grocery giants of today includes the capacity to grant a supplier its very existence or serve it a sentence for its obliteration.

When Walmart floated the idea to Vlasic to retail one-gallon jars of pickles for $2.97, Vlasic couldn't resist the opportunity to supply the world's largest retailer. In short order, Walmart was selling 240,000 gallons of pickles every week out of its 3,000 stores. Walmart only made a penny or two a jar. Vlasic was losing money on the deal. When Vlasic told Walmart they would need to up the price, Walmart refused and threatened to stop buying Vlasic's other products.[146]

The chain retailers have become ruthless in their dealings with suppliers. Interactions like this are conducted behind the shelves of our "neighborhood" grocery stores every day.

To maintain their "power-over" position in the marketplace, a number of stunning practices are almost universally employed[xii] by the dominant grocers — a set of "controls" at the grocery giants' disposal.

Shaping Food — Literally

During my first forays into backyard gardening, I recall an astonishing post-harvest discovery — the food coming out of my garden had significantly *less* shelf life than the grocery-store versions I had grown accustomed to.

The refrigerated lifespan of grocery-variety broccoli is a marvel of the modern world. The stuff will last for weeks! My garden broccoli?

---

xii   Or have simply become business-as-usual

Not so much. Two to three days post-harvest, the yellowing would set in. Same with garden strawberries. Two days tops before they began their rapid descent into the compost.

The durability of "fresh" fruit and vegetables has everything to do with the market power of the grocery giants.[147] Grocery stores have quite literally come to shape the food we eat — the appearance, the texture, the flavor, the nutritional profile, the varieties grown, and the trajectory of most university plant breeding programs, all of it either intentionally or inadvertently. Same goes for government oversight of food production. USDA standards for grades of fresh tomatoes are really just a recipe developed by and for the shelves of the highly coordinated national chains. "Color, size, maturity, firmness, shape, smoothness, freedom from defects and freedom from decay, freezing injury and sunscald," these are the cosmetic requirements of the supermarket. To meet such stringent requirements, growers plant strains that are disease-resistant and have tough skins and a "just-so" shape to make packing them into boxes that much easier.[148]

I remember standing in a tomato field of DiMare Fresh, one of North America's largest growers and distributors of "fresh" tomatoes. It was here where I really learned how subjective one's definition of "fresh" could be. If "fresh" is harvesting a rock-hard, pale green tomato and placing it in a temperature- and humidity-controlled room with just the right amount of ethylene gas piped in to affect ripening, then "yes," these tomatoes were super "fresh"! If you've ever wondered why, rather than being a luscious ruby red, the internal flesh of your tomato is a pale pink, maybe even white — that's why — the tomato has never had a chance to fully ripen, the ethylene gas having never penetrated the interior of the fruit. Not surprisingly, these "factory" tomatoes are almost completely devoid of flavor.

Losses in Flavor

Long-distance transportation requirements were not the only influence on the genetics of the modern tomato. To meet the high-volume, low-cost demands of the emerging grocery giants of the 1940s, growers looked to cut costs and expedite harvesting. Harvesting a field tomato when dark-green presented a unique challenge — visibility. A green tomato is the same color as the leaves, making it more difficult to notice by the people picking the fruit. Enter the plant breeders and their capacity to select genetics that would yield a highly visible, light-green tomato[149] and promote even ripening throughout the individual fruit.[150] It was a remarkable achievement, until ... seventy years later, when it was discovered that the dark green color was responsible for flavor. It was also revealed that by removing the fruit from the plant *prior* to the tomato being fully ripe, flavor was even further reduced. The leaves of a fruit-producing plant or tree are the sugar-producing factories of the fruit itself. Remove the tomato from the plant before it's ripe and sugar production comes to a halt ... and sugar equals flavor.[151] Eaters have effectively handed the keys to flavor over to the most influential grocers.

The long-term ripple effects of the grocery giants' requirements are fascinating. Losses in flavor, phytochemicals, and nutrients have accompanied the genetic development of most fruits, vegetables, grains, and animal products destined for the grocery store shelves.[152] Also lost has been the assurance of safe food.

Cosmetic Requirements and Food Safety

Meeting the cosmetic demands of the grocery giants has been linked to increases in the use of pesticides. As one carrot grower puts it, "We use more pesticides than we'd like to try to meet the cosmetic standards set." Another grower: "They want a perfect product that will keep for a week ... but trying to make quality last a week logically leads to more pesticides."[153]

The correlation between cosmetic requirements and the use of pesticides in the food system has been known for a long time. When the citrus rust mites of 1970s Florida caused oranges to develop superficial blemishes on their skin (with zero impact on internal quality), 87 percent of the entire crop was sprayed with two to three applications of miticide at an annual cost equivalent today of $250 million.[154] The pricey move ignored research from a decade earlier that had demonstrated no change in yields of the oranges receiving the spray compared with those remaining spray-free.[155] Yields were the same, making the application of this chemical purely cosmetic. Today, consumers not only foot the bill for these "non-essential" uses of chemicals, the tightening up of cosmetic standards forces the liberal use of chemicals in the field to protect crops from damage. A greater proportion of the food supply becomes contaminated with residues of insecticides and fungicides.[156]

Genetic Diversity

In a food culture of sameness, the grocery giants have also whittled down the genetic diversity of the global food supply. "If the supermarkets don't want them, the growers won't grow them,"[157] says one grower. With the disposal of diversity, grocers set food's genetic agenda. Sameness is rapidly becoming the global standard in the lab, in the field, and on the shelf. The grocers' trade associations are helping author this future. The Food Marketing Institute (FMI) is the largest trade association and lobbyist for U.S. grocery retail. FMI sets industry standards through its Safe Quality Food Institute (SQF). The slogan for SQF? "One World, One Standard."[158]

Another word for this global vision of sameness? "Boring."

Food Standards as Buyer Leverage

Food-quality standards and requirements can be used as leverage in the buyer-supplier relationship.[159] By drafting up purposefully vague standards, the buyer can use these as a bargaining chip to refuse some or all of a shipment. This (ab)use of power by the retailer further drives the grower to produce a perfect, bombproof product, using whatever means are legally available. With so few retailers to sell to, growers have little recourse but to accept the will of the grocer. The risk of losing access to the market is far too great.

With such high risk in the retailer-supplier relationship, growers also tend to overproduce. As one confesses, "I have to grow for the maximum size of a single order, or else I lose the contract. So I grow on that scale even though the order is usually a lot less. Everything I don't sell, I have to destroy."[160]

Standards and Food Waste

Leeks with eleven inches of white and one inch of green, tomatoes at color stage 5, broccoli with head diameter of seven to twelve centimeters;[161] when we become more aware of the demands placed on food and the people growing it, behold the power of that moment when we select an item from the grocery store shelf.

Supermarkets are driving the evolution of global horticulture and plant breeding, and their requirements are contributing to the epidemic of food waste. Today, half of all produce grown is wasted.[162] That's enough to pull one's hair out over, but remember, there's an already-implemented way out of this cosmetic catastrophe. We're getting there. Next chapters. Save your hair. But sitting with that figure for just one more moment ... let's really let it soak in. If half of all produce grown is wasted, who pays for the wasted food? We do. Farmers do. The environment does. Embedded in the price of our food is the financial cost of food waste. This is the model of the modern grocery industry.

The grocery giants have been swift to pass the food waste blame upstream and downstream. As one retail consortium of grocery giants claimed, "only 1.3 percent of all food waste came from the grocery retail industry."[163] They're only looking within their own walls — refusing to acknowledge the ripple effects of their sourcing policies and practices.

Marching Orders for Suppliers

"They know no loyalty to most of their suppliers. Of course the suppliers cannot say so because they would be talking about their customers, but I can say it. The truth is that supermarkets have distorted the relationship between producer, retailer, and consumer. They have done more than any other agency to damage the business of local supply. Unless the government faces

up to the issue of the unaccountable power of a handful of retailers, we shall not address the problems of
the relationship between producers and consumers or
reestablish in the consumer base a degree of market
intelligence. I suggest that supermarkets have produced
a situation where people neither know the price nor
the value of good food. That needs to be addressed by
this government — or by a government — as soon as
possible."

— U.K. Member of Parliament John Hayes, 2002[164]

Nowhere is the power of the grocery giants more evident, and the
alarm bells for change so loud, than in the strategies used by chain
grocers to maintain power over their suppliers. Because suppliers are
generally terrified at the thought of disclosing any real or perceived
wrongdoing by their own customers, this shadowy world evades the
radar of even the most conscientious of eaters. The British government's Office of Fair Trading calls it a "climate of apprehension among
suppliers."[165]

Thankfully, many examples have surfaced in recent years of bullish
behavior in grocery–supplier relations, particularly in markets with the
highest levels of retailer market concentration.

In 2015, the U.K.'s largest grocer, Tesco, was found guilty of deliberately and "unreasonably" holding back payments to their suppliers.
Some of the practices were made public by the U.K.'s new grocery
watchdog. In one instance, Tesco took "two years [to] repay a supplier who was owed a multi-million-pound sum for products it never
supplied." In another case, "a supplier waited for more than a year for
a £2m repayment due because of duplicate invoicing." In another,
"Tesco deliberately delayed payments at key financial reporting periods to bolster its bottom line, even if suppliers requested payments."
The investigator emphasized how "widespread" Tesco's behavior was.
"*Every* supplier I spoke to had evidence of delays in payments."[166]

Despite the findings, no charges were laid because each of the incidents took place before the watchdog had been officially established.

In 2014, Canada's Competition Bureau investigated the alleged "anti-competitive" policies of Canada's largest grocer. The unifying feature of the policies was that Loblaw "sought retroactive compensation from suppliers when [Loblaw's] profitability was negatively impacted by the competitive activity of other retailers." This was often done without prior agreement with the supplier.[167]

Loblaw's penalization policies fell into three categories:

> Price Competition — If Loblaw found out that a competing retailer was selling the same product at a lower price, Loblaw's policy was to lower its price and deduct the difference from the supplier. For example, if to match the price of a competing retailer, Loblaw reduced its retail price from $2.00 to $1.50, and if Loblaw sold 20,000 units of the product, the *supplier* of that product would be subject to a deduction of $10,000 from a future invoice.

> Non-price Competition — If a supplier offered a product to another retailer without offering, or without first offering, the product to Loblaw, the grocer would seek compensation from or impose deductions on the supplier.

> Margin Shielding — When Loblaw's own margins or profitability of a product fell below a threshold, Loblaw would seek compensation from the supplier to cover the decrease. If the loss was merely the result of low shopper demand for the product, Loblaw would still seek compensation from the supplier.[168]

If this sounds like an abuse of dominance, then your opinion differs from that of Canada's competition regulator, who found "insufficient evidence" to conclude that these policies "prevented competition substantially." Despite the absence of consequences, Loblaw appears to acknowledge wrongdoing(?). In 2016, as the investigation was underway, the company announced they would cease using many of these policies. That announcement came shortly after Loblaw confessed to fixing the price of bread with competing retailers between 2001 and 2016.

These examples only scratch the surface of the grocers' "hard bargaining" (as Canada's Competition Bureau calls it).[169]

In one of the most shocking practices, a British chain will fine suppliers £85 (equiv. $115) every time it receives a customer complaint about their product, even if the supplier is not at fault.[170]

While some may see "hard bargaining," others see a classic case of bullying.

Suppliers Finance Their Own Servitude

In a *Financial Times* investigation into the balance sheets of the U.K.'s grocery giants, results showed that the growth of Tesco and Asda had been financed by their suppliers:

"Working capital in a conventional business is the amount required to finance stock and debtors after deducting the credit made available by suppliers. But food retailing is different, in that stock is turned into cash at the check-out counters long before suppliers have to be paid. Debtors are relatively insignificant and creditors exceed stock by a considerable margin. So there is a negative working capital requirement. Trade credit can end up providing finance for investment in fixed assets. The result is a virtuous circle that has permitted £2bn to be released to help finance a combined £12bn of capital investment in Tesco and Asda over the past five years. For every £1bn of extra sales, these retailers have attracted roughly £100m of extra creditor finance. In effect, suppliers have acted as surrogate bankers to the two groups on a remarkable scale, contributing growing amounts of finance in a period when cash flow from depreciation covered only one-third of the combined investment outlay. This has reduced Tesco's and Asda's need for bank finance and support from the capital markets."[171]

Financial Times, December 6, 2005

Category Management

With the keys to the kingdom, the grocery gatekeepers possess a unique power to delegate roles and responsibilities upstream to their suppliers. Of all strategies used by the grocery chains today, one of the most recent is also the most head-spinning. Most antitrust scholars and authorities are still trying to figure out what to make of category management (CM). The practice itself is not inherently damaging, but the way it's used is highly questionable. For large food manufacturers, CM is an opportunity to become best buddies with the bully and avoid getting their ass whooped at recess.

CM involves assessing consumer demand of an entire category of products and stocking shelves according to that demand. It's a marketing science that analyzes consumer desires, behaviors, values, beliefs, social norms, and preferences. CM effectively turns the management of the entire grocery retail space into a collection of smaller businesses (or categories). The results of the science not only inform the stocking of shelves but aid in the design and layout of the entire retail floor of a supermarket. Whereas some retailers do this work internally, many have come to rely upon their suppliers to make these decisions for them. That's correct, food manufacturers, *not* retailers, are planning the shelves of the grocery stores we shop at.

A retailer will appoint a single manufacturer as a Category Captain and relinquish exclusive control of that category. The Captain will often be an industry leader like Nestlé. In one example, Nestlé has been the Captain for frozen desserts in 22 of the country's 25 largest chains.[172]

Typically, the Captain (manufacturer) will make recommendations and decisions on pricing and promotions, they'll stock and clean the shelves, and will analyze market data. Even more bewildering, a "category" of products comprises more than just the products of the appointed manufacturer. This leaves the Captain with the responsibility to manage the placement of *all* brands, including those the manufacturer directly competes with. "As an antitrust matter, it seems rather strange that you'd have one company advising a store on how to handle the product of its competitors," said former FTC Commissioner Thomas Leary. "Some aspects of category management present high antitrust risks."[173]

A Captain might also be responsible for category managing more than one retailer in the same market. This means that one supplier may be managing their competitors' products across multiple competing retailers in a single geographic region. The blurring of lines goes further. While some Captains will offer these services at no charge to the retailer, some retailers require payment from the manufacturer for the privilege of offering the service. This means that only manufacturers with deep enough pockets are able to compete for the captaincy. As one legal scholar writes, "Category captaincies can result in an exclusive vertical relationship between a retail chain and a single manufacturer. By its very nature, this exclusive arrangement reduces or eliminates competition." He projected that CM practices may, however, pass "unchallenged or even recognized" except for the most heinous of abuses.[174]

One example of "heinous abuse" in 2015 involved the three companies controlling 74 percent of the canned tuna market. The U.S. Department of Justice charged a senior executive at Bumble Bee Seafoods with price-fixing. He pleaded guilty.[175] The charges came only one month after *Progressive Grocer* — the grocery industry's leading publication — awarded a "Category Captain award" to Bumble Bee for having "leveraged a cross-functional team to identify ways to grow the canned tuna category."[176] Turns out, Bumble Bee "grew the canned tuna category" by conspiring with their two competitors to fix the prices of their products and to under-fill cans.

Hopefully, this one "heinous abuse" should not direct attention *away* from the more pervasive day-to-day question-marked "collusion" occurring in the fledgling age of category management. For any eater wishing to contribute to more localized food economies, it's important to see CM through the eyes of smaller foodmakers (growers, fishers, processors, and manufacturers). For them, this is a classic case of the fox guarding the henhouse.

When retail book giant Borders announced its plan to implement CM in its stores by handing over book selection decisions to a single publisher, twenty-seven authors and scholars led by Ralph Nader coauthored a letter to Borders chairman Greg Josefowizc (who had a thirty-year background in grocery retail). "Such pop-tart marketing likely will slash the range of book titles and ideas available to the public," reads the letter. "The Kremlin would have found it difficult to invent a more subtle and effective way of suppressing original view-points and ideas."[177]

Similarly, in grocery, the managing of store shelves by the largest food manufactures reduces or eliminates the chance for food producers to access the eating public. Case in point, an average 22 of 24 ice cream freezer doors are reserved for Nestlé and Unilever. In one store where Nestlé served as Captain of ice cream, Nestlé personnel placed market-ing signage on a freezer that featured products from start-up sugar-free ice cream manufacturer Clemmy's. The signage almost completely blocked visibility of Clemmy's products. In an internal memo, a Nestlé manager wrote about the arrival of Clemmy's products in 2007, "We need to shut this one down."

Clemmy's declared bankruptcy in 2015.[178]

Pay to Play, Pay to Stay

If it wasn't enough to have an ice cream giant muscle a healthier start-up off the shelf, Clemmy's had paid big money to access those shelves in the first place.

No longer are the grocery giants' revenues derived solely from sell-ing products to the eating public. Today, real estate is a big part of the grocery gatekeepers' business model, and *not* real estate by the "acreage," more like by the "inch." Supermarket shelves are said to be the most expensive real estate on the planet, and food and beverage manufactur-ers compete tooth and nail to access the most lucrative placements. The shelves at eye level are the penthouse condo while the checkout aisle is beachfront property.

In what are known as "slotting fees," "contract allowances," and "pro-motional allowances," the grocery chains will often require these fees ("trade spend") from suppliers before agreeing to carry their products.

> Slotting Fees — Initial cost of placing new product on the shelf. No obligation by the retailer to keep it on the shelf. Often non-refundable.

> Contract Allowances — Fee for keeping a product on the shelf for a minimum period of time or when volume threshold is achieved.
>
> Promotional Allowances — Suppliers pay retailer to promote their product. The promotion may be any combination of a temporary price reduction, a feature in print ads, a feature in a flyer, or a preferred location in the store.

Who pays and how much any one supplier forks out is shrouded in secrecy. Agreements such as these are known to often be worked out on an ad hoc, informal basis — no written contracts, no written agreements.[179] "You're talking about a deep, dark secret of the retail world," says one former supermarket chain marketing executive.[180]

What we do know are the total "vendor allowances" filed by publicly held retailers like Safeway (pre–2015) or Kroger. In one year alone, Safeway recorded $2.5 billion in vendor allowances (2015)[181]; Kroger, $8.5 billion (2017). These fees are a "vital source of income for retailers,"[182] and their importance is revealed through a retrospective look at the marketing budgets of food manufacturers. These are divided into two categories: advertising and "trade spend." "Trade spend" involves any payments made to retailers like the three types listed above. In the four decades from 1968 to 2010, the balance of advertising and trade spend among food manufacturers flipped.

Clemmy's was dishing out an average $30,000 per flavor to access the shelves of the chain retailers. In another case, a manufacturer agreed to pay a single chain more than $500,000 for a 52-week deal to have

Marketing Budget of Food Manufacturers, 1968–2010

	Trade Spend	Advertising
1968	28%	72%
1990s	50%	50%
2010	70%	30%

Source: American Antitrust Institute, 2013[183]

its product placed by the registers of its stores.[184] Reports of bribes are also not unheard of. One buyer at a chain retailer asked a California foodmaker for a personal contribution of $10,000.[185]

In 2000, the FTC conducted a public workshop on slotting allowances and invited forty participants from within the industry. One panelist estimated that the "allowances required per item for nationwide distribution might be $4.2 million, so that total slotting allowances on a small product line of four items would be $16.8 million. This was estimated to represent 30 to 50 percent of the total capital cost of bringing the products to market." Also in attendance was a small supplier of canned vegetable products and another small tortilla manufacturer. Both remarked how national brands pay high slotting fees just to keep them off the shelf.[186]

Regulators have stumbled over what to do about slotting fees. When the U.S. Senate Committee on Small Business & Entrepreneurship held a hearing on the subject in 1999, anyone willing to testify hid behind a screen and spoke through a voice-altering machine. "Nothing but a device to exploit money from manufacturers and squeeze all the independent and smaller processors off the shelves and out of business," said one food manufacturer. "I know for a fact that my competition is paying the lease on the buyer's BMW," said another. In response, Senator Christopher Bond instructed the U.S. Government Accountability Office to investigate, but he would later discover that no one from the grocery industry was willing to come forward. When the FTC was then tasked to investigate slotting fees, they too ran into the same challenge.[187] No regulatory action was ever taken.

Is It Bribery?

> Federal law and FCC [Federal Communications Commission] rules require that employees of broadcast stations, program producers, program suppliers and others who, in exchange for airing material, have accepted or agreed to receive payments, services or other valuable consideration must disclose this fact. Disclosure of compensation provides broadcasters the information

they need to let their audiences know if material was
paid for, and by whom.[188]

— Federal Communications Commission

Whereas any payment by a record label or music producer to access
the airwaves must be disclosed to listeners, payments made to grocers
to access their shelves do not receive any such regulatory oversight. The
passive eater standing before a supermarket shelf, beverage cooler, or
frozen foods section is in the dark as to how those foods got there —
none of the financial contributions between supplier and retailer are
disclosed.

The airwaves have historically been vital to the public's access to
information and the creative arts — substantially more so prior to the
advent of the Internet. Disclosing any payments made to access the
airwaves seems entirely appropriate — as would any efforts to control
the content available to users of the Internet. So what about food? Do
our grocery stores deserve the same treatment? They facilitate human
health and community well-being and provide the fuel that makes us
the happy, creative, life-giving people we are. The cost of health care can
be directly correlated to the food available at the grocery store. Should a
marketplace for such an essential human need, regardless of who owns
it, be obliged to inform the public of who influenced the selection of
foods available in a community — particularly when only one or at best
a few retailers are the only accessible options?

The U.S. Department of Justice has answered this specific question
with a resolute "no." What appears on the airwaves, they say, is in the
"public interest," and the airwaves are "owned by the public."[189] Grocery
stores are privately owned. As such, the Justice Department doesn't
think they should receive the same treatment as the airwaves.

This is devastating for the innovating small-scale foodmaker. Just
as exposure on the airwaves is key to making it big in the music industry, so too is exposure on the shelves of a grocery store essential to
growing a food-based business. The myriad of trade fees and retroactive
penalties make accessing eaters insurmountable for many foodmakers.
Should the success of a food product in the marketplace be determined

by consumer demand or the financial capacity to pay the grocery gate-keepers for their shelving real estate?

Some experts on business ethics believe slotting fees come "as close as possible to the line between commercial bribery and economic incentives for exclusion."[190]

Ralph Nader wrote about slotting fees as far back as 1994: "Next time you come upon a supermarket manager while you're shopping, ask him or her what dollar amount of slotting fees are being paid in the store. After all, you're paying for them."[191]

Private Labels (Deliberately Anonymous)

Exclusion of foodmakers from the nation's supermarket shelves may also come in the form of private labels.

Every major grocery chain today maintains its own branded label ("private label"). In the U.S. market, Walmart has "Great Value," Target "Archer Farms," Whole Foods "365." In Canada, Loblaw has "President's Choice," Sobeys "Sensations," Metro "Selection." Smaller retailers may utilize a wholesaler's non-exclusive private label while retailers like Trader Joe's specialize almost exclusively in their own branded products. From the perspective of an eater, a private label equates to one of two things — lower prices or higher quality — but with a little unpacking, private labels reveal the expanding power of grocery retailers. The most apparent expression of this power is seen from the perspective of a food producer or manufacturer — the retailer is both its "customer" *and* its "competitor."

Retailers contract private label production to name-brand or private-label manufacturers, and just like the early A&P, many grocery giants manufacture their own products in their own facilities. In 2017, Kroger reported operating 37 of its own facilities where 33 percent of their private label brands are manufactured.[192]

For the chain grocer operating in an increasingly concentrated retail market, private labels help to differentiate them from their competition, and help to shift their customers from brand loyalty to store loyalty.[193] They've become immensely important to the modern grocery retailer and are a bit of a menace to a truly competitive marketplace.

The most insidious form private labels take are "lookalikes" — a private label that appears unquestionably similar to a popular name brand.

By mimicking the appearance of a name brand, retailers are exploiting the brand manufacturer's significant investment into the research and development of that brand.[194] Name brands can take years or even decades to develop — market research, advertising, reformulations, trial and error, all of this is the lifecycle of a successful brand. The powerful grocery gatekeeper simply sits back, watches, waits, uses the brand as "research and development," then pounces by introducing its *own* private label.

By injecting lookalikes into the marketplace, the grocery giants are distorting competition in the food system and enhancing control over the supply chain.[195] With lookalikes on the shelf, manufacturers of the copied brand may suffer "brand dilution" caused by a "blurring [of] its distinctive character."[196]

Experts in the field of retail competition and supply chain relations also warn of the effect of lookalikes on smaller retailers. Diluting the competitive position of name brands — upon which smaller retailers rely — hurts these retailers.[197] The name brands become less distinctive and the cycle of retailer dominance continues as brand manufacturers are forced to redesign packaging and "over-innovate," leading to higher costs for the manufacturer, higher prices for eaters, and an even smaller piece of the pie for farmers and fishers.

Crying foul on lookalikes has proven to be a lost cause. To date, there is no legal remedy to prevent the practice.[198] "Few food products are protected by patents, and other than trademarks on brand names and logos, retailers have plenty of scope to develop very close lookalikes," says Paul Dobson, an expert in the field.[199] While some complaints to retailers have been successful and often settled out of court, many victims of lookalikes are "reluctant to legally fight against the retailer copycats [out of] fear of being delisted or losing shelf space."[200] The growth of private labels hammers yet another nail into the food system's competition coffin.

The effects of private labels on the supply chain are well established. In his defining of "countervailing power" as an "autonomous regulator of competition," the late economist John Kenneth Galbraith used A&P as a "favorite" example of buyers' countervailing power over sellers. In 1937, A&P commissioned a study to explore vertically integrating into the manufacturing of breakfast cereals. When A&P's cereal suppliers were shown the study, the mere threat of A&P entering into its own production led the cereal manufacturers to drop their prices by 10 percent.[201] A&P's reliance on private labels was well studied as part of the Department of Justice's investigation into the company in the 1940s.

> "[A&P] manufactures no product whatsoever that is not an imitation of a well-known advertised brand which some manufacturer has invented and introduced to the consuming public at great expense."
>
> "In all A&P stores, popular brands are displayed in the most inaccessible places. The fighting imitations are kept in the most conspicuous places and everything possible is done to suggest to customers the disparity in price between the originals and the imitations."
>
> U.S. Department of Justice,
> A&P investigation memos, 1942[202]

By looking to Europe and the most concentrated grocery retail markets in the world, there would appear to be significant room for private label growth in the U.S. and Canadian markets. Not coincidentally, Switzerland has both the highest retailer concentration in the world and the largest share of private labels. The two appear to be closely linked. As markets consolidate, private labels grow.[203]

Private Label Market Share in Select Countries

Switzerland	45%
Spain	41%
UK	41%
Western Europe	25–34%
U.S. / Canada	18%

Source: Nielsen, 2014[204]

What does the future of private labels spell for the name brands? Loss of relevance is certainly part of it. "Trouble in Big Food: America's Cereal, Soda and Soup Companies Are in Turmoil," reads a 2018 *CNN Money* headline;[205] "The death of the 'Big Food' era is imminent," says a 2018 *Quartz* headline. The "turmoil" reached a peak in 2018 when many food manufacturers abandoned their affiliation with the Grocery Manufacturers of America (GMA) — their 110-year-old trade association and lobbyist. Campbell Soup, Nestlé, Dean Foods, Mars, Tyson Foods, Unilever, Hershey, Cargill, and Kraft Heinz, all abandoned the GMA within the span of three months.[206]

Barriers to Entry

Through the many "controls" at the disposal of the grocery giant, an almost impenetrable wall is erected, stifling innovation and barring new entrants at all levels of the supply chain. Slotting fees are one of the highest barriers to entry in grocery retail.[207] According to the FTC, 10 percent of ice cream products in their first year fail to achieve adequate sales to cover these fees.[208] Such barriers to entry are exactly what the Robinson–Patman Act was designed to prevent.[209] Whereas a large manufacturer will be able to pay the cost of any allowances with the help of cash flows from established product lines, new and smaller foodmakers aren't afforded such luxury.

Another marked barrier to entry for new and smaller suppliers are long-term contracts. When a retailer enters into long-term contracts with large well-established suppliers, smaller suppliers can easily be excluded from the market, further contributing to consolidation in the supply chain and increasing buyer market power for retailers.[210]

An egregious example of the effects of coercive long-term contracts and their risks to even the largest of suppliers is the case of the Texas-based chain H-E-B and its former supplier, Delta Produce. H-E-B's market share in southern Texas is one of the highest in the country:

> Delta used to sell ripened produce to Texas-based H-E-B
> and other grocers, and by the mid-1990s distributed all
> the avocados and watermelons and a large percentage

of tomatoes in H-E-B's San Antonio stores [95% of all H-E-B tomatoes came from Delta[211]]. In exchange for being H-E-B's major supplier, Delta agreed not to sell any tomatoes, avocados or watermelons to H-E-B competitors. By 1998, 80 percent of Delta's revenues came from its sales to H-E-B, but H-E-B later began to purchase increased amounts of produce from other sellers, leaving Delta with surpluses. Prospective buyers like Walmart and Albertsons approached Delta, but H-E-B refused to lift the exclusivity restriction, and by the time H-E-B released Delta from the restriction, the distributor couldn't establish relationships with other customers and consequently filed for Chapter 11 bankruptcy in January 2012.[212]

> "Grocery Chain Beats Antitrust Suit Over Produce
> Restrictions," *Law360*, 2013

The demise of Delta Produce offers a stark reminder of who retains the keys to our kitchens. The waves of consolidation happening through-out the food system and its impacts on farmers have been a particular focus for Richard Sexton, Distinguished Professor and Past Chair at the University of California Davis's Department of Agricultural and Resource Economics. Sexton observed that despite attempts among the biggest players in the food system to consolidate operations verti-cally and horizontally, "grocery retailers have emerged as the dominant players in the food chain in most parts of the world." [213]

Setting Food Policy

"We have standards for so many things. Car manufacturers are required to include seat belts and airbags. We need to figure out what the equivalent of a seatbelt or an airbag is in the design of a supermarket." [214]

— Dr. Deborah Cohen, RAND Corporation

Any food store participating in the Supplemental Nutrition Assistance Program (SNAP) in the United States is required to stock a certain level of diversity in the foods they offer. Other than this, the conduct of grocers and their roles and responsibilities in the communities they operate in are more or less left to the wind, with industry itself blowing its own sails. This is particularly true today in the beyond-antitrust era. With little to no restraint, the ever-consolidating grocery giants maintain a level of control over production and prices that effectively appoints them as pseudo-regulators of the food economy.

For people who fear "Big Brother," the transfer of oversight from government to industry is a welcomed development, but Barry Lynn offers a sobering reminder of the irony of such sentiment. "Free-market utopians have long decried government industrial policy because it puts into the hands of bureaucrats and politicians the power to determine which firms 'win' and which 'lose,'" yet, "Walmart picks winners and losers every day, and the losers have no recourse to any court or any political representative anywhere."[215] Herein lies the "con" of the grocery giant — convince the public of the perils of "big government" and, with the smokescreen up, use the grocers' newly minted infantry of eaters armed with spoons and straws to unwittingly usher in the very governing of the marketplace that the army was created to defend against.

With free rein to mold the supply chain to their liking, the grocery giants are effectively appointing themselves as regulators of food production — a task once reserved for nation states. Their reach has gone global through the retailer-founded Global Food Safety Initiative (GFSI) and its affiliated certification bodies (also founded by grocery retailers). The United States is served by FMI and their "Certification for Every Link in the Food Chain" programs. FMI sets the standards in the U.S. food system for livestock housing and feed, animal husbandry, livestock transportation, soil management, and processing of farm goods[216] — all of it under the umbrella of "food safety." Retailers use their buying power to impose these standards on their suppliers and coerce participation in this system of "private food governance."[217] As law professor Paul Verbruggen writes, the aim of GFSI is to "align industry and government in food safety by engaging 'government to recognize and accept GFSI benchmarked schemes.'"[218]

Grocery retail is also no stranger to the all-too-familiar revolving doors connecting industry and government. Former FMI Director of Government Relations Robert Rosado went on to become a staff member of the U.S. Senate Committee on Agriculture, Nutrition and Forestry. Rosado was strategically appointed in 2017 to help usher in the 2018 reauthorization of the U.S. Farm Bill. Prior to his appointment, Rosado managed food and agriculture policy at BIO, the world's largest biotech (GMO) industry trade association. Before BIO, he served in the U.S. Department of Agriculture's Foreign Agricultural Service under President George W. Bush — directing legislative and public affairs related to international food and agricultural exports and trade policy.[219] If you can set the rules, define allowable externalities, and drive down taxes, you maximize profits.

Eaters at the Controls

"In the field of merchandise distribution, a Goliath stands against divided forces plying a powerful weapon with a skillful hand against the vulnerable weaknesses of his opponents.

The Goliath is the huge chain stores. His weapon is huge buying power by the manipulation of which he threatens manufacturers and others with financial stringency or even bankruptcy if they refuse him the prices and terms he demands.

His opponents are not only these manufacturers, not only the independent competitors whom he seeks to eliminate, but the consuming public, whom he hopes to have at his mercy. Their weakness... the disorganized

individualism and hand-to-mouth buying habits of the
purchasing public who cannot realize nor foresee — nor
indeed resist if they could — the merchandising tactics
of the chains — practices which, because of their far-
flung resources, they can concentrate with more deadly
effect in one community at the cost of another."[220]

— Representative Wright Patman, proffered to the
House of Representatives on June 11, 1935,
as part of his bill to amend Section 2 of the Clayton Act

Much of the retailer power described thus far has been power over
suppliers. But what about their direct influence over eaters? Joanna
Blythman conveys the incarceration of the eater quite succinctly:
"When we rely on one supermarket chain for almost all the food we buy,
we can easily be manipulated to accept what they want to give us. As
a consequence, supermarkets' power to shape our shopping and eating
habits is phenomenal, and they know it. The trick is to get us to think
that they are responding to our needs and desires when actually we are
responding to theirs.... The irony of the great supermarket revolution
is that the concept they sold us, 'choice,' has actually become a vehicle
for denying us that. What 'choice' do we really have when all we have
to choose between is an [Amazon, Kroger, Walmart or Albertsons], a
[Loblaws, Sobeys or a Metro]?"[221]

Over the course of the grocery giants' century-long birthing, these
companies have captured the modern age of plant and animal breeding, food production, and food distribution. Their bounty includes the
shopping and eating habits of the Western world. They have become
purveyors of entire lifestyles, and yet, people are generally not all that
happy with the grocery stores in their communities. Shoppers have
been polled at length on their levels of satisfaction with supermarkets. As far back as 1999, one-quarter of all shoppers were dissatisfied
with where they purchased groceries.[222] In another poll, 56 percent
of customers of a major chain retailer were "bored" by the store, 53
percent were "stressed," 52 percent "frustrated" and 51 percent "overwhelmed."[223] Yet another found that 70 percent of respondents would

have preferred to shop locally rather than travel "out of town" to the supermarket.[224]

This often-imperceptible unhappiness seems destined to rear its head in a more substantive way. In recent years, some routine decisions among the chains have revealed this undercurrent of dissatisfaction — and not from "activist" eaters; the backlash has come from mainstream chain store shoppers.

> 2016 — Loblaw stops selling French's brand ketchup across Canada. When consumers learn the ketchup is made with 100 percent Canadian tomatoes, consumers revolt. Within 24 hours, Loblaw reversed its decision.[225]
>
> 2016 — A single photo by a Sobeys shopper of a $4 pre-cut, pitted avocado packaged in plastic and cardboard sparks viral outrage in both the United States and Canada over wasteful packaging.[226]

While at times it may seem we eaters are powerless, we mustn't be fooled — we are immensely powerful. Our sheer numbers dwarf the number of retailers. Just as their consolidation has granted them seemingly limitless powers, that same eroding of diversity upon which they draw strength also makes them all the more vulnerable to the whims of our almighty appetites. Often forgotten in the equation of the food economy is the one sector that likely invests the most time and energy into the planning, acquisition, transportation, and preparation of food — EATERS. And not just any eaters — *organized, consolidated* eaters.

Eaters have been reshaping food systems and culture by eaters for as long as grocery stores have existed. While many eaters have built up tolerances to a culture of sameness, others have chosen to unlock the gates to a far more equitable, nourishing, and downright fun grocery store culture. Yes, grocery stores *are* in the public interest, and yes, they *can* be public institutions.

Where the efforts of antitrust regulation and enforcement have failed, hundreds of communities across the Unites States and Canada are filling the void via community-based ownership in their neighborhood grocery stores. This is "power by the people" in its rawest and, dare I say, most impactful form. The failure of antitrust may be a blessing in disguise. And anyway, all signs seem to point to a system *beyond* salvation — a dominant food culture beyond saving.

> "We can lie down and let the supermarkets take total control of what ends up on our plates. We can stand by, dismayed but passive, as they drive all but the largest farmers and food suppliers out of business by sourcing products from parts of the globe where they buy for even less. Or we can change our food shopping habits and use them to vote for a different sort of food economy, one that supports small, local and diverse, not large, global and monotonous... we can't have both."
>
> Joanna Blythman, *Shopped* [227]

Interlude:
Welcome to What's Possible, North America

"In my dream, the angel shrugged and said, if we fail this time, it will be a failure of imagination. Then she placed the world gently in the palm of my hand."[228]

— Brian Andreas

WHAT'S POSSIBLE, North America, is a place.

It's a place that can live in our imagination, or a place we can call home.

What's Possible is a place where people construct a life based on one's highest values.

The community of What's Possible is whatever we want it to be. What could possibly be more exciting?

Our cities, communities and neighborhoods;

Our local, regional and national food systems;

The grocery stores providing us with food;

... all are only limited by our imaginations — the stories we've inherited, those we tell ourselves and those we tell our children.

"Stories bear tremendous creative power," writes author Charles Eisenstein. "Through them we coordinate human activity, focus attention and intention, define roles, and identify what is important and even what is real. Stories give meaning and purpose to life and therefore motivate action."[229]

What story do you want to be a part of?

Much of what has been revealed in previous chapters remains hidden to most, but not everyone. Certainly not you. Not anymore.

As the previous chapters remind us, immense effort has been made to stave off the present state of our food systems and resist the dominance of the grocery giants. Much of that effort could not hold back the tide. Instead, the prevailing stories of our time, which have constructed the very DNA of our food, carry power of biblical proportions. The resulting food system of over-abundance, of monumental food waste, of ineffective distribution of excess to those most in need is reminiscent of the lessons from the Garden of Eden: a place of imagined and absolute beauty — of heaven on Earth — a place from which Adam and Eve were banished for having taken more than they needed.

How fitting that what was taken from Eden was food.

Eden reminds us of the "more beautiful world our hearts know is possible."[230]

What then of the world of grocery giants?

"Sometimes it is necessary to live a lie to its fullest before we are ready to take the next step into the truth," says Eisenstein.

In taking this next step, food is a required ingredient. Just as an apple ushered in the fall from Eden, food is also being used to help navigate us into new geographies of relationship. Capital city? What's Possible. Population? You!

No doubt, What's Possible will look different to whoever's looking. It may be a low-income community without any grocery store whatsoever — a "food desert" — yet is home to a committed group of people organizing a community-owned grocery store. For others, What's Possible may be a diverse culture and economy of small food businesses, artisan bakers, craft brewers, weekly markets, school gardens, and an abundance of programs providing food and skills to those most in need.

In the remaining chapters, stories will be shared from communities large and small where people have welcomed in this new age by taking ownership of their local grocery stores. Most of these consumer-owned food cooperatives are the lifeblood of their respective communities. Just as the grocery giants send ripples of impact out into the world, so too do grocery co-ops ripple into the lives of so many and touch those most in need — eaters, farmers, fishers, and foodmakers.

What does a community look like that has used food to welcome in this more beautiful world? Be assured that there are many, from large well-connected networks in urban centers to dispersed rural communities — food is contributing to palpable transformations in hundreds of cities, towns and neighborhoods. There are, however, two that stand out —

communities that have been forced to innovate. In these communities, the hollowing out of industry from decades past, the loss of jobs, their distance from major urban centers, and their stories of renewal communicate what *any* community in any city or town might achieve. They communicate in a more carefully packaged way the very same conditions which most communities have either found themselves in today or may in the not-so-distant future. A quick visit to these communities here in this chapter should stoke the imagination, remind us of possibility, and introduce the pivotal role consumer-owned grocery stores can play in community renewal. From there, we can then dive deeper into the movement that is transforming hundreds of communities just like these, and may, with a little imagination, transform yours too.

Welcome to Resisterville (Nelson, British Columbia)

> "We were more interested in creating the society and the community and the values that we wanted for the future than in trying to change the ones that weren't working"[231]
>
> — Bob Ploss, Slocan Valley, BC

The city of Nelson, British Columbia, is one of the most isolated from the country's major centers of food distribution. Nelson lies deep in the Selkirk Mountains — a full eight-hour drive east of Vancouver and a seven-hour drive west of Calgary (and that's only if the mountain passes aren't closed for avalanche control in the winter). With a population of ten thousand, the city is the largest in the West Kootenay — a region with a population of eighty thousand.

While Nelson's isolation deters many from choosing it as a home, others are drawn here for that very reason.

Located on and near the traditional lands of the Sinixt and Ktunaxa people, the Nelson area has attracted a number of immigration waves over the previous hundred-plus years. The first were the city's founders — miners who arrived shortly before the turn of the century. Then, beginning in 1902, and with the help of Leo Tolstoy, a wave of pacifist, vegetarian immigrants from Russia began to arrive in the region. The Doukhobors had refused to swear allegiance to the emperor and resisted conscription by destroying their weapons. They were exiled from Russia. Upon arrival to Canada, they formed agricultural communes, and their descendants today remain a part of the region's social, cultural, and political landscape. A few decades later, a new wave of immigrants was drawn to the isolation of the West Kootenay — Quakers from the United States who opposed the McCarthy-era politics of the early 1950s. Quakers bear a long history of marginalization and persecution. At the time, they were known for their involvement in anti-war movements, for bearing witness to atrocities, and for promoting fair trade. Another wave of immigration followed. The then well-established Quaker and Doukhobor communities played an important role in supporting this next wave of "resistance."[232]

A 2004 headline in *The New York Times* reads, "Greetings From Resisterville." The article drew international attention to the thousands of Americans who had migrated to the Nelson area during the 1960s and 70s.[233] Often called "war resisters," "draft dodgers" or "conscientious objectors," many of them would eventually settle in Nelson and the surrounding area. Even after the end of the Vietnam War, chain migration brought many more idealistic Americans to the West Kootenay. Their arrival would solidify the region's counter-cultural identity. "It was like dropping the population of a large university campus into a remote rural community," writes author Kathleen Rodgers in her book *Welcome to Resisterville: American Dissidents in British Columbia.*[234] The American immigrants were young, educated, middle-class, and urban, and arrived in a resource-based economy with a predominantly working-class population. The culture clash was unmistakable.

While resistance became embedded in the social fabric of the region, it also informed the blossoming of alternative lifestyles — a new story of what's possible. "We were more interested in creating the society and the community and the values that we wanted for the future than in trying to change the ones that weren't working," says local resident and American immigrant Bob Ploss. As Rodgers writes of the Nelson area of today, "the counter-cultural identities and ideas of the 1960s have become institutionalized into the daily life and politics of the town and surrounding area."

Grocery Giants in Nelson

Despite the distinct counter-cultural values visible on every street corner of the city's small downtown, Nelson's grocery store landscape is not so different from that of any town or large urban center. Nelson is home to three grocery giants: a Safeway, a Save-On-Foods, and a Wholesale Club. A small selection of groceries is also found at the local Shoppers Drug Mart and at Walmart (albeit not a Walmart Supercenter). In the shadows of these giants are three natural food stores.

A fun and enlightening exercise for anyone helping to found the community of What's Possible is conducting a scan of the grocers operating in the area. Who are they? Who's behind them? How do they contribute to or extract from the community?

Grocery Giants in Nelson

Store	Parent Company	Headquarters	National Market Share	Key People
Wholesale Club / Shoppers Drug Mart	Loblaw Companies Limited	Toronto, Ontario	29%	Galen Weston
Safeway	Sobeys (Empire Co. Ltd.)	Stellarton, Nova Scotia	21%	Sobey Family
Save-On-Foods	Overwaitea Food Group (Jim Pattison Group)	Vancouver, British Columbia	3%*	Jim Pattison

* Regional market share data unavailable but based on number of stores and average sales per store of Canadian chain retailers, the author estimates Overwaitea commands a 33% share of the British Columbia market.

Source: USDA, 2018[235]

Most fascinating about the grocery giants operating in Nelson are the key people behind their parent companies — more specifically, their wealth.

Using rankings of wealth that include both family and personal fortunes, as of 2018 the Wholesale Club's Galen Weston is the third richest Canadian; Save-On's owner, Jim Pattison, the tenth richest (first in BC[236]); and Safeway's Sobey Family, the thirty-fifth richest.[237]

When *Canadian Business* magazine announced in 2017 that the five richest Canadians held the same amount of wealth as the poorest 30 percent of the country (eleven million people), Weston was one of the top five, and just missing the cut was Pattison.[238] The growing disparity of wealth in the world is playing itself out right on the shelves of Nelson's grocery stores. Every time a Nelson resident buys a box of cereal or an apple at any one of these three giants, the gap between the uber-wealthy and the poorest of Canadians widens.

Nelson's Walmart Resistance

In 2001, when Nelson resident Dave Elliott heard about Walmart's plans to vacate its existing shopping mall location and construct a brand-new standalone Supercenter on a vacant waterfront lot, he and a group of investors cobbled together $1.1 million and acquired the land from underneath the monolithic American retailer.

Elliott was a local business owner and had served on city council for a number of years. He had assumed responsibility for the city's development portfolio. Elliot's ambition was to revitalize the city's waterfront and attract seniors' housing to the area. He only had enough time to introduce the idea before ending his term. His waterfront vision was left in the hands of the incoming council. They had a different agenda. Development of the picturesque waterfront would instead involve attracting a diversity of big box stores. Loblaw constructed its discount Wholesale Club grocery store, and Walmart expressed interest in a vacant waterfront lot for a Supercenter and its own full-service grocery.

One week before the land was put on the market, Elliott put out a call to other business owners in the community. In "no time" he had the $1.1 million needed to purchase the land. "Some investors were so committed to keeping Walmart from developing the land, they even borrowed money against their homes to do so," recounts Elliott.

The move infuriated Walmart's Nelson employees, but residents were generally relieved to have the land remaining in the control of the local consortium.

With no other land options in Nelson available, Walmart has remained at the mall to this day in their smaller non-grocery format.

Elliott became so popular for his grassroots protectionist move, he was elected mayor in 2002 and began the work of reversing the council's big-business agenda.[239]

The Regional Food Movement

In the shadows of Nelson's grocery giants is a counter-culturally rich local food economy. In a city of only ten thousand people, more than forty locally owned restaurants and cafes line the streets. In the middle of the workday, the small downtown is reminiscent of the streets of Seattle or Vancouver. There's no other place like it in Canada. As one visitor remarked while looking out the window of the Full Circle Cafe onto Nelson's crowded Baker Street, "Doesn't anybody here work for a living?"[240]

Farmers' markets are a weekly happening in almost all West Kootenay communities. Nelson alone hosts two of them each week, with one shutting down an entire block of the city's downtown.

A few blocks up from downtown is a 120-year-old building home to a number of delicious food and drink manufacturers, including the Nelson Brewing Company — one of Canada's first certified organic breweries; Oso-Negro — a fair-trade organic coffee roaster that distributes its products across Western Canada; Kutenai Chai — supplying restaurants, coffee shops, and retailers with chai tea; Silverking Soya Foods — organic tofu; and in the basement, a cooperatively owned flour mill where shareholders freshly mill organic grains grown in the nearby Creston Valley. Adjacent to this aromatic hive of edible activity is the Nelson Food Cupboard's urban farm where vegetables are grown exclusively for their food bank clients.

The Nelson area's food access programs are some of the most innovative rural services of their kind. In the nearby village of Kaslo — with a population of only 1,000 — the Kaslo Food Hub successfully worked with their village council to adopt a community food charter. Over the course of its history, the food hub has launched a food bank, gleaning programs, a community root cellar, a community garden, a tool lending library, and a resource center of cookbooks and how-to gardening guides. It has become a critical resource for the community.

A few minutes up the road from the Nelson Food Cupboard's garden is Organic Matters — a highly praised distributor of dry organic goods. From its small warehouse, OM supplies hundreds of food-buying clubs and small retailers across Western Canada.

Outside the city exists an unusually large number of organic farmers. In the nearby Creston Valley, a locally grown grain economy has emerged, bolstered by the formation in 2008 of Canada's first CSA (community supported agriculture) program for grain. In its second year, the Kootenay Grain CSA was delivering 100-pound shares of organically grown heritage wheats, oats, lentils, and dry peas to 450 families and a dozen businesses. In a few of the CSA's early years, a local sailing association gathered upwards of a dozen sailboats to transport the grain along the waters of Kootenay Lake — a three-day round-trip journey from the Creston Valley to Nelson's municipal pier.

With the West Kootenay region once famous for its fruit orchards, the West Kootenay Permaculture Co-op Association supports the orchardists of today by coordinating a mobile juice press to travel between communities. The WKPCA also organizes annual conferences with sector-specific themes like "livestock and meat processing" or "herbs and plant medicines." They coordinate monthly educational activities like local root cellar tours and operate a mobile classroom.

Food festivals are commonplace in the region. One of the country's largest garlic festivals — the Hills Garlic Fest — attracts over ten thousand people to the one-day event. Hills is adjacent to the village of New Denver — a genetically engineered (GE) free community. Along with the communities of Nelson, Rossland, and Kaslo, New Denver participated in the country's first adoptions of municipal policies restricting the cultivation of genetically engineered plants and trees within their borders. The Nelson-led effort spread across the province, inspiring policies later adopted in dozens of other British Columbia towns and cities.

Once a year, more than forty local food businesses sponsor a multi-day food documentary film festival centered in Nelson and hosted in other West Kootenay communities. The festival curates films that will inspire residents to be more active in the region's food culture and economy. Nelson's only oyster grower, Brent Petkau, has been a staple presence at the annual festival. Petkau cultivates, harvests, and transports oysters from the Pacific coast to Nelson.

As with any thriving local food economy like this, a "hub" is necessary to help incubate, communicate, and centralize activity. For Nelson, that hub has long been the Kootenay Co-op — a grocery store formed in 1975 and today owned by more than thirteen thousand West Kootenay residents. The co-op has in one way or another partnered with all the businesses and organizations just mentioned, by either incubating them, purchasing from them, or donating food or financial resources to them. No other food organization in the region has been so integrated into *all* aspects of the region's food economy. Whereas other local food economies may require the support of a nonprofit, a charity, or a food council of volunteers (all of whose futures depend on the precarious nature of government funding, grants, and donations), the West Kootenay's food system is reinforced by the most important link in the chain — a grocery store.

From its roots in the resistance movements of the 1970s, the Kootenay Co-op has played one of the most important roles of any business in helping nourish the ongoing development of What's Possible, British Columbia.

Viroqua, Wisconsin

Resistance movements in America have helped form hundreds of communities similar to Nelson that are nourishing the growth of local food economies. One of them is Viroqua, Wisconsin.

As the county seat of a rural agricultural community, Viroqua's population of 4,400 has used food to stave off the decimation of the farm economy and the hollowing out of the town's businesses and employers.

Today, the region surrounding Viroqua is home to more organic farms per capita than anywhere in the country.[241] The community's success was not, however, spontaneous. It grew out of a "culture of collaboration that had been built in a sustained manner since the 1970s."[242] The region's cooperative roots in food and farming date back to at least 1903, when the Westby Cooperative Creamery first formed.

When farm prices began falling in the 1980s and the American food system began heavily consolidating, farmers were forced to either scale up or get out. A group of farmers began pooling organic vegetables to sell in local communities. What began as the Coulee Region Organic Produce Pool (CROPP) grew into what today is known as Organic Valley — a cooperative owned by more than two thousand farmers in 35 U.S. states, Canada, Australia, and the United Kingdom. The cooperative is one of the country's leading producers of organic dairy, soy, egg, and produce products. OV is Vernon County's largest employer with their three facilities in the region employing most of the co-op's over 950 employees.[243]

The region's knack for turning challenge into opportunity came again when Walmart arrived in 1987. The town quickly responded with a state-funded downtown revitalization initiative. In the few years after Walmart's arrival, rather than send shopkeepers packing, the number of downtown businesses increased. In 1992, *Smithsonian Magazine* named Viroqua "The Town that Beat Walmart."[244]

Another blow struck in 2009, when tech giant NCR shuttered its factory. Eighty jobs disappeared. When the Chamber of Commerce failed to attract new owners to the facility, the Vernon Economic Development Association acquired the property and turned the 100,000-square-foot factory into a Food Enterprise Center. Today, the center supports 23 food-based businesses with dedicated and shared space for food processing, distribution, and storage. Some of the tenants include Wisco-Pop — organic craft-brewed soda; Community Hunger Solutions — consolidator and distributor of food to area food banks; B&E's Trees — bourbon barrel-aged maple syrup; Plovgh — an agricultural coordinator connecting the region's farmers and foodmakers; and Fifth Season Cooperative — distributor of local food into institutions and restaurants across the Midwest.

Just like Nelson, Viroqua is home to a thriving consumer-owned grocery store — the Viroqua Food Co-op. Founded in 1995, the co-op has been growing steadily ever since and today is owned by more than four thousand member–owners, churning out $7.5 million in annual sales. The co-op has served as a testing ground for the many food-makers operating out of the Food Enterprise Center and maintains a steadfast commitment to carrying predominantly organic and local foods out of its 9,200-square-foot store. The co-op projects $12 million in sales by 2020.[245]

Like many consumer-owned grocery stores, the Viroqua Food Co-op acts as a beacon for people looking to migrate to the community of What's Possible.

Enter the Co-op

"No thoughtful person, who brings a dispassionate mind to bear upon the subject, can doubt that, in due course, the machinery of production, distribution and exchange of wealth will be administered on a just and equitable basis for the use, comfort and convenience of the people as a whole instead of, as now, for the private aggrandizement... of a few. The period and the form will depend upon the extent to which, and the rapidity with which, the mass of the people are capable of moral and intellectual improvement, and the reception of the associative spirit. That is, we believe, the orthodox co-operative view."[246]

— George Keen,
Co-operative Union of Canada, 1911

AT A GROCERY STORE IN TORONTO, the calendar of in-store events is unlike most.

On May 11, participate in a sauerkraut and kimchi workshop in the store's teaching kitchen. On May 13, shoppers are encouraged to place bulk orders for grass-fed beef from a Mennonite farm 100 miles out of town. At $7.85–$8.00 a pound, the beef prices are on par with most conventionally raised equivalents. May 16 is monthly customer appreciation day; all items in the store are 15 percent off regular prices. On May 17, beef orders are ready for pickup. On May 23, learn to make naturally fermented soft drinks (kombucha). On May 29, commence the first of eight workshops and get trained in the art of preserving the local harvest ... pickled asparagus, apricot jam, and tomato sauce are all on the menu. On May 30, take a class to acquire the traditional skills for homemade sourdough bread.

This grocery store is not a Kroger, nor a Publix, nor a Loblaw. It's a co-operative — owned by the people who shop there. This cooperatively owned grocery store was a product of the most recent wave of community-owned grocery stores that began appearing in the United States and Canada around 2008.[xiii] This latest wave is one of a number of distinct periods in history when communities have come together en masse to develop community-owned grocery stores.

The late economic historian Karl Polyani predicted such periods as a natural reaction to an overly liberalized economy. After witnessing early attempts to institute free markets in late nineteenth-century England, Polyani observed the rise of "counter-movements" — society's attempt to repair the disruption inflicted by the "free market." For Polyani, the "disruption" he witnessed was social — a subordinating of society to the market economy[247] — a devaluing of pre-existing patterns of social organization.[248]

The opposing forces of the counter-movement called for greater economic democracy — and not only through the will of government. Grassroots economic democracy has also crystallized as a response to the failure of autonomous, self-regulating, "free market" economies.

In the United States and Canada, just as Polyani would have predicted, waves of cooperative enterprises like credit unions, fishing and farmer cooperatives, and community-owned grocery stores have closely followed the rise and fall of liberalized market economies.

- ✳ As an outcome of the rise of monopolies during the turn-of-the-century Progressive Era, co-ops followed.
- ✳ In the aftermath of the wealth of the "Roaring '20s" and the ensuing Great Depression, food co-ops followed.
- ✳ In the aftermath of the economic prosperity and disparity of the 1950s and 1960s, a wave of food co-op development followed.

---

xiii   The co-op was the West End Food Co-op in Toronto. Despite closing its doors in 2018 due to challenges securing affordable real estate, it remains a shining example of "what's possible."

✳ After the fallout of 1990s grocery merger-mania, rampant globalization, and the ensuing financial crisis of 2007–08, yet another wave of community-owned grocery stores began appearing.

Co-ops are like the "pioneer plants" that first appear on the landscape following a forest fire — society's fireweed and morel mushrooms.

In this way, co-ops reflect a community's health and well-being. As Canadian co-op leader Brett Fairbairn says, "Each [co-op] is a microcosm of what is happening to communities, and each offers insights into community response to challenge."[249]

What Is a Co-op?

> "A co-operative is an autonomous association of persons united voluntarily to meet their common economic, social, and cultural needs and aspirations through a jointly owned and democratically controlled enterprise."[250]
>
> — Statement on the Cooperative Identity,
> International Co-operative Alliance

Most simply, co-ops are businesses or organizations founded and owned by the people who directly benefit from their products or services. Co-ops are created to meet member and community needs.

Contrary to some beliefs (mostly of decades past), a cooperative is not some form of communist or socialist experiment; nothing could be further from the truth. Participating in a co-op is 100 percent voluntary. This arguably makes participating in a co-op an even *more* "democratic" social relationship than that of our *required* participation to fund public institutions and services. This is probably why early twentieth-century cooperators were so adamant on replacing the state and capitalism with co-ops. As cooperative leader Tom Webb says, "Cooperatives are the radical center ... whereas capitalism and communism have a history of consolidating power into fewer and fewer hands, cooperatives spread power around."[251]

Today, these democratic forms of bottom-up organizing are a global movement spanning every sector of the economy. From worker-owned factories to grain mills owned by farmers to outdoor apparel shops owned by consumers, the co-operative model of democratic ownership is thriving. According to the International Co-operative Alliance, one in every six people on Earth (that's 1.2 billion people) are members of at least one of the world's three million co-ops.[252]

As globalization reduces individual and community autonomy to effect change, co-ops respond by "opening up public spaces," says Fairbairn. In cities and towns of any size, when the places people shop, work, and entertain themselves are *not* rooted in the community, people can easily be left to feel an absence of autonomy and of hope for the future — the creative spirit is suppressed. This can lead to feelings of hopelessness and maybe even depression. Alternatively, when our cities and towns are filled with spaces that we can claim as our own, people can feel a sense of value and purpose — living from a place of freedom and possibility.[253] This is the human side of cooperatives.

There are many types of co-ops. Worker co-ops are owned by the people who work there. Producer co-ops are often oriented toward marketing, distribution, or processing and owned by the businesses that sell into them. Credit unions are cooperative banks owned by their customers. Housing co-ops are residential developments owned by the people who live there. Consumer co-ops — the type of co-op featured in this book — are businesses owned by their customers. REI in the United States and MEC in Canada are two examples of large consumer co-ops. Some co-ops are hybrid or multi-stakeholder, meaning they use two or more of the above models.

Members will most often invest equity into their co-op in the form of a share. The investment is returned to the member when they leave the cooperative. Member equity is a valuable source of capital for co-ops, particularly in their start-up phase. A share in a co-op grants the member the right to vote, but unlike a shareholder in a company, voting control is linked to membership and not to the number of shares held.

Shareholders in a co-op will usually vote annually for their board of directors. A director's term varies from co-op to co-op but usually ranges from one to four years. Some cooperatives rely on volunteer boards while others offer compensation in the form of cash or credit within the business. Members of a co-op may also be asked to vote on matters of significance to the co-op. The criteria for decisions to be made by the membership or by the board are written into a co-op's bylaws (or rules of association).

Many co-ops issue a financial return to their members at the end of the business year. The return is a portion of the co-op's profits. In a consumer co-op, this may come in the form of a patronage return — determined by the value of purchases the member made in the previous year.

Mission-Driven and Transparent

Unlike their primarily profit-driven counterparts, co-ops (which also may happily enjoy a profit) are first and foremost mission-driven organizations.

In the world of retail grocery co-ops, the Seward Co-op in Minneapolis, Minnesota, writes into their "Ends Statement" that they will "sustain a healthy community that has:

1. Equitable economic relationships;
2. Positive environmental impacts; and,
3. Inclusive, socially responsible practices"[254]

Quite a different type of grocery store!

The nearby Wedge Community Co-op strives to "Build community by developing a strong local food system."[255]

At the Great Basin Community Food Co-op in Reno, Nevada, their annual report to their member–owners includes a detailed description of where the previous year's profits will end up. Some of it will be put into the "construction of the store's new cafe," some will be invested in a new "security camera system," and some into their "crumbling patio."

Co-ops are highly transparent. They're also astoundingly resilient.

Resilience

> "It turns out that the things co-operatives do success-
> fully in good economic times are the same things that
> sustain them in bad times."[256]

> — Brett Fairbairn, Center for the
> Study of Cooperatives, University of Saskatchewan

Co-ops generally last longer than private-sector businesses. In one Canadian study, it was found that more than six out of ten co-ops survive more than five years compared to four out of ten private-sector businesses.[257]

The International Labor Organization of the United Nations has shown how financial cooperatives (customer-owned banks like credit unions) "out-performed traditional investor-owned banks before, during and after the global financial crisis of 2007/2008."[258]

By utilizing member capital to expand the business rather than borrowing from a bank, co-ops further reduce their risk and increase their resiliency.

Resilience is not a proven characteristic of the dominant economic model. Contrary to the promises of the self-regulating economy, some of its most ardent champions are no longer convinced.

> When former U.S. Federal Reserve Chairman Alan
> Greenspan testified before Congress in October 2008,
> he told American lawmakers that the economic melt-
> down had revealed a "flaw in the model" that he had
> not expected — that banks operating in self-interest
> would not self-regulate to protect their shareholders
> and institutions.[259]

> — John Restakis, *Humanizing the Economy.*

There is nothing resilient about repeating the same cycles of boom, bust, and bailout.

For the pioneers of What's Possible, fixing the broken system is not the way forward. You won't find them repeating the mistakes of the past by reaching for the energy of resistance nor calling for a reforming or rewriting of policy (at least not as a first line of defense). Rather than confront the challenges of the market economy via the breathtakingly clumsy political process, co-ops instead offer an *immediate* engine of political and economic transformation that works within the market economy itself. Reaching for the tools of cooperation turns out to be a far more expedient approach when the evolution of the market can outpace the political process seeking to reform it. By the time any corrective action is prescribed, the process may have already been rendered obsolete. Co-ops allow for change to emerge from *within* the system and at the evolutionary pace of the system itself.

> "According to Darwin's *Origin of Species*, it is not the most intellectual of the species that survives; it is not the strongest that survives; but the species that survives is the one that is able best to adapt and adjust to the changing environment in which it finds itself. Applying this theoretical concept to us as individuals, we can state that the civilization that is able to survive is the one that is able to adapt to the changing physical, social, political, moral, and spiritual environment in which it finds itself."[260]

> — Leon C. Megginson (1963)

History of the Co-op Movement

> "What truly conditions how people live and what societies will become is the degree to which people can exercise control over their lives. Economics is central to this."[261]
>
> — John Restakis, *Humanizing the Economy*

In his account of Tesco's rise to dominance in the United Kingdom, author Andrew Simms writes, "The original purpose of the corporation was to encourage people to invest in projects of public interest." He continues, "It is time to re-invent the corporation so that it works to the benefit of the whole of society."[262] The book was published in 2007, and yet, centuries earlier, and for the very same reasons, people were calling for just the same thing — for a re-inventing of the industrialists' enterprise and their purely profit-driven motivations. Rather than reform the industrialists (the corporations), workers conceived of the cooperative as a business model that could act in the "public interest."

To be sure, the cooperative model was nothing new — more like a formalizing of old ways. Various forms of cooperative organizing were practiced among ancient and tribal societies, long predating the first co-op.[263] There was, however, one particular group credited for bringing some level of formality to the cooperative model. In 1761, at the dawn of the industrial revolution, a group of weavers in Fenwick, Scotland, began cooperating in the acquisition and sharing of materials and looms. By 1769, the group expanded their cooperating into the purchase of a sack of oatmeal, selling each other smaller quantities at a reduced price.[264]

The industrial revolution began to transform British society, leading to an exodus of the population from the food-producing countryside into the cities. Villages were depopulated and subsistence lifestyles were replaced with dependence. Industrialists introduced a culture of profit maximization. Workers were replaced with machines.[265]

Alongside the wealthy elite, the working poor suffered from deplorable conditions: child labor, exploitation, poverty. No longer able to feed themselves off the land, the poor lived with the threat of hunger, which emboldened the industrialists to drive wages to inhumane levels. In extreme cases, the poor would work without pay and instead receive clothes and food in exchange.[266] In response to such extreme economic disparity, people began to organize.

The counter-movements were substantial. Out of the industrial revolution came the luddite movement of 1811 (objection to automation in factories) and the rise of the labor movement in the 1830s. The cooperative movement began with industrialist Robert Owen's commitment to end poverty through "villages of cooperation." William King began publishing *The Cooperator* — a monthly "textbook" for the movement.[267]

The first lasting success of a cooperative came in 1844 when a store opened on Toad Lane in Rochdale, England, with a supply of butter, sugar, flour, oatmeal, and candles. Tea and tobacco were added months later, followed by a flour mill that ensured members had access to unadulterated, freshly milled flour. The store promoted "honest weight" and "fair dealing" and believed in education as a tool for strengthening community. A classroom was built above the store to serve this purpose.

The store was owned by the Rochdale Society of Equitable Pioneers — a group of 28 cotton weavers who each contributed one pound sterling to build the store ($153 equivalent in 2018). Before opening the store, the workers had been demanding better wages from the mills. The stores in the mill towns were often owned by the mills themselves, and the prices of goods were high and quality of foods low. When their demands proved unsuccessful, the cotton weavers turned to innovative forms of consumption as a means to survive on such low wages.[268]

To secure the people-centered values that they had embedded in their cooperative business, the Rochdale Pioneers cemented a set of principles that would become the forebears of today's globally accepted Seven Principles of Cooperation. The Seven Principles set co-ops apart from other forms of business and bind the movement together.

Today, "while the co-operative model parts company with capitalism, it remains firmly connected to the notion that the market can be made responsive to human needs," writes John Restakis in his book *Humanizing the Economy.*[269]

The success of the Rochdale model caught on, and more than four hundred consumer co-ops were operating in England by the mid-1800s.[270] Today, a sign leading off the highway into the town of Rochdale reads, "Birthplace of cooperation."

The Seven Principles of Cooperation[271]

1. Open and Voluntary Membership
2. Democratic Member Control
3. Members' Economic Participation
4. Autonomy and Independence
5. Education, Training, and Information
6. Cooperation Among Cooperatives
7. Concern for Community

The First Consumer Co-ops in Canada and the United States

"The absence of democracy in economics is a permanent threat to the survival of democracy in politics."[272]

— John Restakis, *Humanizing the Economy*

Waves of immigrants from many parts of Europe to North America
brought cooperative ideals with them.

The first consumer cooperative store in Canada was established by
British immigrants in the coal-mining town of Stellarton, Nova Scotia,
in 1861.[273] The larger Canadian cooperative movement, however, was
first established by dairy farmers, who developed more than 1,200
cooperative creameries and cheese factories between 1860 and 1900. In
1900, Alphonse Desjardins created the first cooperative banking institution, and by 1909, the first national co-op association was formed
to support the sector.[274] On Malcolm Island in British Columbia, a
Finnish community started the Sointula Co-op Store in 1909. It
remains the longest-running cooperative in Western Canada and the
longest-running food cooperative in North America.

In its early days, the co-op model brought relief to many of Canada's
farming communities. Oligopolies had formed in sectors of the food
system like grain processing. To gain increased power in the marketplace, farmers responded by creating cooperatively owned mills and
grain-handling facilities. Cooperatively owned banks gave farmers
credit when banks were unwilling.[275] Today, Canada has the highest
per capita membership in credit unions and *caisse populaires* (people's banks), with over one thousand of them now serving ten million
members (one-third of the population). Vancity is Canada's largest
community credit union, having formed in 1945 to address the lack
of access to financial services in the low-income neighborhood of
Vancouver's East Side.

Ironically, Canada's largest grocery chain today traces its roots to the
early cooperative movement. In 1919, the United Farmers' Co-operative
hired T.P. Loblaw to develop a chain of centrally managed cooperative
grocery stores. The effort failed, but Loblaw took this experience and
founded what would become Loblaw Companies Ltd.[276]

Similar to Canada, some of the first cooperatives in the United States were agricultural and organized by dairy farmers. Consumer co-ops also emerged. By 1866, most industrial cities were home to a consumer cooperative. The first of these co-ops emerged out of labor organizations (as a response to worker exploitation). The Workingmen's Protective Union in Boston coordinated bulk food purchases for its members and in the 1850s maintained 400 protective unions in the northeastern U.S.[277]

One account of the first food co-op in the United States is in New York City in 1822,[278] but the first consumer cooperative based on the Rochdale principles is understood to be the short-lived Union Cooperative Association #1 in Philadelphia (1864). It's said to have contributed greatly to cooperative ideology in the U.S.[279]

Another important and often overlooked area of early cooperative development was among segregated black communities. The Colored Farmers' National Alliance and Cooperative Union (CFACU) was formed in 1886.[280] By the late nineteenth century, CFACU branches had opened up retail stores in Virginia, South Carolina, Alabama, Louisiana, and Texas. Members could purchase goods at reduced prices.[281]

One of the most influential figures in the formation of black cooperatives was W.E.B. Du Bois, who, in 1907, documented 103 African American-owned distribution or consumer cooperatives. Du Bois viewed cooperatives as a promising response to racial economic inequality.[282]

The Empowered Consumer

As the monopolists of industry rose to power in the turn-of-the-century Progressive Era, so too did the empowered consumer. The National Consumers League founded by middle-class women in 1899 pioneered early conceptions of consumer rights and supported producers by encouraging conscientious consumption.[283] In the eyes of early cooperators, however, the ethical consumer alone was not revolutionizing the economy, but was simply reforming it — continuing to enable the maximization of profit in the capitalist system.

This became the raison d'être of the first national cooperative association, the Cooperative League of the USA (CLUSA) — to transform

America by replacing both the capitalist economy and the state with co-ops. It was an entirely new forum for the ethical consumer. To be certain, this was *not* socialism. As the founding president James Warbasse of CLUSA wrote in 1920, "[Socialists] want the government to take over business; we want the people directly to do it." Co-ops, as they were understood, could achieve socialist aims *without* the state.[284]

Operating today as the National Cooperative Business Association (NCBA), the CLUSA has been the most influential organization in the last hundred years of cooperative development in America. In its early days, CLUSA drew its base of support from the labor movement. The group believed that a more people-centered America would require the efforts of laborers *and* consumers. By itself, CLUSA saw the labor movement as constrained without the capacity to control consumption. If the labor movement was to successfully achieve higher wages, the point of consumption needed to also be protected so that any gains in the workplace would not be extracted in the marketplace. As CLUSA saw it, the labor movement would never "truly be free of capitalist exploitation if they limited their demands to higher wages, reduced hours and better working conditions."[285]

> The constructive function of the consumers' cooperative movement was to awaken the working class to the complete exploitative nature of capitalism and train the class to lead the cooperative economy that would slowly replace capitalism until that economic system's eventual demise.
>
> Labor, CLUSA argued, had learned that through striking they could "paralyze the machine" and "stop things." However, "Labor must take the next step, and learn how to start things."[286]

CLUSA's vision for a labor-led cooperative movement was only mildly effective. Labor unions *did* establish hundreds of consumer cooperatives between 1916 and the end of the 1930s, but there was a "general absence of a strong and meaningful relationship" between the two movements — they were generally incompatible. The labor movement was still seen to be legitimizing the capitalist economy while Warbasse was convinced that capitalism would fall. As he saw it, the cooperative economy would need to be built from the ground up. But unlike the socialist and communist visions at the time, the cooperative economy did *not* need to wait for collapse to commence construction. The cooperative vision was one of patient evolution, not one of "disruption and chaos."[287]

The Food Co-op Waves

> "Sensing this transfer of power from the government to corporations, which is a hallmark of the emerging global neo-liberal order, protestors have decided to focus on brands rather than on policy makers to get things done. In keeping with this change, it is almost as if citizens have outsourced their politics from the voting booth to the supermarket.
>
> This does not represent a retreat from politics, but a shift in venues."[288]
>
> — Bryant Simon, Temple University

THE "FOOD FOR PEOPLE NOT PROFIT" MANTRA is a principal feature marking the waves of food co-op formation in North America.

Whereas the first wave of consumer co-op activity leading up to the Great Depression was generally led by the labor movement, a new movement gained strength between 1930 and the 1950s, this time led by consumers. The cooperative movement began to see consumers, not workers, as central to social change.[289]

The Consumer Wave

The labor movement's interest in consumer co-ops continued into the 1930s, particularly as a result of the Great Depression. Membership in consumer cooperatives doubled between 1933 and 1936.[290]

As a distinct movement from other food co-op development, African Americans were also successful in establishing co-ops as an instrument to rise above the economic struggles of a segregated nation. W.E.B. Du Bois believed self-segregation would be necessary to achieve equity for black Americans. For Du Bois, retail co-ops could be what he referred to in 1917 as the "economic way out, our industrial emancipation."[291]

> "There exists today a chance for [blacks] to organize a cooperative State within their own group. By letting Negro farmers feed Negro artisans, and Negro technicians guide [black] home industries and [black] thinkers plan this integration of cooperation, while [black] artists dramatize and beautify the struggle, economic independence can be achieved. To doubt that this is possible is to doubt the essential humanity and the quality of brains of [black people]."[292]
>
> — W.E.B. Du Bois, 1935

In 1934 in Gary, Indiana, a successful African American buying club was formed and within three months had become a fully-fledged grocery store. The Negro Co-operatives Stores' Association had 400 members in their first year and did more business than any other black-owned retailer in the country.[293]

Housing projects in 1930s Harlem also became home to food co-ops like the Pure Food Co-operative Grocery Store that in 1934 was owned by 350 Harlem families. In one case, a Harlem food co-op was so successful, the local A&P was forced to closed.[294]

Meanwhile CLUSA welcomed the Roosevelt administration's efforts to reconstruct the economy by placing increased power into the hands of consumers, but saw it as only a short-term measure to "ease the pains of poverty" and "give time for thinking things through and organizing the new cooperative economic order."[295]

At American colleges and universities, interest in the study of cooperatives grew and is likely why many consumer co-ops began to appear in college towns. Some of the more notable co-ops were connected to the University of Chicago (1932), Cornell University (1932), and Dartmouth College (1936). In Dartmouth's home of Hanover, New Hampshire, seventeen families (mostly Dartmouth faculty) formed what would become the Hanover Consumers Co-operative Society. Unlike many Depression-era co-ops, Hanover continues to this day as one of the largest and most successful food co-ops in the country.

According to Hanover's historical records, it's clear that the consumer co-op movement was "catching on like wildfire," says Hanover's Allan Reetz. "There was this rabid collegiality of one co-op quickly reaching out to help another newcomer to this model of selling groceries to consumers."[296] Hanover's founders clearly relied on the wisdom and experience of already-established co-ops operating elsewhere. "Cooperating among cooperatives" was then, as it is today, a foundational principle to the growth of the movement.

At its incorporation, sixty-two families committed the capital required to start the store, and a manager was hired. The Hanover Co-op would purchase foods in bulk and pass on savings to members. From its beginning, the co-op was committed to purchasing from local producers and distributors.[297]

After the war, 2.5 million people across the United States had become members of retail co-ops.[298] The thrust of the movement, however, began to change. In its vision for a cooperative commonwealth, CLUSA began to scale back its approach. Instead of replacing capitalism, the movement would set its sights on challenging the monopolies and would do so as a sector *co-existing* within a capitalist economy.[299, 300]

As the first co-op supermarkets began to appear, the grocery giants sensed a new threat. The chains launched attacks on food co-ops, calling them "un-American, subversive and communistic." One newspaper headline read; "Retailers Plan Nation-wide War on Co-ops."[301]

Just as the big grocers used low prices to drive out the smaller independents, co-ops were not immune to their wrath. Many co-ops failed. CLUSA's director in Washington, DC, said that the failure of co-ops was the result of them "competing against a false price level established by chain stores."[302]

While many co-ops failed, many prospered. By the 1950s, there were twenty thousand co-ops with six million members. In San Francisco, one quarter of the population were members of the Berkeley Food Co-op (1939).[303]

Early Consumer Food Co-ops Still in Operation

1909 — Sointula Co-op Store — Sointula, BC

1935 — Adamant Cooperative — Adamant, VT

1936 — Hanover Consumer Cooperative Society
(Co-op Food Stores) — Hanover, NH

1937 — Swarthmore CO-OP* — Swarthmore, PA

1941 — Putney Food Co-op — Putney, VT

1943 — Niskayuna Co-op Market — Niskayuna, NY

* Began in '32 as produce buying club

In their efforts to grow, remain relevant and compete, many food co-ops in the 1950s began to resemble their capitalist counterparts. It was hard to distinguish old-wave co-ops from supermarkets.[304] Member participation in the co-op democratic process decreased, and many co-ops across the globe entered into what John Restakis calls a "phase of conservatism."[305]

In Canada, this era brought about what today is the country's largest network of consumer co-ops — Federated Co-operatives Limited (FCL) — while the now-defunct Co-op Atlantic became a strong force in Canada's eastern provinces. These stores are and were markedly different from those that are the focus of this book, those which were formed in the early 1970s. Whereas the 1970s co-ops operated on a parallel course to the conventional chains, the mid-century co-ops competed head-on.

Today, the mid-century co-ops have retained their more conservative roots and resemble conventional grocers, but they're certainly worth mentioning as a unique application of the cooperative model. Whereas many of the co-ops under the FCL umbrella are financially stable, Co-op Atlantic's demise offers a cautionary tale of what *may* happen when a food co-op or federation of co-ops drinks the conventional Kool-Aid. This will be explored in a later chapter.

Hanover, New Hampshire — Main Street Parade, with Co-op Store in the background. ca. 1961. SOURCE: HANOVER CONSUMER COOPERATIVE SOCIETY

In the United States, one food co-op that got its start in 1953 stands on its own. The Puget Consumers Co-op of Seattle (PCC) began as a buying club of fifteen families and would grow to become a leader in the natural food co-op movement. In 1967, PCC opened its first store, marking the beginning of what today is known as "The New Wave" of food co-ops.

The New Wave

Whereas the 1940s through '50s saw a transition of food co-ops from being a working-class movement to a middle-class movement, the late '60s through '70s marked the entry of a new and predominantly middle-class and price-conscious cooperator — the counterculturalist. This new wave of community-owned grocery stores would end up playing an important role in the growth of the organic, fair-trade, and local food movements and would increase public awareness of healthy food, food quality, and many food issues. The largest and most successful community-owned grocery stores in the United States and Canada today are mostly a product of this counter-movement. An estimated five to ten thousand food co-ops (or "food conspiracies") were started in the 1970s.[306]

Out of the prosperity of the '50s and '60s came a number of well-organized resistance movements to the economic, racial, and gender disparities of the time. Civil rights, women's rights, and the anti-war movements had created a highly organized counterculture. Two other significant global events deepened the counterculture's commitment to food as an engine for change: the end of cheap energy precipitated by the OPEC oil shock, and the global food shortage caused by the devastating harvests of 1972 and 1974. Like their earlier twentieth-century revolutionary counterparts, the '60s and '70s revolutionaries began to envision economic systems that would replace capitalism. But the next wave of food co-ops wasn't driven entirely by the desire for a new economic order. The 1960s was a time of increasing awareness of diet and nutrition, and many had begun turning to vegetarianism and unprocessed whole foods. Privately owned alternative natural food stores served this new demand, but their prices were high.

To secure greater control over their food while ensuring it was nutritious and affordable, people organized food co-op buying clubs and storefronts across the U.S. and Canada. "You could go to an anti-war meeting and then go to a food co-op discussion and half of the room were the same people," says longtime food co-op leader Dave Gutknecht.[307] In one case, the People's Food Co-op in La Crosse grew out of a class on whole foods at the University of Wisconsin.

Most co-ops were initially financed with little capital. Access to traditional forms of capital was hard to come by. Commercial lenders were hesitant to lend to zero-profit cooperative businesses. Over 60 percent of established co-ops at the time were refused financing.[308] Most relied on truly bottom-up democracy and depended upon members for both financing and labor. Member labor kept prices low.

Co-op buying clubs and storefronts came to support craft food production, organic farming and provided healthier alternatives to highly processed "corporate food." Food was the vehicle for a new way of life. "Selling food isn't our goal, it's just a pretext for building, living, and breathing models of revolutionary change," said one member of Washington, DC's Field of Plenty Co-op of the late 1970s.[309]

The New Wave co-ops became progressive neighborhood community centers. Outpost Natural Foods Co-op in Milwaukee, Wisconsin, was open twenty-four hours a day, "not just to sell more food, but because people wanted a place to hang out," says founding member Steve Pincus. "There was often a faint odor of marijuana, and the spacey checkout clerks sometimes made incorrect change." For many food co-op founders, food would become the ground zero from which society could be transformed. "We wanted to set up an alternative, parallel system to just about everything, and food was a good place to start."[310]

The spaces food co-ops grew into, however, were far from bastions of storybook utopian vision. Many of today's most successful co-ops first set up shop in the basements of houses and churches. Stores were often cramped and unkept and lacking air conditioning. Unlike the linear design of supermarkets, the layout of food co-ops was often more maze-like. The Buffalo Mountain Food Co-op in Hardwick, Vermont, shared a roof with a gun shop and a liquor store. "Under one roof you could purchase a "pistol, a pint of Jim Beam, and a pound of tofu," says founding member Annie Gaillard.[311]

The governance of the early co-ops was haphazard, often intentionally so. They rejected the supposed benefits of formalized structure for the "intimacy of spontaneously occurring and situationally flexible leadership."[312]

Members of the new wave co-ops were proud of their grocery stores. They used slogans like "we own it" and placed co-op bumper stickers on their vehicles. "How many supermarket customers are willing to put Safeway bumper stickers on their cars even if these were offered free of charge?" remarked one researcher studying food co-ops in 1982.[313]

As hubs of community activity, food co-ops often became the only places providing the economic and political resources for groups working on strategies for alternative living. They became the best place for "leaflets, collecting signatures and discussing issues." They were highly social environments. When researchers studying food co-ops in 1982 approached shoppers at both co-ops and supermarkets for interviews, customers at supermarkets "were more likely to avoid eye contact and walk away when approached." Overall, they found higher rates of interactions at co-ops between shoppers and between shoppers and workers — a level of intimacy that for people "habituated to the impersonality of commercial supermarkets" was understood as "threatening to non-members."[314]

The new-wave consumer co-ops had arrived without any formal ties to the early cooperative movement.[315] They were also noticeably different from the larger, more conventional food co-ops of the previous decades. "The tone of business [was] friendlier, warmer, looser," wrote William Ronco in his 1974 book *Food Co-ops: An Alternative to Shopping in Supermarkets.*[316]

Mountain Avenue Market (Fort Collins Co-op), Fort Collins, Colorado, ca. 1978–1980.
SOURCE: MOUNTAIN AVENUE MARKET

To facilitate the rapid rise of co-op buying clubs and storefronts, distribution co-ops were established to increase buying power of the individual co-ops and to centralize food storage and distribution. Iowa's Blooming Prairie Co-operative Warehouse of 1976 would eventually service food co-ops in five states and offer direct support to groups interested in starting co-ops or transitioning from a buying club to a storefront.[317] Many of the distribution co-ops were owned by the individual co-ops being supplied.

The importance of new food co-ops to the ideologies that spawned them is best captured by the violent clashes that took place in the Twin Cities of Minneapolis–St. Paul between rival factions of cooperators. Yes, an oxymoron! In one case in 1975, food co-op organizers battled over control of the People's Warehouse — a food co-op distributor. On one side were the anarchists, on the other, the communists. The firebombing of a delivery truck, Molotov cocktails through the window of Bryant Central Co-op, a violent takeover of Seward Co-op — the formation of food co-ops in the Twin Cities was impassioned, albeit an isolated extreme among food co-op formation.[318] Cooperative combat aside, the Twin Cities and surrounding communities became a hotbed of food co-op activity.

In Canada, two particular distributors were instrumental in supporting the formation of co-op buying clubs and storefronts. In 1976, the Ontario Federation of Food Co-operatives & Clubs was founded by eleven co-ops and clubs to provide distribution to their groups. The federation would become the Ontario Natural Food Co-op and for decades would serve buying clubs and natural food stores across the province.[319] Two small Ontario consumer co-op storefronts that have stood the test of time are the London Food Co-op in London (1970) and Karma Co-op in Toronto (1972).

In British Columbia, CRS Workers' Co-op of Vancouver formed Fed-Up Co-operative Wholesale in 1972 to serve ten BC co-ops and clubs.[320] By 1975, it was servicing more than fifty groups. At the Fed-Up warehouse, labor came in the form of a rotation of volunteers who would travel from member buying groups from all over Western Canada. The volunteers would prepare and package foods for distribution. For volunteers from the West Kootenay, this meant a sixteen-hour round-trip.[xiv] This level of commitment validates how the establishing of cooperative food-buying groups was about more than just access to better-quality food. To borrow the concepts of American sociologist Wini Breines, food co-ops held the potential to build community in "lived action and behavior."[321] For Breines, the vision of a future society arises when people construct institutions that become the sites of "alternative sources of power."[322]

The people generating such sources of power through food co-ops believed they were also actualizing something that was culturally appropriate. Similar to many of the co-ops of previous decades that had opened along ethnic lines, the cultural and social values espoused by the counterculture were simply not being met by conventional grocers.

Many of the food-buying clubs in the West Kootenay were developed by American counterculturalists, some of whom had previous experience launching co-ops in the United States. Jon Sheppard, an American immigrant to the region who had been a founding member of the Food Conspiracy buying club in Berkeley, California, helped establish three buying groups in the West Kootenay. For him, the co-ops challenged "the hegemony of the grocery fascists in the region."[323]

Helping support the rise of the region's counterculture was *The Arrow,* a community newspaper that provided alternative perspectives not represented in mainstream local news. Food was a prominent topic of discussion in the paper, which often included concerns about the area's chain grocers and their lack of natural and vegetarian foods. "A member run co-op is forming in your area," reads one ad found in a 1975 edition. "Its aims are to provide an alternative to the Super-Valu-Safeway way of buying food. The co-op is a political organization designed to educate its members of the economics of food production, packaging, distribution and consumption."[324]

---

xiv   Buying clubs from as far away as Saskatchewan and Manitoba also sent volunteers to the Vancouver warehouse.

The area's mainstream newspapers seemed far less interested in covering the subject. When a journalist working for the *Nelson Daily News* approached his editor suggesting he could pen a piece on the area's emerging food co-ops, he was told that no such story would be run because the supermarket chains were advertisers and would disapprove.[325]

The New Wave Grows Up

By the late '70s, many buying groups had begun to merge. In Vancouver, a dozen clubs supplied by Fed-Up joined with CRS to acquire a storefront and open up the East End Food Co-op.[326] In the West Kootenay, buying groups there merged to form what would become the Kootenay Co-op in Nelson — today, Canada's most successful consumer food co-op from the era.

Eventually, Fed-Up folded and was superseded by CRS, which maintained a commitment to supporting communities. "We do not want to change our grocers. We want to change our lives," reads a 1977 CRS report.[327] CRS grew into privately owned Horizon Distributors and became Western Canada's leading distributor of natural foods. Today, Horizon supplies small buying clubs, co-ops, natural food stores, and the largest of the chain grocers.

Once the early '80s had arrived, many food co-ops found themselves at a crossroads. Many co-ops had already grown into successful businesses with managers and boards of directors, while others had retained strong opposition to any formalized structures that resembled capitalism. Paradoxically, the *non*-model approach to cooperation was seen by many as *anti*-democratic compared to more formalized models of intentional planning, delegation, and consenting of decisions. The participatory management approach resulted in meetings dragging on "interminably" with "nothing seeming to be settled." "The same issues arise, get discussed, voted upon, only to appear again in the same or another form." This level of dialogue strengthened the co-ops but also contributed to member burnout.[328] The need for change was in the air. In a 1984 article in *The New York Times*, Ron Cotterill, a professor of agricultural economics at the University of Connecticut, proclaimed that the "general blush of social and cooperative spirit that was present before 1980 is gone." Cotterill believed it was time for co-ops to become more "practical" and "businesslike." It was time to learn that "capital" was different from "capitalism" and being profitable meant staying in business."[329] If they continued to rely on a non-traditional, erratic approach, co-op members could "burn out this hopeful alternative and doom the national movement to obsolescence," said one member of a co-op.[330] The greatest threat to co-ops at the time was themselves. "You can't be an economic alternative if you're not around," said food co-op leader Karen Zimbelman in 1985.[331] If the co-ops could *not* make it, the alternatives to eaters were the conventional supermarkets. Many co-ops chose to avoid such demise.

For those willing to evolve, this was no easy transition. Co-ops would need to balance the ethics and values of their members with the realities of running a business. Weavers Way in Philadelphia was well ahead of the early '80s curve. They had already had a dialogue in 1974 to decide whether or not to retain the existing "go with the flow" approach and have the co-op's entire existence as a viable business depend on a few people's "physical and emotional energy."[332] The majority of members chose to evolve into a more consumer-oriented board and management structure that could keep them functioning well into the future. Today, Weavers Way is one of the most successful and inspiring co-ops in the country.

For the co-ops that "grew up" through the early '80s, it was far from "selling out." "They did not suddenly morph into free-market, profit-fixated corporations, as many collectivists feared."[333] Co-op managers at the time understood that if they deviated at all from the market's "competitive fringe by imitating the supermarket chains' model of growth," they would become more vulnerable to the market power of the big chains.[334] Co-ops understood the niche they operated in and the value their position brought to their cause. "Growing up," however, threatened the low prices that co-ops had become well-known for.

The early new wave co-ops had kept food prices remarkably low, thanks to the energy and effort of volunteers who carried out tasks that would otherwise have been performed by paid labor. To keep prices low, many co-ops maintained their roots as "participatory co-ops," requiring members to commit labor to the functioning of the store. Many of these co-ops had evolved to have paid managers, but with on-the-floor tasks performed by members. The participatory approach was effective at keeping prices down — generally 25 percent lower than conventional stores.[335]

Some co-ops made member labor a requirement, while others made it optional. Choosing to invest one's time granted access to lower prices. An estimated three thousand of these participatory co-ops existed in 1982.[336] Not surprisingly, requiring member participation at co-ops was precarious. Most co-ops who emerged successfully out of the era relied completely on paid labor, or made member-labor optional.

This era of change reduced the total number of food co-ops in the country, but total volume of sales among co-ops remained steady. Some of the co-ops that had weathered the period chose to open up second and even third stores, like North Coast Co-op in Arcata/Eureka, California, and PCC in Seattle.

Modernizing co-op stores with cash registers, refrigeration, management teams, and boards opened up new possibilities. With stronger frameworks in place for running a grocery store, co-ops could expand their creative potential and begin to truly develop their bigger picture visions — particularly, placing greater attention on the foods they were selling. Their power to effect change was strong. Co-ops boycotting products was not uncommon nor was the introducing of previously restricted foods. With many co-ops having grown up as vegetarian stores, some began to introduce meat. The Brattleboro Food Co-op in Vermont held a referendum in 1985 with members voting 51 percent in favor of carrying meat.[337] At the Wedge Community Co-op in Minneapolis, convenience foods and frozen dinners also began to appear on the shelves.[338]

The co-ops that made it into the '90s had deservedly entered into a period of abundance. Interest in vegetarianism and organic food was growing, and co-ops were well-positioned to serve this rising demand. Conventional stores, on the other hand, were not yet prepared to compete on these products and knew very little about this peculiar market of conscientious consumers.

Member-Owners of Twin Cities (MN) Food Co-ops

Year	# Retail Stores	# Members	% Change	Average # Members
1992	13	10,655		820
2002	15	36,157	239%	2,410
2012	17	91,102	152%	5,359
20-year gain	4	80,447	755%	4,539

Source: CDS 2014[339]

The Newest Wave

There was very little new food co-op development in the 1990s and early 2000s, but many existing co-ops thrived.

As the new century commenced, so did increased awareness of food politics. With it came a renewed interest in the model of community-owned grocery stores, and another wave of food co-op formation followed.

One of the first co-ops of the new wave was the River Valley Co-op in Northampton, Massachusetts, population 29,000, which opened in 2008. A 1970s food co-op in Northampton had failed in the tumultuous early '80s, with the arrival of the Bread and Circus natural food chain sealing its fate. In 1992, Bread and Circus was acquired by Whole Foods.

Of the small number of independent natural food stores in the city, none were able to serve shoppers' full range of grocery needs. A local consumer-owned, full-service grocery store became the most attractive alternative among a group of residents who first met in 1998. The store they envisioned would help to build the local food movement and support the local economy. It would need to be "large enough to meet your needs and small enough to meet your neighbors."

By 1999, the co-op was incorporated, but it would take almost ten years before the store would open its doors. Founding members engaged in community outreach by tabling at local events and standing on street corners to recruit new members.

By 2001, with three hundred members on board, the co-op hired Rochelle Prunty as general manager. Within six months, membership had grown to one thousand. The original preferred site had fallen through, and the search for an alternative led them in 2002 to a piece of land adjacent to the Potpourri Mall. All seemed to be in place until a tentacle of grocery giant dominance emerged from the depths in the form of a deed restriction. It turned out in the early 1960s, Stop & Shop — a now-Dutch-owned multinational — offered many nearby landowners attractive funding in exchange for deed restrictions to prevent other competitors from opening and operating grocery stores anywhere near their store on the main commercial strip into Northampton. This restriction included the land by Potpourri Mall. Naturally, the co-op approached Stop & Shop and requested that the restriction be lifted. After six months of meetings, Stop & Shop informed the co-op, quite bluntly, that "[they] consider retail a war and if the co-op opens, we will use every weapon in our arsenal to protect our market share."

Undeterred by the threat, River Valley secured another suitable location in an abandoned rock quarry. "There was no deed restriction there," jokes Prunty. The project was eligible for New Markets Tax Credit funding, making what had at first seemed like an impossible project look feasible with an additional $1 million in funding from the co-op's founding owners in the form of member loans. With that assurance, lending institutions pooled funds to bring a total $7.3 million in funding for the new venture.

In 2008, the co-op opened in a 17,434-square-foot space with 2,500 members and 74 staff. After a challenging first year, River Valley still managed to achieve break-even by the one-and-a-half-year mark. By 2011, the co-op was turning a profit, and in 2014, it was purchasing over $3.7 million in local foods, generating $20 million in total sales and employing 130 people who served over 6,700 members. In its first ten years, the co-op purchased over $40 million in local foods and directed $750,000 in contributions to and sponsorships of local nonprofits. Of its 167 staff, over 90 percent are full-time, and all are eligible for the co-op's $15-an-hour minimum wage — introduced four years ahead of the state-mandated $15 minimum wage. As of 2018, a second store is being explored to serve its ten-thousand-plus owners.[340]

River Valley is an example of a highly successful newest wave co-op that formed at a time without a very well-developed support system for start-up food co-ops. But once the local food movement took hold, interest in co-ops exploded. To nurture and support this wave of interest, organizations like the Food Co-op Initiative (FCI) were formed with the support of the national food co-op sector. FCI focused on organizing the movement, CDS Consulting conducted planning and feasibility studies for co-ops, and National Co-op Grocers' development co-op focused on operations. Between 2008 and 2018, 134 new co-ops opened in the United States with a 74 percent success rate. This represents 160,000 new member–owners of community-owned grocery stores nationwide. As of 2019, another 100 are in the works.[341]

In Canada, a food co-op development initiative was launched in Ontario in 2009, and many of the co-ops there, like The Mustard Seed in Hamilton (2014) and the Berry Road Food Co-op in Toronto (2019), have promising futures.

With more support for food co-op development, many of these newest wave co-ops have launched directly into storefront formats. Others have followed in the footsteps of the 1970s buying clubs. In Reno, Nevada, the successful Great Basin Community Food Co-op began as a buying club in 2005 — aligning their purchases with a weekly CSA box program. With the two groups combined, it only took a year before it was realized a storefront would better serve members. The co-op now generates $4.35 million annually with 2.4 percent profit margins. In 2017 alone, Great Basin welcomed 1,483 new member-owners.

The most surprising feature of the newest wave of co-ops has been their resilience through an incredibly challenging economic climate. Natural food chains have burst onto the scene, and conventional chains are dedicating more square footage to many of the same foods that co-ops have traditionally carried. The success of many co-ops in this new competitive climate indicates that there's something different about co-ops that draws eaters' interest.

The launch of the Portland Food Co-op (PFC) in Portland, Maine, helps tell this story of ambition and resilience in the face of seemingly impossible odds.

When it opened in 2014, PFC wasn't the first food co-op to have operated in the city; the previous one had closed its doors in 1997. This left eaters who were interested in alternatives to the big grocers to rely on the Portland Public Market, The Whole Grocer (a privately owned natural food store), and one location of the Wild Oats natural food chain (which, by the way, to much disdain, had opened literally next-door to The Whole Grocer in 2003). Then, in 2006, the Public Market closed and Whole Foods moved into town. Whole Foods staked its claim by purchasing The Whole Grocer and commencing construction on a megastore that opened the following year. Whole Foods shut down The Whole Grocer location, then announced its nationwide plans to acquire the Wild Oats chain. Portland's Wild Oats location was soon shuttered.[342] Whole Foods had effectively colonized the alternative food scene in Portland, Maine.

Rather than surrender to the Texas-based grocer, in 2008, residents launched the Portland Food Co-op — a buying club that relied on distributors like UNFI, Frontier Natural Products Co-op, and local suppliers. By 2012, 350 member–owners were purchasing $200,000 a year through the co-op's online ordering system. In their move toward a storefront, a core group of fifty members began forming committees in 2013, and by 2014, membership had grown to two thousand. The required $1.3 million was raised to open the store — $800,000 of it provided by members, with the remainder contributed by the Cooperative Fund of New England and the City of Portland. The store opened in 2014.[343] A pretty incredible story of "what's possible."

Beyond Natural Foods — Co-ops for Low-Income Communities

Joining as a part of the newest wave are two new breeds of food co-op.

In one new stream are co-ops offering a blend of conventional and natural foods. In another stream is an interest among communities that find themselves in "food deserts" — low-income neighborhoods devoid of any full-service grocery store whatsoever. Difficulty accessing a nearby full-service grocery store may exist in any neighborhood regardless of income levels, but the impact among low-income communities is considerably greater due to the comparative lack of access people with limited financial means have to transportation. Because of the promise that the cooperative model holds for this second stream, an entire chapter is dedicated to this (hopeful) next generation of co-ops. There are inspiring stories of food co-ops being established in food deserts and in mixed-income neighborhoods lacking easy access to healthy food. The chapter dedicates particular attention to some of the astounding efforts in Cincinnati, Ohio, and Greensboro, North Carolina.

Whether one lives in a low- or high-income neighborhood, an urban center, or rural countryside, or whether one shops for conventional or organic foods, grocery stores owned by their shoppers hold the possibility for *all* people to democratically control access to good food.

Consumer Food Co-ops Today

"Over the last twelve years at my co-op, I have learned to see what a child raised the 'co-op way' looks like: bright-eyed, curious, engaged, polite, verbal, and rosy-cheeked. Watching people make great food and lifestyle choices at my co-op has convinced me that providing a child with real food, and helping them see the connection that their food makes with soil, people, water and the economy, makes for a great kid." [344]

— Crystal Halvorson, General Manager,
Menomonie Market Food Co-op, Wisconsin

I N THE COMMUNITY ROOM at the People's Food Co-op in Portland, Oregon, members are invited to attend a talk on psychedelics hosted by the Portland Psychedelic Society. This is 2018, but the event is reminiscent of the food co-ops of the 1970s.

Characteristics reminiscent of the formative years of food co-ops can still be found at today's co-ops, but for most shoppers, the cues that were once stereotypically "food co-op" have mostly been shed. Many food co-ops today are high-functioning modern grocery stores. They're also much more than just places to purchase food. This entire chapter is dedicated to the contributions food co-ops make *beyond* the shelves.

There's Nothing Cookie-Cutter About Food Co-ops

Food co-ops come in every shape, size, and color. They can be found in the thick of a dense urban metropolis, smack in the middle of a residential neighborhood, or at the crossroads of rural country roads. They're found from Fairbanks, Alaska, to San Diego, California, from

Florida to Maine, and from British Columbia to Nova Scotia. They live in historic schoolhouses, suburban malls, and multi-story condominiums. They range in size from less than one thousand square feet to well over twenty thousand, and from single-store locations to entire chains. Some co-ops have moved locations more than a half-dozen times. Others like the People's Food Co-op in Portland have been in the same building since 1970. Co-ops adapt as needed to their communities.

Geographically, there are some areas of higher-than-usual food co-op concentration: the American Midwest (particularly around the Great Lakes) and New England are the most concentrated of any regions. At a more local level, the Twin Cities of Minneapolis–St. Paul have eight co-ops comprising fifteen locations (and many more in nearby cities and towns). In Seattle, Central Co-op has one location, and PCC has twelve, with another five planned.

No other co-op has anywhere near the number of stores as PCC. Of the other co-ops that have gone "chain," like Outpost Natural Foods in Milwaukee, La Montañita Co-op in New Mexico, New Pioneer in Iowa, or Weaver Street Market in North Carolina, all of them operate between two and five stores.

In small cities and towns, the food co-op may be the only grocery store in the downtown core, helping to draw residents to other independent downtown businesses. The Kootenay Co-op in Nelson, BC, is the city's only downtown grocer, as is the Monadnock Food Co-op in Keene, NH; North Coast Co-op's Eureka, CA, location; and both locations of the People's Food Co-op in Rochester, MN, and La Crosse, WI.

Generally, the physical size of a cooperative grocery store pales in comparison to the modern supermarket's average size of 45,000 square feet. This is an important difference that helps to ensure co-ops don't outgrow the smaller, more personalized experience that sets them apart.

Annual sales at food co-ops range from as low as $1 million at a single store to as high as $277 million at PCC's eleven locations.[xv] But by *all* grocery store standards, many single food co-op locations pull

---

xv   2017 fiscal when PCC had 11 stores

Food co-ops range in size from large modern stores to smaller neighborhood markets. Pictured here are Sacramento Natural Foods Co-op (Sacramento, CA) and Alberta Co-op Grocery (Portland, OR). Credit: Sacramento Natural Foods Co-op / Jon Steinman

off staggering sales relative to their size. City Market's downtown location in Burlington, Vermont, moves $42 million of product out of a 12,000-square-foot retail space. With 240 employees at that one location, a 24-hour staffing schedule is required to manage such high volumes in such a small space. At Brooklyn's Flatbush Food Co-op, they sell $17 million in only 4,500 square feet; at the nearby Park Slope Food Co-op, $56 million in only 6,000 square feet.

The process to become a member–owner at a food co-op usually takes five to ten minutes. After making an equity investment of between fifty and two hundred dollars, the new member obtains a share in the co-op. Should the member ever choose to leave the co-op, the share is refunded in full. For people unable to afford the full investment, most co-ops offer more accessible monthly payments.

As for the products on the shelves, food co-ops fit no template, though for much of the previous few decades, they have become almost synonymous with organic and natural foods. While it is true that most co-ops continue to fall within this category, natural and organic are not a requirement of any food co-op constitution. Canada is a great example of this, where most food co-ops (like those of the Federated Co-op family) are visually indistinguishable from conventional supermarket chains. In the United States, where the sector is predominantly rooted in the 1970s "new wave," none have gone nearly so far as to resemble conventional stores, but many have evolved their product selections to reflect the needs of their members and the demographics of their neighborhoods.

- The Sevananda Natural Foods Market in Atlanta is a strictly vegetarian co-op.
- The produce section at the Sacramento Natural Foods Co-op is 100 percent organic, whereas Weavers Way Co-op in Philadelphia has a product mix that is 50/50 natural and conventional.
- At City Market (Onion River Co-op) in Burlington, Vermont, 72 percent of sales are conventional foods, but 40 percent of sales are still from local suppliers.

- The Brattleboro Food Co-op in Vermont began as a natural/organic store but introduced conventional over time.

> "As a mixed income neighborhood that has over 300 shareholders enrolled in our needs-based 10% discount program, we must continue to lower prices in any way possible. We are not omitting non-GMO and organic but trying conventional where it sells and then expanding if need be. Our co-op is for everyone and we must deliver products that meet all people's needs."[345]
>
> — Jon Megas-Russell, Marketing & Community Relations Manager, Brattleboro Food Co-op

What all the food co-ops featured in this book have in common is their success in transmitting one of the core cooperative principles directly on to their store shelves — *Concern for Community*. More on that later.

Food Co-ops as Community Centers

> "We're not serving the community, we are the community."[346]
>
> — Leila Wolfrum, Durham Co-op Market, North Carolina

Grocery stores are one of the most frequently visited businesses within our weekly routines. This makes them ideally positioned to be hubs of community activity and connection. So how do the chain stores in your community fare? Are they reminiscent of a community center? Do they draw people in to their scheduled educational programs? Are they actively supporting your community?

Food co-ops are generally bustling hives of social activity. Even academic research has demonstrated a higher number of social interactions in food co-ops than in conventional stores.[347] Co-op shoppers already know this. The co-op shopper who is *not* feeling social (or is in a rush) may choose to avoid the co-op on occasion and grab a few things at another supermarket. But for the more experienced of co-op shoppers, keeping one's eyes on the shelves greatly reduces the chances of getting held up. This is a wonderful "first-world" problem.

Beyond the intrinsic community center that food co-ops are, it's more common for food co-ops than chain stores to have community rooms directly in the store. Such spaces are symbols of a co-op's strong relationship to its community. At the Franklin Community Co-op in Greenfield, Massachusetts, both a meeting room and a dining room are available to reserve at only fifteen dollars an hour. At the Upper Valley Food Co-op in White River Junction, Vermont, a resource library and reading room is found upstairs with more than two hundred books and films on topics related to alternative living. At City Market in Burlington, Vermont, prior to constructing their second store in 2018, the neighborhood requested a gathering space for community groups. Without hesitation, the co-op included a community room in its new store to fill the void.

Education

Education comprises one of the Seven Cooperative Principles.

At Community Food Co-op in Bellingham, Washington, their educational events read like a continuing education calendar of a community college:

> Monday: Cybersecurity — Learn the basics of cyber-security. We'll talk about how ads, data mining, and Google affect your online experience. FREE

> Tuesday: Solar Energy — Overview of latest solar energy options. FREE

> Wednesday: Co-op Walk, Nutrition Talk — Join a Registered Dietitian for a healthy eating discussion and store tour highlighting ways to balance nutritional, bud-getary, and ecological concerns. FREE

> Thursday: Kids Can Cook — A lunch menu kids can learn to make for the whole family.

> Friday: Pakistani Vegetarian Cooking Class

Not your typical grocery store!

At the Brattleboro Food Co-op, some of their educational offerings extend *beyond* the store and into local schools, hospitals, and museums. At Outpost Natural Foods, a learning education center is made available to groups like the local farmers' market that uses it for farmer training. At Weavers Way, the co-op owns and operates two farms that offer ongoing educational programming and workshops.

Kitchen Skills Training

The healthiest meals are generally made at home with the freshest ingredients available, so it's standard practice for food co-ops to offer classes and workshops that empower people in their home kitchens.

Many co-ops construct teaching kitchens directly in the store, while others like Davis Food Co-op in California have a teaching kitchen in their own dedicated building. Attend a class at the Davis teaching kitchen and receive a complimentary glass of wine or beer! Sweet.

At Sacramento Food Co-op, a fully-fledged "Cooking School and Community Learning Center" was constructed on the upper level of their store and hosts almost daily classes with cooking guides on site. The co-op partners with local nonprofits to provide low-income residents with nutrition education and cooking classes at no charge. At PCC in Seattle, a teaching program began in 1983 and today offers 1,600 classes a year at six of the co-op's locations. At Berkshire Co-op in Great Barrington, Massachusetts, every Saturday morning is a class for kids — vegetable spring rolls, stir-fries, and homemade lip balm are all on the menu. On a budget? Seward Community Co-op in Minneapolis offers free classes to low-income members on basic scratch cooking and how to prepare meals that feed a family of four for under ten dollars.

Children's Programming

At food co-ops, children receive a lot of attention. It's a longstanding tradition for children to receive a free piece of fruit every time they visit the store. Starting around 2016, quite a few chains have followed co-ops' lead and are now offering this in their stores as well.

Harmony Co-op in Bemidji, Minnesota, hosts a monthly Co-op Explorers program for kids twelve and younger. It includes farm tours, ornament making, and an annual harvest festival.

Brooklyn's Park Slope Food Co-op offers free childcare to members while they shop. As Park Slope is a participatory co-op requiring a few hours of member labor per month, childcare is also offered to members during their work shifts.

Co-ops in Schools

Many food co-ops work directly with area schools. Oryana Natural Foods Market in Traverse City, Michigan, designed ten interactive lessons about food, farming, and nutrition for middle- and high-school students, including "Packing a Healthy Lunch," "Smart Snacking" and "Don't be Fooled — Food and Advertising." Berkshire Co-op runs programs that send staff directly into schools, camps and community centers to teach kids about healthy food. Viroqua Food Co-op provides the food for Wisconsin's first organic hot lunch program.

Food Access

Food co-ops have long suffered from a stigma of being overpriced and only accessible to those who can afford to shop there. There's both truth and myth to this, which will be explored later in this chapter. Whether true or just a question of perspective, the story behind food prices really doesn't matter to anyone unable to afford food or healthier, higher-quality options. We can debate food prices till we're blue in the face, but there's no debating the immediacy of food accessibility.

Some co-ops have excelled at making food more accessible — particularly those that are members of National Co+op Grocers, a co-op of co-ops owned by 145 food co-ops across America. Through NCG's Co+op Basics program, individual co-ops use their combined purchasing power to access incredibly low prices on packaged foods through their national distributor, UNFI.

To make membership at most food co-ops more accessible, many permit members to pay their share over longer periods rather than in one lump sum. Bloomingfoods in Indiana offers a 24-month payment plan of \$3.75/month. At Mariposa Food Co-op in Philadelphia, an "owner fund" invites member–owners, shoppers, and local businesses to donate to help offset the share cost for other members.

On everyday purchases, many co-ops offer discount programs to low-income members ranging from 10–20 percent off most items in the store. Most require proof of enrollment in income assistance programs; others, like Central Co-op in Seattle, do not, placing their trust in their shoppers' own definition of "need." Bloomingfoods, Mariposa, and Mississippi Market (MN) offer 10 percent discounts every day, while Central Co-op offers it two days a week. Sacramento Food Co-op's needs-based discount is 15 percent, and Durham Co-op Market offers the highest in the nation, at 20 percent. At Durham, 400 members are signed up to receive the discount, representing 10 percent of their membership. At Mississippi Market, 1,500 members use their discount, which equates to over \$119,000 in annual savings. At City Market, discounts total over \$181,000.

Food co-ops are also prodigious supporters of food access programs beyond their store walls. At NCG's 145 member co-ops alone, 1.5 million pounds of food was donated in 2016 — an average 24,100 pounds per store. At Hanover's Co-op Food Stores, their Willing Hands Round-Up Program invites shoppers at the checkout to round up to the nearest dollar. The program brings in twenty thousand dollars a month, 60 percent of which ends up at food access programs. Round-up programs are common at food co-ops. Weaver Street Market raised \$260,000 in 2017, primarily through their round-up program. The funds are used to purchase food for those in need in Orange County, NC. Weaver Street sources the food and handles all the logistics of delivering the food to food agencies. At Swarthmore CO-OP in Pennsylvania, round-up dollars are put toward Sunday Suppers. The program coordinates volunteers to cook every Sunday for seniors in need of food. Recipients receive three or four nutrient-rich meals each month, made from ingredients purchased through the co-op and cooked in the store after hours.

At La Montañita, the co-op delivers groceries free of charge to any member who is housebound for any reason. At Isla Vista Food

Co-op in California, advocates from the state-supervised Cal-Fresh food stamp program visit the store twice a week to sign people up for the program. This has increased purchases at the co-op through the program by over $100,000 in less than three years.

The West End Food Co-op in Toronto (which sadly closed its doors in 2018) excelled at offering a diversity of food access programs in the mixed-income neighborhood of Parkdale. Other food co-ops should take note. Parkdale residents are 13 percent unemployed, 34 percent low-income, and 21 percent on social assistance. In partnership with local nonprofits, the co-op ran a co-op cred program — inviting low-income residents to help out in the store, kitchen, and local community gardens in exchange for co-op credit. The program was estimated to have helped participants by increasing their purchasing capacity by seven hundred dollars a year — the equivalent of two and a half months of food costs. It also provided participants with employable skills.

Inexpensive Meals for Community Building

A relatively new happening at food co-ops are inexpensive community meals. The meals embody so much of what food co-ops stand for. Bloomingfoods offers three-dollar dinners weekly at two of their locations. At Weavers Way's new Ambler store, four-dollar dinners are offered at a long table set up in the freezer aisle with live music and local beer available. Durham Co-op Market's three-dollar weekly dinners have become one of the most popular events in the city with 500 to 700 people attending (members and non-members alike). BBQ sandwiches with chips and slaw, Brunswick stew, and chicken legs with rice and beans are just some of what's appeared on the weekly menu. The meals are so popular that the co-op is now offering a five-dollar weekly lunch.

Community Giving

The generosity of food co-ops in the communities they operate is substantial. A portion of every dollar spent at most co-ops directly supports nonprofits. In 2017, the Kootenay Co-op contributed the equivalent of $196,625 toward affordable housing initiatives, food access services, schools, choirs, gymnastics programs, sports associations, and wildlife rehabilitation services among others — 185 groups in total.

An average 4 percent of profits at conventional stores are devoted to charitable donations compared with 13 percent at food co-ops. Viroqua Food Co-op's Jan Rasikas recounts, "One year Walmart bragged about giving away $500 to community groups in the town while in that same year our small co-op had given away $9,000."

Round-up programs are often dedicated to nonprofit groups. Mississippi Market's round-up program supports one nonprofit every month with an average $10,000 donation. Three Rivers Market in Knoxville, Tennessee, raises $7,000 each month. At City Market, where $309,000 is contributed annually to community groups, their round-up program alone contributes $27,000 per month to area nonprofits.

Some co-ops use ecological incentives to support nonprofits. Franklin Community Co-op donates five cents for every reusable container or bag a customer uses. Rewarding shoppers for "greener" shopping is common at food co-ops.

Some co-ops offer grants. The North Coast Co-op with its two locations in Arcata and Eureka, California, established a permanent endowment fund in the 1990s. The fund is fed by direct donations, their round-up program, and a 10-cent charge for every paper bag purchased at the checkout. It has granted more than $400,000 to projects that promote sustainable agriculture, nutrition and food security.

At almost every food co-op in North America, people are directly supporting their friends and neighbors with their food purchases. The family you are supporting with your purchases may just be the next person in line at the checkout.

Nonprofit Arms

A number of food co-ops have established their own nonprofits to carry out their missions.

At The Merc Co+op in Lawrence, Kansas, their Community Mercantile Education Foundation (CMEF) 501(c) (3) provides hands-on nutrition education. CMEF's Growing Food Growing Health project works with youth to create school gardens that act as living classrooms. The project tends to over 14,000 square feet of gardens at schools and a residential drug treatment facility for women and their children.

The slogan for Weavers Way's nonprofit, Food Moxie, is "We Dig What We Eat." Food Moxie coordinates experiential programs focused on urban agriculture, nutrition, and the cooperative economy. In 2009, they began offering programming at a homeless shelter to teach residents about gardening and nutrition. Included is a culinary program on how to eat healthy on a budget. In 2014, they launched an urban farm for students with intellectual disabilities and autism. Food Moxie brings more than three hundred students at an area high school to the Weavers Way farm every year. The program includes paid summer internships and an out-of-school time (OST) component.

Positive Workplace

In their earlier years, food co-ops developed a reputation for not paying well. This is not surprising as many early food co-ops were participatory and weren't formed with an intention to create meaningful employment. With the co-op culture of today being primarily rooted in those participatory co-ops of the 1970s, the lines between volunteering and fair pay have taken decades to be clearly drawn. Today, food co-ops are predominantly staffed by paid labor and on average pay a dollar more per hour than conventional grocers, and a higher percentage of staff are eligible for health benefits.[348]

A rather heated and public debate helped move Wheatsville Co-op overnight from an entry-level wage of $9.50 to $13.01. At Central Co-op, entry-level wages of $15 meet the city's newly established living wage. At Hunger Mountain Co-op in Montpelier, Vermont, Valley Natural Foods in Burnsville, Minnesota, and Outpost Natural Foods, 100 percent of their staff earn a living wage as a minimum.

While the workplace at food co-ops is not immune to the same challenges experienced in other places of employment, food co-ops are generally more positive work environments. "I get paid to have fun," says one employee of Durham Co-op Market.[349] It's also not uncommon to find lifelong employees at food co-ops. Many have worked their way into managerial positions without having received any formal training. At Outpost Natural Foods, General Manager Pam Mehnert joined the co-op in 1980 as a customer service clerk and from there became assistant grocery manager, then marketing manager and then GM in 1987. Mehnert became a leader in the national food co-op community. With food co-ops often locating *within* communities rather than *around* them, their staff generally have a shorter distance to travel to work. At Outpost, 58 percent of the staff live within walking or biking distance.[350]

Working Members

With the exception of the Park Slope Food Co-op (1973) and a little more than a handful of smaller co-ops, today's food co-ops rely almost entirely on paid labor. The days of co-ops being exclusive to those who participate are mostly a thing of the past. But that doesn't mean Park Slope has been asleep at the wheel. The co-op has successfully preserved a model that returns substantial benefit to eaters. If anything, the co-op should receive some sort of heritage designation to protect the model as an example of "what's possible." Park Slope's core team of 77 staff are paid to run the store, but that only accounts for 25 percent of the co-op's labor. The other 75 percent comes from the co-op's 17,000 members, each of whom works a mandatory 2 hours 45 minutes every four weeks. Miss a shift? You owe two. Fail to complete the two, you're suspended from shopping until you do. The benefits of this model are huge. Labor is one of the largest expenses at food co-ops — representing anywhere between 18–30 percent of sales. By eliminating 75 percent of Park Slope's labor expense, members are rewarded with 20–40 percent savings on their food purchases — all for less than three hours of work commitment per month.[351] That's a highly worthwhile investment, and the demand for it is high. The co-op became so busy it was forced to cap its membership at seventeen thousand. In 2018, Park Slope finally announced plans for a second store.

In the film *Food Coop* by Tom Boothe (2016), a Park Slope member comparison shops identical products between Whole Foods and the Park Slope Food Co-op.

	Co-op	Whole Foods
Bread (loaf)	$4.30	$6.99
Cheese (Gruyere)	$14.41/lb	$21.99/lb
Pepper (orange)	$2.43/lb	$4.99/lb
Chocolate Bar	$1.65	$2.50
Total (2 weeks of groceries)	**$293**	**$419**

The comparison shop resulted in 40% savings. This works out to annual savings of $3,000. Over 10 years, savings amount to $30,000. All for less than 36 hours of work commitment per year.

SOURCE: FOOD COOP FILM (2016)[352]

Among the other co-ops that have offered a member labor option, most have done away with it in the face of more active enforcement of state minimum wage laws and the Fair Labor Standards Act. While some co-ops have "gotten away" with substituting what would otherwise be paid labor, others have been investigated for the practice. Rather than risk prosecution, most co-ops have retired their volunteer member labor programs. The loss of these programs is considerable. Whereas, at some co-ops, coordinating member labor might have been seen as onerous and inefficient, for others, it returned important benefits. Member labor has historically enhanced the survival of food co-ops. As far back as 1978, researchers had drawn this conclusion for two reasons: member labor "familiarizes the shopper with the co-op and its products," and as a result, shoppers are less inclined to change stores, even if the competition begins offering lower prices. These programs also offer a service that is not offered by the chains — an arrangement which permits trading labor for lower prices.[353] Four decades later, there is still truth to this.

Weavers Way in Philadelphia is committed to maintaining its optional member labor program. One third of its members participate by committing only six hours annually. In exchange, they receive a 5 percent discount on all purchases. For a couple spending $150 per week on groceries, this works out to annual savings of $390. Volunteer labor doesn't save Weavers Way any money, but they use it to engage their member–owners. To be sure, the co-op reviewed the shopping patterns of members enrolled in the program and discovered that they shop at the co-op twice as often and spend more. Member labor "encourages feelings of purpose and solidarity and the social atmosphere of the store is improved."[354]

Discounts can also be higher than 5 percent. At Buffalo Mountain Food Co-op, members who choose to work receive a 10 percent discount per month for every hour worked; at Mariposa Food Co-op, 10 percent for every three hours worked per month.

Some co-ops have gotten innovative with the retiring of their member labor programs. In 2015, City Market rolled 90 percent of their member labor into their support for community nonprofits. Instead of working at the store, members are encouraged to commit their time to a nonprofit. In its first year, co-op members contributed 17,379 hours of labor with twenty different groups such as school food programs, community gardens, and local food system organizations. This was the equivalent of supplying over eight full-time workers. Members receive a discount at the food co-op for their time invested.

Cooperation with Local Businesses

At many food co-ops, membership has perks beyond the walls of the store. Quite a number of them have extensive partnerships with local independently owned businesses. Wheatsville Co-op features a full directory on its website of businesses owned by their members. Three Rivers Market maintains a comprehensive guide of locally owned food based businesses on its site. As a symbol of incredible selflessness, the guide includes a section of competing locally owned grocery stores.

At many co-ops like Central Co-op, Moscow Food Co-op (Moscow, Idaho), and Open Harvest Co-op Grocery (Lincoln, Nebraska), member-owners receive discounts and benefits at dozens of local businesses. This level of cooperation helps insulate community-owned businesses from the pressures of non-local chains.

The Co-op Footprint

The most far-reaching impacts of food co-op shopping come from the food found on the shelves. Food co-ops have shrunk the distance from farm to plate unlike any other grocers, and their sourcing of more ecologically minded food has led the grocery retail industry. Co-ops are often the first to carry products with new sustainability certifications. Same goes for their impact beyond the shelves. PCC's Redmond store was the first in the nation to earn LEED Gold certification (2006) for its building. In 2007, PCC was one of the first to eliminate plastic shopping bags from their stores. In 2013, two PCC stores were the first to house WISErg Harvesters — enzyme-driven digesters that repurpose food scraps into liquid organic fertilizer. Today there are harvesters in five stores.

City Market diverts 83 percent of its waste to compost and recycling and sells 142,535 gallons of bulk water per year — the equivalent of 912,224 twenty-ounce water bottles. Community Food Co-op in Bozeman, Montana, partners with an organization that picks up food scraps from their two stores and their central kitchen/bakery. The hundred thousand pounds of scraps end up at Strike Farms to be used to grow veggies for the co-op's produce department and kitchen.

Isla Vista Food Co-op successfully crowdfunded solar panels for its store. Monadnock Food Co-op launched a community-supported solar project that they will buy outright in the next ten years. The Merc Co+op is home to the city's largest solar installation — providing 29 percent of the store's energy needs.

Outpost Natural Foods publishes what amounts to an encyclopedia of its sustainability achievements and is ranked among the U.S. Environmental Protection Agency's (EPA) Top 30 Green Power Retailers. At their store in Mequon, Wisconsin, rainwater catchment irrigates their kitchen gardens, and their toilets reuse waste water with a reverse osmosis system. The Kootenay Co-op was the first business in the city of Nelson to offer electric car charging stations. North Coast Co-op employs a sustainability coordinator to track its use of natural resources, guide its recycling and composting efforts, and provide them with environmentally responsible alternatives for packaging.

By the Numbers — Food Co-ops vs. Conventional

	CO-OP (Consumer-Owned)		CONVENTIONAL (Privately or Investor-Owned)
LOCAL IMPACT	157	Local foodmakers woking with each store	65
	20%	Locally sourced products sold	6%
	13%	Percentage of income devoted to charitable donations	4%
	38%	Revenue spent locally	24%
HEALTHY & SUSTAINABLE FOODS	82%	Organics as a percentage of produce sales	12%
	48%	Organics as a percentage of grocery sales	2%
EMPLOYEES	$14.31	Average employee earnings including bonuses and profit sharing	$13.35
	68%	Employees eligible for health insurance	56%
	19%	Revenue spent on local wages and benefits	13%
ENVIRONMENTAL IMPACT		Recycling rates	
	96%	Cardboard	91%
	81%	Plastics	29%
	74%	Food waste	36%
	82	Average Energy Star score out of 100	50

SOURCE: NATIONAL CO+OP GROCERS, 2012[355]

Community-Owned Good Food Media

A usual by-product of a community-owned grocery store is a publication celebrating good food. In many cases, food co-op newsletters are a community's *only* food periodical. They're often in the form of monthly or quarterly newsletters. Some publications at larger co-ops like New Pioneer's *Catalyst* and Seward's *Sprout!* are beautifully crafted magazines.

Park Slope's *Linewaiters Gazette* has been published since the co-op first formed in 1973. Some publications have great names like *The Bullsheet* and the *Natural Inquirer.*

Middlebury Natural Foods Co-op's *Under the Sun* is a dense read filled with articles like "Decoding Meat Labels" and features on seasonal foods. In an issue of *Cultivate* from the recently merged Linden Hills Co-op and Wedge Co-op in Minneapolis, the cover article features women of the local food system. French Broad Food Co-op's *Buzz* is heavy on recipes.

Through these publications, food co-ops become the voice of the community and of the local food system.

College Town Co-ops

Young people feel less confident in the kitchen than older generations.[356] Ask the manager of your local chain grocer what they're doing to support young people to get cooking, good chance you'll get a blank stare. Ask what your local food co-op is doing, and they might even hand you a pamphlet about it.

A disproportionately high number of food co-ops are found in college towns, leaving them in a great position to set young people up on a path to self-sufficiency in the kitchen. One co-op leading the way is Isla Vista Food Co-op (IVFC) in Santa Barbara, California — home to the University of California Santa Barbara (UCSB).

Located ten miles north of the city, Isla Vista may very well be located on the mainland, but with only two entrances off the highway to the north and an ocean bordering it to the south, Isla Vista is virtually an island. Of the 23,000 residents, 19,000 of them are students, and all of them packed into less than one square mile. Isla Vista Food Co-op's General Manager, Melissa Cohen, has seen this as an opportunity; "90% of our shoppers are 18-24 years old... they're with us for 2–5 years, then they leave." IVFC likely has the most transitory membership of any American food co-op. "We're always losing our customers," Cohen adds.[357] But this is how it's always been for IVFC. Students built the co-op in 1972 as a spin-off of a sociology class project. Today, IVFC does $3.5 million in sales out of 3,200 square feet.

As an island of teenagers and twenty-somethings, with many deep in debt, food affordability is front and center — 48 percent of undergrads are at some level of food insecurity, 6 percent of them are homeless, and 400 of them are undocumented and therefore unable to access bene-fit programs. IVFC responds to this from all fronts. They've piloted a grocery voucher program that uses funds from the State of California to pay for gift cards so students can shop the co-op. The funding was so successful that the University decided it was only fair to bring other grocers to the table, but when students were surveyed, it was clear that the food co-op was where they most wanted to shop.

To support students' kitchen phobias and food affordability fears, IVFC runs programs to equip students with the right foods, the right skills, and at the cheapest prices possible. Their "Grocery Store 101" store tours offer simple and effective recommendations like "make a list." This eliminates impulse purchases. "When purchasing fresh pro-duce priced by the unit, make sure to grab the biggest one." "When purchasing by the pound, focus on produce that doesn't go bad quickly like potatoes." Tips are provided on how to store produce properly to avoid spoilage. At the entrance to the store, students can pick up a two-page list of 170 low-priced items currently available.

Shopping on a budget of less than $50/week? IVFC publishes shop-ping lists that come in under $50. The guide walks students through the setting up of their "pantry" in week one, and then focuses on fresh foods for the remaining three weeks.

Community-owned grocery stores in college towns help power the food co-op movement. "Students are incubated into the world of food co-ops at a young age," says Cohen. We want these kids to understand that they *do* have the capacity to hold their own future and it doesn't have to be corporate, it can be cooperative." Her vision is working. Many IVFC staff have left Isla Vista and gone on to become fully-fledged food cooperators. Ashley Audycki became Coos Head Food Co-op's Community Outreach Coordinator. Osunkoya Chavon became the first paid worker at the start-up Long Beach Grocery

Co-op, and Anbareen Shefa is working on the merging of a housing and food co-op in East Lansing, Michigan.

Governance and Ownership

The dominant ownership model at North American food co-ops is the consumer co-op — a co-op entirely owned by its customers. There are, however, quite a few successful food co-ops in the United States and Canada that are entirely owned by their workers, like The Big Carrot in Toronto and Rainbow Grocery in San Francisco. Among the consumer food co-ops, a small number are what are known as hybrid co-ops —

Profiles of Board Directors at Food Co-ops

The most engaged members of food co-ops are those who offer their time and energy to the board of directors. The diversity of people who have taken on this responsibility helps to communicate the local community-driven leadership of food co-ops.

Andrea Stanley, *River Valley Food Co-op (Northampton, MA)* — Andrea started Valley Malt with her husband to fill a gap in the local food system and bring local grain to local beer. They farm 80 acres of organic crops like barley, wheat, black beans, sunflowers, and popcorn.

Scott Hess, *Hunger Mountain Co-op (Montpelier, VT)* — Scott was a trader on the floor of the New York Mercantile Exchange (NYMEX) and served on NYMEX's board of directors for ten years. He moved to East Montpelier and shortly thereafter was elected to Hunger Mountain's Co-op Council.

Beth Hopping, *Durham Co-op Market (Durham, NC)* — Beth is co-director at Food Insight Group (FIG), a Durham-based food systems research organization. She holds a PhD in nutrition intervention and policy from UNC–Chapel Hill. Beth works with farmers, grocery retailers, schools, nonprofits, foundations, and community development financial institutions to research and implement ways to strengthen community food systems.

owned by two categories of members, workers *and* consumers. One of the most established hybrid co-ops is Weaver Street Market, where 217 of their 250 staff are worker–owners. Central Co-op joined the hybrid ranks later in the game with 90 percent of members voting in 2015 to introduce worker ownership. The now-closed West End Food Co-op in Toronto was operating under a *multi*-stakeholder model — owned by consumers, workers, *and* food producers.

Governance at food co-ops is vested in a board of directors (or board of trustees) elected by the member–owners. Boards are usually made up of seven to eleven directors serving two- to three-year terms. Many consumer co-ops will also provide a seat on the board for a member of the staff who is elected *by* the staff. In some cases, general managers are also members of the board. While many co-op board directors serve as volunteers, many others receive a modest stipend, store credits or store discounts, or some combination of the three. At larger co-ops like The Wedge, directors receive stipends ranging between $9,128 and $12,778. Other co-ops may simply offer a couple of hundred dollars of store credit per month.

Engaging Members in Their Co-op

On the retail floor, a well-informed and empowered member is an engaged member. To achieve this, some co-ops host store tours for their members. Seward hosts over thirty of them each year.

Behind the scenes, voting for your grocery store's board of directors is a huge opportunity to participate in a co-op's democratic underpinnings. The power of this one act should never be underestimated.

Beyond governance, most co-ops actively engage their members in dialogue during periods of substantial change like expansion planning, changes to bylaws, or significant financial decisions. This becomes increasingly important for co-ops that are growing their impact in their communities by increasing the sizes of their stores. As stores get larger, keeping members democratically engaged in what feels like a less-personalized space can be challenging.

Some co-ops build member engagement directly into their ongoing operations. Franklin Community Co-op hosts member participation circles to keep members talking about the future of their grocery store. During its new store development, the Kootenay Co-op held free weekly lunches for members to casually discuss their co-op with board directors and management. At many co-ops, members are invited to more formally participate on committees. At Park Slope, the Animal Welfare Committee educates members and influences the store's product selections. At Weavers Way, their Food Justice Committee has 50 participating members, and at their Ambler store, landscaping and youth committees welcome member participation. Each committee at Weavers Way has a staff liaison, and their work helps steer the future of their store.

Member engagement at co-ops is highest in the day-to-day interactions between members and staff. Food co-op shoppers are an opinionated bunch. There's no two ways about it. It's what keeps co-ops relevant. Melissa Cohen is actually inspired by shoppers who get upset: "It means people still care."[358] She believes the future of food co-ops depends on healthy conversations with members. This is what separates co-ops from the chains. Through dialogue, trust is established. Opinions and requests really do make a difference. Many co-ops will happily order a single item for a member. No chain does this. Seward

Member-owners of Hanover Co-op Food Stores vote in favor of opening another store in Lebanon, New Hampshire, ca. 1996. Source: Hanover Consumer Cooperative Society

even tracks their shoppers' influence on product selection. In 2017, 419 product changes resulted from customer requests. No customer has anywhere near the power to influence what's on the shelf of a grocery store that shoppers do at a food co-op.

Diversity

It's true that the majority of food co-ops serve a predominantly white clientele, but many food co-ops are serving and employing an increasingly diverse base of members.

When the Seward Co-op announced plans to open a new store in the Bryant neighborhood of Minneapolis, the community challenged the co-op to hire staff that would reflect the racial diversity and income of the people living nearby. The population of Minneapolis is 39 percent people of color. In Bryant, it's 66 percent (mostly black and Latino), many of whom are low-income. The concerns were not unfounded. In the neighborhood of Seward's first location, people of color represented 44 percent of the population but only 14 percent of staff.[359] People of color are disproportionately impacted by employment discrimination in Minneapolis.

If the Bryant store didn't reflect the neighborhood, people feared it would harm the community by gentrifying it. In response, Seward successfully updated its needs-based discount program, and when the new store opened in 2015, 61 percent of employees were people of color, most from the immediate neighborhood.[360]

North Carolina's Durham Co-op Market serves a neighborhood that includes a wide range of races, incomes, and religions. To the north of the store is a predominantly white residential area; to the south, predominantly people of color. To welcome people from both sides, the entrance to the store was intentionally designed to face not north, not south, but east.

Social Cohesion

Without question, food co-ops contribute to greater social cohesion within communities. The "age of reunion" is alive and well inside a food co-op.

Food co-ops contribute to social cohesion in a diversity of ways, and there's a particular recipe that enables this to happen:

- Co-ops are Autonomous: Most food co-ops are autonomous, independent businesses. This necessitates social cohesion by forcing co-ops to look *inside* not *outside* of their communities for the resources and support they need.
- Community Connections: Food co-ops are well connected to other businesses and organizations in the community and support local cultural and sporting activities as well as schools and hospitals.
- Enriching Workplace: Employees of food co-ops are also customers and therefore owners of the co-op too, leading to a stronger connection and commitment to their place of employment and to their communities.
- Member Participation: Food co-ops encourage their customers to participate directly in their stores' futures.

With these ingredients for social cohesion, co-ops act as a shared symbol of "community." The aroma from this recipe can be intoxicating. Across the United States and Canada, some people deliberately choose their place of residence because of its proximity to a food co-op. No other type of grocery store can claim to be such a fundamental consideration for someone deciding where to live. And in the current frenzied climate of chain store closings, openings, and shufflings, no one should risk considering their place of residence by its proximity to a chain store when the future of that location is at the mercy of a distant head office.

Activism

Food co-ops were notoriously "activist" organizations from the 1970s through the early part of the new century. Hosting protests out front of the store, boycotting products that didn't ethically align; this was business as usual at food co-ops. While there are still some expressions of this form of activism, much of it has been absorbed directly into the day-to-day operations of food co-ops today. Supporting nonprofits and the development of co-ops, adhering to strict buying guidelines — this is the activism of the modern food co-op. Many of the earlier "causes" have also been institutionalized. The Non-GMO Project is one such example, with most major manufacturers now including the Non-GMO label on products free of genetically modified ingredients. Food co-ops were some of the first retailers to actively support this organization. The Kootenay Co-op was the first grocery retailer in Canada to financially support The Non-GMO Project.

On Prices

> "There is no such thing as cheap food. The real cost of the food is paid somewhere. And if it isn't paid at the cash register, it's charged to the environment or to the public purse in the form of subsidies. And it's charged to your health."[361]
>
> — Michael Pollan

The price of food at food co-ops is a persistent topic of conversation. To be fair, food prices are top of mind for most shoppers, regardless of where they shop. But for food co-ops, there's a strong "overpriced" stigma. So is it true?

There are many dimensions to the food price conversation. Let's just get a bigger-picture one out of the way. Unlike a privately owned or publicly traded grocer, food co-ops *cannot* possibly gouge their customers. Food co-ops are owned *by* their customers. Any store profits are customer profits. Those profits might be returned back into the store to improve operations and grow the co-op's impact. Profits may go back into the community through the co-op's giving programs. In many cases, profits are returned right back to customers — literally. With this closed loop, no matter the type of food on the shelf, prices at food co-ops are a better reflection of the *true* cost of grocery store food. Beyond the closed loop of the store itself, "true cost" is also determined by food production methods. It simply costs more to pay a local farmer a living wage to harvest local strawberries than it does to pay a seasonal migrant laborer living in cramped and sometimes deplorable conditions.

Then there is transparency. Financial statements of food co-ops are available to all member–owners. There are no secrets. Wish to speak with a board director or manager about the co-op's strategies and practices? Never a problem. The head office of an independent food co-op is usually right there in the store itself.

Then there is food quality. Food co-ops are *not* required to carry higher-quality foods nor foods that simply cost more to produce. These are choices that are ultimately determined by member–owners. Whether members wish for a more expensive artisanally produced local food or a highly processed conventional name brand — a food co-op can choose to carry it if members decide that this is what they want their store to provide. So it's simply not true that food co-ops as a grocery store model are more expensive than non-co-op stores. Food price comparisons are reserved for *what's* on the shelves, not the type of store.

From a smaller-picture perspective, there are two (mostly) distinct conversations — one is highly subjective, the other pretty cut-and-dried.

The highly subjective one is for eaters who have the luxury of *choosing* how much of their income to devote to food. For those who have such choice, the food price conversation can't possibly be had without first identifying the value one places on food relative to all other expenditures. Food becomes less a question of "affordability" and more a question of what's more important, the $100 monthly cellphone plan or the $50 plan and $50 of food. For those in *this* category, the value placed on food, and food "affordability," are inseparable. One determines the other.

Of the "cut-and-dried" conversation — for eaters spending the *bare minimum* on housing, living expenses, childcare, and any other necessities, what's left over to spend on food is non-negotiable. Food affordability is *not* subjective but a hard and objective reality. In this case, "yes," the prices at a grocery store that specializes in more natural foods might very well be out of reach. For those in this category wishing to access healthier, local, and natural foods, a much wider socioeconomic conversation is required to address the *full* spectrum of reasons why so little disposable income is generally available for good food. Until that conversation can adequately address this, food co-ops are leading the way among grocery stores at making good food more accessible to more people and by supporting organizations in their communities that serve those most in need.

In addition to their efforts to support food access for lower-income eaters, food co-ops have become proficient at passing along substantial savings to members. Many co-ops do this through periodic "case-lot" sales. For usually no longer than one week, popular foods are available in wholesale sizes at prices either at or near cost. Some co-ops require pre-orders of wholesale items, like River Valley Co-op, which requires members to pre-order for their three-day "Truckload Sales." Ten-pound packs of local ground beef for 39 percent savings. A case of Annie's Mac & Cheese for 48 percent off. Nature's Path breakfast cereal by the case for 51 percent savings. Substantial.

As another approach to member savings, a small number of storefront co-ops like Berkshire Co-op (MA) and Potsdam Food Co-op (NY) have maintained their buying club roots. Throughout the year, members can order cases at small markups above wholesale prices.

Some co-ops have confronted the "price myth" head-on by publishing comparisons of shopping baskets between competing retailers. Every year, Community Food Co-op in Bellingham (WA) undertakes a rigorous price comparison of identical products at nearby stores. In 2018, the co-op was consistently cheaper than its competition.[362]

Community Food Co-op (Bellingham, WA) — Price Comparisons

	Co-op Savings	# Identical Items Compared*
Co-op vs. Haggen (Albertsons)	$101	230
Co-op vs. Whole Foods (Amazon)	$70	306
Co-op vs. Fred Meyer (Kroger)	$37	392

* Final number of products compared was determined by the competitor's product selection. If it was on the co-op's list and the competitor sold it, it was included in the comparison. The product selection was not edited to improve comparison.

SOURCE: COMMUNITY FOOD CO-OP, 2018

Unleashing Potential

The goal of every chain store is to maximize profit for *distant* share-holders. For food co-ops, their goals are to serve the interests of *local* shareholders — which happen to be the people shopping in their stores — maybe even you. This chapter captures many of those areas where food co-ops may be of service to their member–owners and communities, but no single food co-op will excel in *all* of these areas. It's a substantial undertaking to be more than just a grocery store. What *is* certain, however, is the striving among most food co-ops to be of service in all, if not *most*, of these areas of impact. It remains entirely possible (and quite likely) that the incredible impact food co-ops are having today is only a taste of what's possible. As the food co-op movement grows, so too will the potential for our neighborhood grocery stores to be generating stations of community health and well-being. The possibility of this future is entirely in the hands and mouths of eaters.

Co-ops as Food Desert Remediation

"If you don't have a place to buy healthy food, it makes
you feel like you've been forgotten."
— Allison Karpyn, University of Delaware[363]

WATER. FOOD. SHELTER.
With the exception of the public management and distribution
of drinking water, the provision of food and shelter in North America
has been left almost entirely in the hands of the private sector.

Nowhere is the failure of the private sector to provide this essential
human need more glaring than in low-income neighborhoods, which
frequently lack the level of grocery store competition found in middle-
to higher-income communities.[364] Many are completely reliant on a
single chain store while others have no grocer at all. In those places
devoid of a grocery store, food is often purchased at convenience stores.
Former Guilford County (NC) Commissioner Ray Trapp describes a
typical meal in a food desert as a "cup of noodles as your entree, Cheetos
or some other form of chip as your side dish, a sugary desert, and a sugar
drink to wash it down."[365]

Lower-income neighborhoods are hardest hit because of access to
transportation. Automobile ownership is lower among people on low
incomes, and if public transit is available (and adequate), people are still
restricted to however many shopping bags they can carry on the bus or
subway. Seniors are especially challenged.

Transportation is only part of the problem. Grocery store profitability is consistently lower in low-income areas, and chains are generally
hesitant to operate in them. In today's retail climate of razor-thin
margins and ruthless price wars, chains will waste no time closing

down their least profitable locations. No community consultations, no forewarning.

When Piggly Wiggly closed its West Beltline Boulevard location in Columbia, South Carolina, in 2016, the surrounding neighborhood became a "food desert"— a term used to describe a low-income neighborhood lacking access to affordable fruits, vegetables, whole grains, and other foods that make up the full range of a healthy diet. Residents, joined the nineteen million other Americans experiencing what the USDA defines as "low-income, low-access" — people who are more than one mile from a supermarket or large grocery store. In rural areas, the distance is more than ten miles.[366]

Columbia's West Beltline neighborhood is one of a long list of food deserts in the United States and Canada. It's also one of a growing number of communities that aren't waiting for the private sector to come to the rescue. With support from the City of Columbia, a group of residents began exploring what it would take to open a community-owned grocery store.[367] Lucky for them, they're not alone.

In communities across the country, the food co-op model is being turned to as a promising alternative to food deserts (or any neighborhood lacking easy access to good food). Food co-ops can also solve more than just food access. Community-owned grocery stores have led the way in providing education on nutrition, kitchen skills, and shopping on a budget, as well as making food more affordable to those most in need — all of which are critical to addressing food insecurity in lower- and mixed-income communities. Thankfully, because food co-ops are a people's movement and cooperation among cooperatives is coded right into their DNA, there are plenty of resources available for communities to begin this journey. Communities of "What's Possible" are appearing everywhere.

Greensboro, North Carolina

On October 14, 2016, the doors opened to the Renaissance Community Co-op — in the northeast quadrant of Greensboro, a city with a population of about 290,000. Renaissance was the first of its kind and sadly closed its doors in January 2019. Yet it remains an incredible story of dedication, perseverance, and possibility.

Before opening their doors, the roughly 38,000 residents of Northeast Greensboro had been living in a textbook food desert for eighteen years. The nearest grocery store was a Food Lion 1.8 miles away. For the 17.5 percent of area households without an automobile, taking (the infrequent) public transit involved a round-trip that would take at least one-and-a-half hours (not including walking distance to and from the bus stop).[368]

The predominantly black neighborhood's per capita income of $13,468 is half the country's average. Unemployment is 18.4 percent. SNAP (Supplemental Nutrition Assistance Program) participants comprise 28.6 percent of households. The area is heavily populated with fast-food and gas station "food marts." Obesity affects 38 percent of area residents; diabetes, 15 percent; high-blood pressure, 41 percent. Access to healthy food through the creation of the Renaissance Community Co-op was literally a life-saving development.[369]

The neighborhood had become a food desert in 1998 after grocery chain Winn-Dixie shuttered their store in the Bessemer Center — a 45,000-square-foot shopping plaza that was the "hub of the community." Grocery stores are anchors of a neighborhood's commercial center, so with the departure of Winn-Dixie, other businesses went with it.

Just before it closed, residents had organized themselves into the group, Concerned Citizens of Northeast Greensboro (CCNG). Their efforts weren't enough to convince Winn-Dixie to stay.

The closure of the Winn-Dixie location was part of the Florida-based company's plans to consolidate stores. According to those involved in the co-op's early development, the Winn-Dixie store was actually profitable, just not as profitable as the chain's other locations. The location's profitability left residents believing another grocer would move into the vacant space. None did. Winn-Dixie's departure was part of a wider trend of grocery chains abandoning the least profitable neighborhoods.

What happened next is a wonderful story of "what's possible," and it's not so surprising given its location. Greensboro, North Carolina, has a long history of "what's possible." It was in Greensboro in 1960 that four African-American college students sat down at a white-only lunch counter in a Woolworth department store and refused to leave.

The Greensboro sit-in sparked a six-month-long protest and contributed to the passage of the Civil Rights Act of 1964. It also led to the chain retailer removing its policy of racial segregation.

That same commitment to social justice remains. From 2009 to 2011, CCNG had been working to keep a proposed landfill from being re-established in the neighborhood. By the time they won that fight, they had developed some serious community organizing muscles and political clout. At the same time, the Greensboro-based Fund for Democratic Communities (F4DC) had begun focusing its attention on cooperative economics. F4DC founders had been connected to the landfill fight and also participated in some of the earliest meetings of CCNG in the late '90s, as the residents of northeast Greensboro struggled to fund a grocery solution. F4DC floated the idea of a cooperatively owned grocery store at a CCNG community meeting and handed out "how to start a food co-op" pamphlets published by National Co-op Grocers. Many people showed interest.

In 2012, F4DC sponsored a field trip of 25 Northeast Greensboro residents to Company Shops Market — a food co-op that had just opened in nearby Burlington. The trip was enough to convince the group to move forward on a food co-op for Northeast Greensboro, and a founding committee was quickly established. The Renaissance Community Co-op was incorporated in 2013, and steering committee member Sadie Blue became member #001.

The committee's first line of work came unexpectedly. The City of Greensboro had purchased the shopping center after Winn-Dixie had left, and in late 2014 was prepared to sell it to one of two developers. It became clear to the committee that the developers were *not* willing to accommodate a community-owned grocery store in any authentic way. When the City awarded one of the developers the contract, the committee and more than a hundred ardent neighbors kept close watch over all the promises and proceedings, and ultimately succeeded in forcing the developer to withdraw. In entered Self-Help Credit Union — a cooperatively owned financial institution. Through one of their funds, the credit union purchased the Bessemer Center with a plan to have the co-op as the anchor tenant.

A low-interest loan from the Community Foundation of Greater Greensboro enabled the co-op to hire a full-time fundraising and membership coordinator, and an Indiegogo crowdfunding campaign raised another $16k from 600 people.

> Our community has spent the past 16 years court-ing a number of grocery store chains, none of whom have opened a store in the Bessemer Shopping Center. We decided that a cooperative would prevent us from depending on large grocery chains, keep the profits in our control, and ensure that the store is accountable to our community.
>
> — Renaissance Community Co-op,
> Indiegogo crowdfunding campaign, 2014

A market research firm determined that within a two-mile radius of the proposed location, residents spent $1.34 million on groceries every week. If the co-op could capture 5 percent of this, the numbers added up to confidently build a 10,530-square-foot grocery store.

It took $2.53 million to open the store. Funding came from many sources. In 2015, the co-op was awarded a $250k economic development grant from the City of Greensboro. Another $90k came in the form of grants from two local churches — one deeply rooted in the black com-munity and a largely white church from the other side of town. More than $143k in loans came from the co-op's 1,200+ member–owners. Each of those members also invested $100 into their member shares. Grassroots investor group Regenerative Finance secured over $250k in 0 percent loans from 29 investors. Other financial partners supporting the co-op's launch included Fund for Democratic Communities, Cone Health Foundation, Community Foundation of Greater Greensboro, Shared Capital Cooperative, and The Working World. The co-op also relied upon the support of CDS — a network of food co-op consul-tants — and Uplift Solutions, an organization supporting communities across the United States who are challenged with access to full-service grocery stores.

Renaissance Community Co-op opened in 2016 with 32 jobs filled by people living in the neighborhood.

The health impacts of food desert remediation are considerable. Studies have shown how easier access to grocery stores is associated with greater fruit and vegetable intake. It has also been shown that the closer one is to a grocery store, the lower one's body mass index is.[370] These are important factors in reducing the risk of obesity and diabetes. But food access is only part of the equation. The *types* of foods found on the shelves is also a determinant of health, as is access to the skills and education needed for healthy eating. Food co-ops are well-positioned to meet these needs. Across the continent, they have proven that a grocery store can be more than just a purveyor of food.

Getting Rich from Struggling Supermarkets in Low-Income Communities

The pulling out of Northeast Greensboro by Winn-Dixie reveals a deeper pattern of institutionalized wealth extraction from struggling grocery stores in communities that need them most.

Winn-Dixie was a struggling chain. There's no two ways about it. Pulling out of Greensboro was the beginning of a company-wide Hail Mary. In 2002, four years after leaving Greensboro, Winn-Dixie closed its 76 stores in Texas and Oklahoma, and two years later it closed another 156 stores — mostly in the Midwest. In 2005, the company filed for bankruptcy and got rid of another 326 stores. By the end of 2011, the chain was sold to Bi-Lo for $530 million. Bi-Lo continued to purge stores before filing for bankruptcy itself on March 15, 2018. More stores were closed or sold off.

Most affected by these monumental corporate restructurings are the people who rely on the stores as a source of food and a place of employment. But what about the companies involved? How do they fare in these transactions? Enter the private equity firm. Private equity loves a struggling retailer.

Lone Star Funds had invested $150 million in 2005 in the buyout of Bi-Lo. They invested another $275 million in the 2011 purchase of Winn-Dixie. In the years leading up to Bi-Lo filing for bankruptcy in 2018, LSF paid itself at least $800 million and collected even more in management fees that were paid for by the retailer.[371] While Bi-Lo was sinking, LSF was cashing in on the failing company. It was akin to a few industrialists on the sinking *Titanic* turning a profit by selling off the furniture and fixtures — except in this case, LSF had a lifeboat reserved just for them.

This is the private equity business model. "Borrow money to buy a company, load the company up with debt, use the debt to pay yourself and — with interest rates at rock bottom — issue more debt and pay yourself more."[372] With their steady cash flow, grocery stores are a great target for this approach. Another analyst summarizes the strategy as "buy, clean up the balance sheet, and suck up the cash and profits."[373] The retailer is left with the debt.

With retailer price wars, the rise of e-commerce, and Amazon's purchase of Whole Foods, analysts predict more of these predatory investments in the grocery sector.[374] The hardest hit will be the smaller regional chains and the lower-income communities they operate in. Even natural and organic chains are an expected target. It's almost certain that benefiting from a community's loss of a grocery store will be the vultures of private equity.

Cincinnati, Ohio

The largest traditional grocery chain on the continent is Kroger — its headquarters in Cincinnati, Ohio.

Not to be outdone on its home turf, the company claims a 60 percent share of Cincinnati's grocery retail market. That's unheard of in any major urban center. As one Kroger executive puts it, "We use Cincinnati as a benchmark for our fill-in strategy."[375]

Kroger has been accused of causing widespread desertification of communities across the country, Cincinnati included.

In February 2018, after the company closed two stores in Memphis, Tennessee, and another in Clarksdale, Mississippi, civil rights leader Reverend Jesse Jackson got involved. The three closures, plus many other Kroger closures from the previous year, were all in predominantly black neighborhoods. Jackson called for a national boycott of the company and received substantial press.[376]

Jackson traveled to Cincinnati where he organized a protest in front of another vacated Kroger store that closed in 2017 in a predominantly black neighborhood. Following the store's closure, residents were required to travel to Kroger's newly expanded location 1.3 miles away. From the perspective of the company, it was a brilliant move, and one that has been carried out by most chains for the past few decades — exchange smaller stores for larger ones. The chains are effectively unloading the higher costs of operating smaller stores onto consumers. Rather than the company incurring the higher cost of supplying *many* stores, the consumer is left to absorb those costs through their personal expense of transportation and time required to travel to the larger-format stores. Isla Vista Food Co-op's Melissa Cohen calls it "oppression." "If you're a low-income person living in a city, just by the virtue of the technology of a 48,000-square-foot store, you're not going to be able to access it if you don't have a car. Just that alone leads to oppression by the virtue of its existence."[377]

Mega stores and food deserts have become the landscape of Cincinnati. The city needs ten additional grocery stores to meet the national average.[378]

This makes Cincinnati a perfect home for a co-op revolution.

Cincinnati's modern food co-op revolution began with a *non*-storefront food co-op — Our Harvest Co-op, a worker-owned cooperative that eventually went hybrid by inviting consumer–owners into the mix. In only five years, the co-op of fourteen staff was managing two farms, working with twenty-two local producers, wholesaling to ten retailers and cafés, distributing to eaters at eleven pickup sites in ten neighborhoods, and operating its own distribution center with two refrigerated trucks.[379] In addition to fresh produce, the co-op retails pasta, pasta sauce, salsa, soup, beans, eggs, and honey among other staples.

The first storefront food co-op in the city opened its doors in 2017.

Clifton Market — A Cautionary Tale of Hope

Cincinnati's Clifton neighborhood has a population of 8,300 and a small commercial center made up of a few blocks of mostly independent businesses.

The community's IGA grocery store had been operating there since 1939. When it closed its doors in 2011, Clifton residents found themselves over one mile from the nearest grocer. Other businesses saw their sales plummet.

After a few years, residents began to organize. In 2013, a group of fifteen people met and out of that a core group became the founding board of what would become Clifton Market — a retail food co-op with conventional and organic foods.

At their first public meeting in 2014, they sold a hundred shares. After launching a member loan campaign, the co-op raised $300k in the first month. When they attended the national Up & Coming conference for start-up food co-ops, they realized that they had become the fastest-growing start-up in the country.

In 2015, the co-op purchased the building of the former IGA and began throwing house parties to drum up support. Five hundred yard signs were scattered throughout the Clifton neighborhood. The signs soon became a "status symbol," one founding member recalls. Before opening, the co-op had pulled together 1,400 member–owners whose investments totaled $1.8 million. The remaining funds came from financial organizations like National Cooperative Bank and Shared Capital Cooperative.[380]

Clifton Market opened in 2017 with eighty-one new jobs. The efforts were hopeful and inspiring and remain a story of 'what's possible'. Once on the ground, however, and right out of the gate, the challenges of running a successful grocery store became evident. The co-op was only selling half of its projected weekly sales of $256,000, The store was losing money and there was insufficient cash on hand to keep the shelves fully stocked. Conflict on the board of directors was severe enough that attorneys were brought in. But the co-op remained hopeful and kept its doors open through November 2018. The situation, however, did not improve enough. On November 30, co-op members voted overwhelmingly to sell the store to a local restaurant owner.

As of writing, the sale is pending and it remains too early to draw conclusions as to why the co-op couldn't make it. Lack of grocery retail experience on the board, spending too much cash to renovate the building, and the challenge of re-patterning residents' shopping patterns after six years without a neighborhood grocer have all been suggested as contributing factors.

Apple Street Market

In the Northside neighborhood of the city, another food desert had been created with the almost-overnight departure of Save-A-Lot, a discount chain based out of Missouri. When the owners of the building told the grocer's parent company that their lease was coming up for renewal, Save-A-Lot decided to just close shop. Four of the six surrounding neighborhoods were also without a grocery store, making the impact to residents even more substantial. Some residents without cars simply chose to pack up and move. Others turned to food banks. The two-hour-each-way bus ride to the nearest Kroger was basically out of the question.[381]

The prospect of another grocer coming to the neighborhood was slim. Capital expenses are high for any private sector grocer wanting to open a new store and lacking access to grant money. Grocery margins are also thin.

The prospect for a food co-op, on the other hand, was much higher. Cincinnati is home to a network of community councils that receive small allotments of money from the city. Those that are well-organized can have considerable influence. Northside's council was aware of the work of the Cincinnati Union Cooperative Initiative to help form Our Harvest Co-op. CUCI was asked to conduct a feasibility study. The results were promising.

The Apple Street Market Cooperative was established as a hybrid worker–consumer co-op with an initial board selected by CUCI. Once one hundred consumer and seven worker shares had been committed, the co-op's governance would be turned over to the co-op itself with one seat reserved for a CUCI selection. Christopher DeAngelis, an experienced food co-op manager, was hired as the general manager. An angel investor stepped in to purchase the property as a temporary measure, and a neighborhood nonprofit began pursuing funding to take over ownership in late 2018.

DeAngelis was excited by the hybrid worker–consumer model. "Worker ownership improves the quality of work," he says. With labor being a grocer's greatest expense, employing people who are fully invested in the future of their workplace makes a whole lot of sense. The hybrid model was also seen to increase the chance of widespread neighborhood support.

To rally support for the co-op, a core group of twenty members became "block captains" who went door-to-door to inform people about the co-op. Without a storefront yet, Apple Street saw an outreach opportunity that could support the food access crisis immediately. Through an agreement with the local farmers' market, the co-op set up a stand where they offered a selection of dry goods for sale. Residents could now visit the market and walk away with ingredients to make a well-rounded meal. The co-op sold those foods at extremely low margins. The initiative was inspired by a similar program at the Davis Food Co-op in California.

In another innovative move, Apple Street partnered with nonprofit Churches Active in Northside. By subsidizing the $100 co-op shares with $90, the group enabled low-income residents to become co-op owners for only $10.

To meet the mixed-income needs of the community, products would be a blend of local, higher-end and cheaper conventional. This model has proven to be more sustainable in an industry with such low margins. The higher-end products help subsidize the cheaper ones. The co-op would also be home to a teaching kitchen directly on the retail floor.

Unexpectedly in January 2019, just as Apple Street was readying itself to enter into the development phase, some of its key financing fell apart. It was enough to force a pause in the co-op's momentum and it served as a hard reminder of the reliance many grocery initiatives in lower income communities have on subsidy to get out of the ground. At the time of publication, co-op member-owners remained committed to moving forward.

Other Stories of "What's Possible"

Food deserts have sadly become commonplace in the age of grocery giants. For these communities, the promise of food co-ops is very real. When Kroger closed two stores in Peoria, IL, in 2018, food co-ops were floated as one of a number of options.[382] Same in North Charleston, SC. After Piggly Wiggly pulled out of plans to construct a store in late 2017, city council began discussing the food co-op option immediately as a solution to the federally recognized food desert.[383] Across the country, established food co-ops and start-ups are already well on their way to remediating food deserts and areas severely lacking neighborhood grocers.

Moran, Kansas

When the one grocery store in this rural farming town announced plans to close, residents formed a co-op and bought out the store. The Marmaton Market opened its doors in June 2018.

South Bend, Indiana

Purple Porch Co-op began in 2009 in an underserved area of the city's downtown. After first operating as a buying club in the basement of a Montessori school, the co-op opened a storefront in 2014 in a small, 3,300-square-foot space. The store does $1.15 million in sales, with 30 percent of sales coming through the co-op's café. An impressive 30 percent of their products are sourced from within 60 miles of the store. Mayor and presidential hopeful Pete Buttigieg is a proud co-op member–owner.

Austin, Texas

To relieve the city of Austin of its food deserts, the Wheatsville Co-op coordinates pop-up markets that act as one-stop shops for members with SNAP benefit cards. Fresh produce and staples are offered.

Ambler, Pennsylvania

In 2012, residents of Ambler began discussing the need for a community-owned grocery store in a food desert. They formed the Ambler

Food Co-op. Initial conversations gathered steam, but then something unexpected happened the following year — a Bottom Dollar grocery store came to town. Co-op enthusiasts were undeterred. They understood the precarious nature of chain grocers. Sure enough, when German grocery giant Aldi bought the Bottom Dollar chain in 2015, they shuttered the Ambler location and left the community once again as a food desert. The co-op's organizing efforts were successful, but co-op members wanted to speed up the process. They reached out to the experienced Weavers Way Co-op in nearby Philadelphia, and after much discussion, Weavers Way agreed to absorb the Ambler Co-op. In 2017, Weavers Way opened their third location in Ambler in the former Bottom Dollar building.

Detroit, Michigan

Half of Detroit residents live in a food desert. The Detroit Food Commons is a planned 30,000-square-foot complex for the city's North End where 92 percent of residents are black and 40 percent have a household income of less than $15,000. Spearheaded by the Detroit Black Community Food Security Network, the project will become home to the Detroit People's Food Co-op — a full-service grocery store, an incubator kitchen for food entrepreneurs, a café, and a community space. "We're modeling how cooperatives can become a vehicle for intentionally dis-invested communities to build community empowerment; to circulate wealth within those communities, as opposed to having it extracted; to create employment; and, most importantly, to create ownership," says DBCFSN founder Malik Yakini.[384]

Denver, Colorado

Denver's predominantly Hispanic Westwood neighborhood has the largest youth population in the city and the highest rate of childhood obesity. Despite having the highest density of people in Denver, Westwood has no grocery store. In the absence of a neighborhood grocer, organizers estimated $13.5 million in food dollars were leaving the community. With the support of local nonprofit Re:Vision, the Westwood Food Cooperative was formed in 2014. Mayor Michael

Hancock became a vocal supporter of the initiative. The vision for the co-op is a mixed-used development with the co-op as the anchor tenant. The WestwoodHUB will feature a one-acre urban farm, greenhouse, incubator kitchen, fitness center, and civic plaza. Until the co-op opens in 2019/2020, a pilot store is providing residents with fresh food and staples.

Starting a Co-op Isn't a Shoo-in for Success

Opening food co-ops comes with its challenges, but as more communities carve a path, the likelihood of finding success only increases.

Particularly in low-income neighborhoods, food co-ops are still up against the same reality experienced by the chains — a grocery store culture built on razor-thin margins and cutthroat competition. Traditional banks see food co-ops as too high a risk, and the prevailing governance model continues to rely on volunteer board members who may or may not possess the professional expertise to help navigate the turbulent waters of grocery retail.

After opening, both Renaissance and Clifton experienced lower-than-projected sales. Board conflict weakened Clifton in its early years, and in 2018, sales and cash flow were not adequate to sustain the store and the co-op defaulted on its mortgage. At Renaissance, low customer counts forced a reduction in the number of staff from thirty-two down to sixteen. Renaissance was eventually forced to close its doors in January 2019 and the sale of Clifton Market to a private owner was pending as of February 2019.

In areas that were once food deserts, start-up co-ops are faced with the challenge of re-patterning eaters to shop at the new store. This became one of the biggest obstacles identified at Renaissance — convincing people to break eighteen-year-old shopping habits.

Start-up food co-ops are also up against a culture that doesn't yet fully understand the importance of community-owned grocery stores. But with 75 percent of start-ups making it, the odds of success are in food co-ops' favor, and a number of national organizations are establishing industry best practices, working with co-ops across the country to help them manifest their visions.

Food Co-ops and the Local Economy

"Nowadays it may be more apt to distinguish places not according to how locals earn their money, but by how they spend it."[385]

— Joanna Blythman, *Shopped*

Food co-ops are veritable economic engines for communities. By the simple virtue of what they sell, they enable more widespread social and community development to take place.

Among those who sought to resist the rise of the grocery giants in the early- to mid-twentieth century, it was understood that the chains posed a significant threat to a well-rounded and balanced community. In the 1934 film *Forward America*, the filmmaker set out to expose the "anti-American business methods" of the chains. The film profiles the American housewife, who, by patronizing the chain, is "sending her money away from home, trading her husband out of his job, destroying the value of her home, and adding to the national problem of unemployment."[386]

Money and how we spend it has always been integral to the formation of "What's Possible." The 35 member co-ops of the Neighboring Food Co-op Association (NFCA) purchase more than $60 million worth of product from local businesses in the northeastern United States. They employ more than two thousand people and pay wages of over $49 million.[387] In the metro area of Minnesota's Twin Cities with a population of 3.4 million, fifteen co-ops with seventeen stores[xvi] serve 91k owners and another 50k shoppers. Sales of local products at those

---

xvi   2014

175

co-ops amount to $54 million — of which $30 million passes through the farm gate.[388] All of this translates into social impact.

The economic and social impact of food co-ops begins with their interest and capacity to support small-scale farmers. The contribution of small farms to the social fabric of communities was well understood as early as 1946. A study commissioned by the U.S. Senate compared two California farming communities[389] that were "similar in population, shared value systems, and social customs." Where the two communities differed was in the size of farms. One community was made up of small farms, the other large. The study's author set out to determine whether or not "other aspects of society, economy and culture" were affected by this. He observed noticeable differences. The "large industrialized farming communities lacked solidarity, leadership, prosperity, permanent settlement, adequate educational facilities, and in general, a life of their own." These characteristics were reversed in the community with smaller farms.[390]

Many regions across the country are also topographically constrained. Hilly, rocky, mountainous — these characteristics can constrain farm size and limit the type of production. By providing easier access to the marketplace for small-scale farms, food co-ops can ensure viability of farming in these geographically diverse areas.

Easier Access to Eaters

Food co-ops are providing foodmakers a level of access to eaters that is often unavailable through the large chains. Smaller-scale farmers simply cannot supply the volumes necessary for the national wholesale distribution the chains require or favor, and many are unable to meet the long list of fees. Food co-ops, on the other hand, are often happy to accept direct deliveries at their loading docks — and slotting fees are *not* part of their culture.

Of all grocery categories, the local foods sold most often through food co-ops are meats, eggs, fresh produce, and dairy.

True Local

Before the explosion of interest in local food, food co-ops had already embedded a strong commitment to ensuring well-stocked shelves of

2012–2013 Retail Co-op Local Sales and Purchases by Grocery Category in the Twin Cities

Category	% of Total Sales	Category $	Local Sales %	Local Sales $	Local Purchase / Farm Gate (1)	Category as % of Farm Gate (2)
Meats	9%	$15,877,065	72%	$11,433,529	$7,412,644	24%
Produce	20%	$35,239,181	25%	$8,955,740	$5,315,262	17%
Refrigerated (incl. dairy)	11%	$19,254,322	45%	$8,702,914	$5,730,777	19%
Packaged	21%	$37,374,622	8%	$2,850,325	$1,695,058	5%
Deli (incl. cheese)	13%	$23,561,964	51%	$11,910,407	$5,010,472	16%
Health & Beauty Care	10%	$18,478,158	8%	$1,560,909	$781,749	3%
Frozen	4%	$7,469,678	8%	$604,372	$361,345	1%
Bulk	9%	$15,349,364	30%	$4,625,988	$2,616,022	8%
Bread	2%	$4,325,842	60%	$2,587,307	$1,714,540	6%
Other	1%	$1,627,144	42%	$681,983	$214,474	1%
Total all metro stores	100%	$178,557,339	30%	$53,913,476	$30,852,343	100%

(1) Farm gate is the income that is paid to farmers. Farm gate income is calculated here as retail sales minus retail and distributor margins.
(2) This column shows the percent of total local farm gate (income to producers) for each grocery category. Meat, Produce, Refrigerated/Dairy, and Deli are the strongest local categories in total dollars purchased in this system, accounting for 76 percent of total farm gate.

SOURCE: CDS 2014[391]

local products. Today, the average co-op carries a range of 15 to 42 percent local product.[392] For small-scale foodmakers, food co-ops are a critical market that helps ensure their survival. Among local producers selling into co-ops in the Twin Cities, food co-ops represent between 25 and 90 percent of their customer base.[393]

Great Basin Community Food Co-op in Reno, Nevada, works with 101 local suppliers, selling 10,327 pounds of local meat, 3,904 pounds of local honey, and 4,444 pounds of local tomatoes each year. Local food is important enough to this grocery store that they track and celebrate their sales to the nearest pound.

Local Suppliers at Food Co-ops

	Number of Local Suppliers	Annual Sales of Local Products
Brattleboro Food Co-op (VT)	450	$4M
Co-op Food Stores (NH/VT)	300	$13M
Hunger Mountain Co-op (VT)	500	$8.7M
Middlebury Natural Foods Co-op (VT)	300	$4.7M
Monadnock Food Co-op (NH)	374	$3.7M
River Valley Co-op (MA)	403	$6M
Viroqua Food Co-op (WI)	200	$2.5M

SOURCE: INTERVIEWS WITH FOOD CO-OPS

Food co-ops have also become victims of their own success. At one point, it was easy to label a product as "local" and have customers understand what that meant, but when the chains got wind of the opportunity, the definition of "local" became ambiguous. During the "wild west" era of "big food's" attempts to cash in on "local," Unilever went all out with its Canadian marketing of Hellman's mayonnaise. In 2007, they launched The Real Food Movement — a series of advertisements claiming Hellman's as a "local" product. But for Unilever, "local" meant *all* of Canada. The campaign slogan of "Eat Real, Eat Local" was followed with "Choose Canadian."[394]

Federal and state regulators have since stepped in to help define boundaries for the marketing of "local," but the range of definitions from region to region is quite broad. In New Hampshire, "local" is defined as from within the state.[395] The moment a food crosses state lines, it's no longer "local." That's a bit limiting for the many communities that straddle the border of such a small state, but it protects local foodmakers from imposters. At the other end of the spectrum is British Columbia. When Canadian regulators set out in 2013 to redefine the marketing of "local" from its previous requirement of 50 kilometers (31 miles) from point of origin, they chose to expand the definition to being from anywhere within the entire province (or from 50 kilometers across provincial borders).[396] Between New Hampshire and British Columbia, these are two enormously differing standards. Whereas in New Hampshire, "local" is defined as coming from an area no bigger than 9,349 square miles, the geographic range of "local" in British Columbia is over forty times that. This means that a jar of honey from Vancouver Island can be sold in a store in Nelson, 500 miles away, and be marketed as "local." For the Kootenay Co-op and its community of *truly* local foodmakers, this posed a problem. The Kootenay Co-op had already defined "local" as being from within a distinct bio-region. For the co-op, "local" involved no more than a distance of 60 miles as the crow flies.

When the Canadian government expanded the definition, the big chains jumped on board immediately. Some even stretched the defined limits. In one instance, meat from producers in Alberta was being shipped to a processing facility near Vancouver, BC, turned into private-label Western Family hamburger patties, and then shipped to the Save-On-Foods store in Nelson where it was marketed as a "local" product. Total distance traveled — about 1,100 miles. The Kootenay Co-op refused to play the same game. In June 2013, at a rally held in front of the co-op were Nelson's federal Member of Parliament, Alex Atamanenko, provincial Member of the Legislative Assembly, Michelle Mungall, and the president of the National Farmers Union, Colleen Ross. They were there to draw attention to the government's redefining of "local" and to help launch the co-op's new labeling initiative, "True Local." From that point forward, all products in the store that came from within the co-op's longstanding "local" region would now be affixed with a "True Local" label. The Kootenay Co-op was regulating itself. The effort was a success and remains the namesake of the co-op's local sourcing program. In 2018, the co-op paid $2.6 million to True Local suppliers, representing 18 percent of its total payments.

The True Local program employs two staff who work directly with local suppliers to support them in growing their businesses. It's more than just a marketing program — it's a political statement, an incubator of the local food system, and an economic development initiative unlike

Sales of True Local Products — 2018

Organic Milk & Cream	85,000 liters
Bread	37,000 loaves
Organic Eggs	46,000 dozen
Organic Potatoes	27,000 lbs
Organic Kale	8,000 bunches
Meat	53,000 lbs

Source: Kootenay Co-op

any found within a Canadian grocery store.[xvii] In the larger food co-op community, the Kootenay Co-op is not alone in its work to strengthen its local food economy. At Hanover's Co-op Food Stores, public relations director Allan Reetz maintains ongoing communication with government officials. While the chain stores were lobbying the federal government on the 2018 Farm Bill, Reetz was traveling with a group of Northeast farmers to Washington, DC, to protect the interests of small-scale agriculture in their communities.

Food co-ops are truly invested in protecting and growing their local economies.

The Language of "Economic Development"

Though credit is due to the local food movement for helping connect the dots between local food and local economies, the language of "economic development" was never quite at the forefront. Instead, it found itself comingling with the languages of "justice," "policy," "globalization," "genetic engineering," "climate change," "human rights," and "animal welfare." For the uninitiated, these *other* languages carried an air of confrontation and of conflict — all of them well-positioned to spark debate between widely differing perspectives and values. The promise of local food to local economic development tended to be buried within the diversity of "causes." In many instances, the language

---

xvii   The Big Carrot Community Market (a worker co-op) with two stores in Toronto is another impressive grocery retailer that has been a relentless supporter of southern Ontario's local food system.

of "economic development" remains in the shadows. But the movement is young and the opportunities plentiful.

There's a secret to the language of "economic development" ... it's quite free of confrontation. Even better, it's a language that the wider population understands. Mention "policy," "justice," "rights," and you've already limited your audience substantially. By no means is "economic development" any more provocative, but we're not talking complex economic theory here, we're talking simple economics — "jobs," "income," "affordability," "security." We're talking about keeping money circulating locally. Everyone understands this. It's a language we all speak. No translators required. No matter what type of food ends up in our refrigerators, everyone in a city, town, or community can rally behind an initiative that stands to support job retention, job creation, and local business development. The economic development opportunities provided by food co-ops is a conversation that can bring an entire community together — red and blue, black and white, granola munchers and microwave meal poppers — all within the same circle.

Beyond the entry-point of economics are the substantial social impacts that arise from stronger local economies. This also makes for an easy and compelling conversation. The social components of economics were understood as far back as the Renaissance in central Italy, when the conduct of economics was an "expression of social values" and an integral part of the "civic humanism" of the time.[397]

For these reasons, the language of "economic development" might hold the greatest potential for all food movements. In fact, it *may* just be the mother of all "causes." Food co-ops embody this potential and put it into practice every day. As co-ops strengthen local food economies, there is a corresponding influence on food policy, animal rights, and climate change, to name just a few of the causes food co-ops use their economic impact to influence. As co-ops multiply and grow, so does their impact. Every grocery store, no matter the type, is an economic engine that has lasting effects on people and the planet; food co-ops are just more intentional with their impact and use their economic position to effect positive change. The movement for more local, clean, and healthier food would be well served to put more resources behind community-owned grocery stores. Same goes for all food movements: farmer welfare, equitable trade, the environment. Fewer resources could be put toward fending off the destructive tide of the grocery giants and redirected into the creation of a new economy and a new food paradigm — one that food co-ops are already helping usher in. We already know it works. The first entry-point into a food co-op conversation does not have to be about pesticides, GMOs, or factory farming. It can start with "economic development," and the rest will follow.

The start-up Westwood Food Cooperative in Denver understood this when they first pitched their co-op vision by referencing the over $13 million worth of food dollars that eaters were transporting out of their neighborhood every year to the chain grocers.

Anyone can calculate this. Pick a geographically defined area — a county, a city, a town, or a neighborhood. Determine its population and then multiply that by per capita annual food expenditures. In short

Per Capita Food Expenditures
(food purchased for the home)

Canada — $2,472 (CAD dollars) *(2016)*[398]

USA — $2,512 (U.S. dollars) *(2017)*[399]

Per Capita Food Expenditures
(all food purchases — for the home and away from home combined)

Canada — $3,516 (CAD dollars)[400]

USA — $5,033 (U.S. dollars)[401]

Note: These are national averages. Per capita food expenditures vary between province/state and even more so between communities.

SOURCES: *USDA ERS FOOD EXPENDITURES SERIES; STATISTICS CANADA 2016 — PER CAPITA FIGURES CALCULATED USING NUMBER OF HOUSEHOLDS,[402] FOOD EXPENDITURES,[403] NATIONAL POPULATION[404]*

order, you have a figure of potential — a numerical representation of the town of "What's Possible."

In the bioregion defined by the Kootenay Co-op as "local," for instance, the regional population of 80,000 spends $198 million on at-home food purchases or $281 million on total food purchases. With sales of locally produced foods representing less than 5 percent[405] of total food purchases, that remaining 95 percent represents a whole lot of potential.

Food Co-ops as Economic Development

When the River Valley Food Co-op opened in Northampton, Massachusetts, at the height of the financial crisis in 2008, one dairy farmer told the store that they likely would have lost their farm had the co-op not opened and featured their brand. The loss of the dairy would have put one more notch in the belt of "big food" and siphoned one more pool of community wealth and social capital off to a distant head office and distant shareholders. In their first year, River Valley's purchases of local product exceeded $1 million. Ten years later, local purchases had tripled.

A more penetrating way to understand the impact of consumer purchases of local food is the multiplier effect — the increased spending that ripples out of an initial injection of income.

Weaver Street Market has tracked the multiplier effect of their purchases of local products. For example, among many local foods, the co-op sells 1.44 million local eggs, 29,050 containers of local berries, and 212,643 loaves of local organic bread each year. The people involved in producing, processing, and distributing those foods then go on to spend more money locally. Regardless of where we spend it, our food dollar initiates waves of further spending, but it's become clear that the purchase of a local product at a food co-op has a stronger multiplier effect in a local economy than that of a food dollar spent at a chain. For all of Weaver Street's local purchases, they track an extra $10 million of additional spending compared to the same dollars spent at chain stores.[406]

In one British study, it was calculated that for every ten pounds sterling spent at an establishment carrying products from local foodmakers, another twenty-five pounds is generated in the local economy because of the other businesses the foodmakers are in turn supporting. Alternatively, at a chain supermarket, that same ten pounds only generates fourteen pounds of community benefit.[407] Buying locally produced foods is an effective drain-stopper — it prevents food dollars from leaking out of a local economy.

Locally-produced foods aside, when Civic Economics was commissioned in 2017 to study the recirculation of *all* consumer food dollars at Central Co-op in Seattle, their results were compelling. "Recirculation" included labor costs, product purchases for retail sale and internal use, and charitable giving. For every dollar spent at a conventional store, 23 cents was recirculated locally. At the average co-op nationally? 36 cents. At Central Co-op? ... even higher: 52 cents — that's more than twice that of the average conventional store.[408]

Revenue Recirculated in the Local Economy

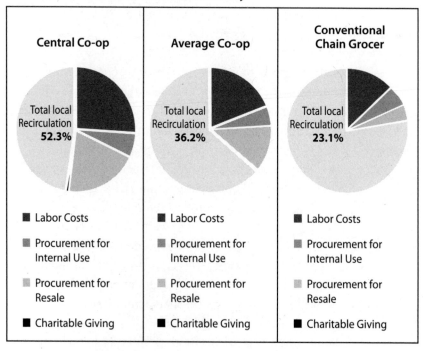

SOURCE: CIVIC ECONOMICS, 2017[409]

Compensation Comparison

	Central Co-op	Typical Co-op	Conventional Chain
Wages/Benefits as % of Sales	26%	19%	13%
Average Hourly Wages (Indexed)*	158.7	107.2	100.0
% of Full-Time Employees	81%	61%	43%
% of Employees Eligible for Benefits	87%	68%	56%

* The wages for the Average Co-op and Conventional Chain reflect national averages. Due to Seattle's Minimum Wage Ordinance, it is likely these numbers would be higher locally, but exact numbers are not available.

SOURCE: CIVIC ECONOMICS, 2017[410]

Local Food System Stimulation

Beyond the store shelves, food co-ops have become incredibly proficient at stimulating development of local food systems.

Some co-ops like Vermont's Putney Food Co-op host farmers' markets directly on site. Other co-ops have positioned themselves as pickup locations for CSA box programs like Eastside Food Co-op and Mississippi Market. The Merc Co-op has been a pickup location for three hundred members of the Rolling Prairie CSA since 1994. Mississippi Market is a pickup location for a CSB (community supported bakery).

Valley Natural Foods in Burnsville, MN, hosts an annual farm festival that draws more then two thousand people. Seward Co-op has hosted an annual CSA Fair since 2001. The event links eaters up with CSA farms. In 2018, twenty-seven farms participated.

While it might seem odd for a business to support its competition, food co-ops recognize that a stronger local food system involves farmers having a diversity of channels to sell their products through. By supporting these channels, co-ops are in turn supporting the very existence of their suppliers. When all venues for the sale of local food are strong, so is the food co-op. By investing in the local food system, co-ops are securing their own future.

The ripple effects do, however, support the competition. In Nelson, BC, Save-On-Foods has become a unique example of a single location of a large chain that creates space for local foods. The Kootenay Co-op helped incubate all of their suppliers, like Tipiland Organic Produce, which credits their existence to the co-op. Today, Tipiland supplies both the co-op and Save-On-Foods.

Food co-op managers are also engaged in food system development by participating in organizations outside of their own. Viroqua Food Co-op's general manager, Jan Rasikas, has been involved in the local food broker initiative Fifth Season Cooperative. Outpost Natural Foods GM, Pam Mehnert, is founder and board chair of Local First Milwaukee, a cross-sector alliance of independent locally owned businesses.

Another initiative emerging within consumer food co-ops is micro-lending. At Chequamegon Food Co-op in Ashland, Wisconsin, a micro-lending program was developed in 2008 to provide loans to local foodmakers looking to expand their businesses. Loans have supported a drinkable yogurt product from a local dairy, the acquisition of a grain mill, and a poultry processing trailer. The co-op caps loans at $5k with three-year terms. Viroqua Food Co-op's lending initiative awards one loan per year. In 2017, the program funded Deep Rooted — a local certified organic farm that supplies $18,775 of tomatoes to the co-op between May and October. The one-year, no-interest loan of $3,500 helped them construct a walk-in cooler on the farm so they could expand production into greens, vegetables, and cut flowers and extend the shelf life of their produce. At City Market, a $40k, five-year, no-interest loan helped support the Vermont Tortilla Company, a corn chip manufacturer that uses 90 percent Vermont corn. Since 2000, Bellingham's Community Food Co-op has dedicated a portion of its budget to food and farm projects. With the support of other local funding agencies and credit unions, the fund has financed fifty projects to the tune of $245k.

Food co-ops will even go so far as to finance their suppliers in times of need. Following the recession of 2007–08, North Coast Co-op partnered with Tofu Shop Specialty Foods by fronting them the money to purchase organic soy beans in bulk. Tofu Shop applied a credit to their invoices to pay back the investment.

Co-ops also use grant monies to support their local food systems. Monadnock Food Co-op launched a Farm Fund in 2017 in partnership with their regional municipality. The fund has awarded grants to local farms producing dairy, pork, beef, and root crops. At the Kootenay Co-op, one day per month, a percentage of sales is donated to a local nonprofit. The Kootenay Organic Growers Society (KOGS), which represents twenty-five local farmers, receives 25 percent of its annual budget from that one donation day.

The preservation and development of farmland is another way in which food co-ops engage in food system stimulation. Through their support of One Farm at a Time, Sacramento Natural Foods Co-op made it possible for Good Humus Produce to purchase an easement to protect their land in the Capay Valley for generations to come. In 1999, PCC founded the PCC Farmland Trust, an independent nonprofit. The Trust saved its first farm in 2000 and has now conserved twenty farms across Washington, totaling 2,030 acres. At Outpost Natural Foods, they saw an opportunity in the growth of urban farming in Milwaukee. Their efforts led to the creation of the Milwaukee Farmers Union — a network of a dozen urban farmers who are consolidating plots of land to grow produce for the co-op.

Food distribution is one of the most recognized "missing links" in local food systems and is yet another area of co-op involvement. In 1999, The Wedge started Co-op Partners Warehouse (CPW), a stand-alone certified organic distributor for one hundred local producers. CPW serves more than four hundred customers in the Upper Midwest that include grocery stores, restaurants, food processors, and educational institutions. CPW relieves many local foodmakers from the burden of direct delivery, allowing them to focus on what they do best, production. CPW's services includes a cross-dock program that picks up product at the producer's place of business and delivers direct to customers. Unlike many distributors who prohibit their suppliers from delivering directly to their customers, CPW permits this practice.

Other co-ops incorporate wholesale distribution directly into daily store operations. The Great Basin Community Food Co-op has staff dedicated to operating a food hub. Food hubs are "businesses or organizations that actively manage the aggregation, distribution, and marketing of source-identified food products."[411] The idea for DROPP (Distributors of Regional and Organic Produce & Products) began at Great Basin not long after they opened their doors. Produce staff had been receiving a steady stream of inquiries from local restaurants and schools with requests to order large quantities of local product. Rather than burden the produce department, the co-op launched DROPP in 2012. DROPP quickly learned that their customers were also restricted from ordering dry goods from national distributor UNFI. Their customers' businesses were too small to meet UNFI's minimum order thresholds. DROPP expanded to begin offering this important service, and now facilitates the sale of $550k of product to area businesses and another $250k sold directly into the co-op. The program has become a critical component in Reno's local food system. When one foodmaker supplying DROPP was "dropped" by national foodservice distributor Sysco, DROPP provided them much-needed access to the local market.[412]

Co-ops are also facilitating programs for shoppers to purchase local products in wholesale formats. At the now-closed West End Food Co-op in Toronto, their Buy the Bushel program coordinated wholesale orders of seasonal local foods including rhubarb, strawberries, Roma tomatoes, beef, and turkeys.

Incubating and mentoring foodmakers is another important role played by some food co-ops. Outpost Natural Foods hosts weekly Makers Markets — an opportunity for new food businesses to get in front of potential customers. Trueman McGee's Funky Fresh Spring Rolls is one such business. Without Outpost's support, McGee doesn't believe his business would have been able to grow the way it has.

At City Market, "gaps" in the local food system are identified — a list of foods that they would like to sell but are not yet being produced locally. The "gaps" are published directly on their website to inspire new or existing foodmakers to fill the void.

Another area where food co-ops are helping ensure more of a community's food dollars remain in the local economy is in the ready-to-eat market of prepared foods. With over 50 percent[413] of American and 30 percent[414] of Canadian food dollars going toward the purchase of foods to be consumed *away* from the home, food co-ops are increasingly positioning themselves to capture some of this market. They use "commissary kitchens" to produce ready-to-eat meals and prepared foods for their store shelves or in-store cafés. Weaver Street Market is home to one of the most extensive of these kitchens. Housed in an 18,000-square-foot space, WSM's Food House includes a bread and bagel bakery, a pastry bakery, a kitchen facility (for grab-and-go items and food for the hot bar and salad bar), a sushi kitchen, and a meat-processing facility. Adjacent to the Food House is a large warehouse space. The kitchen does more than just prepare food for their four locations, it also sends products to other sister co-ops in the area. With this facility, WSM was able to introduce cross-docking. Small farmers and distributors deliver their products to the Food House where they are sorted for delivery to the co-op's four locations.

Commissary kitchens are further enabling food co-ops to develop an "ecosystem" within the store. When foods being sold in the retail space are in surplus or nearing their best-before dates, the kitchens are able to convert those foods into immediately saleable items, helping to reduce food waste. Whereas grocery stores of decades past had kitchens like these located directly within the stores, the chain stores of today receive almost all of these prepared foods from centralized facilities in distant cities. This results in a greater portion of consumers' food dollars leaving local economies.

Anchors for Main Street

> "Communities are held together by thousands of threads that directly connect people in social, cultural and economic interactions; but real, face-to-face human relationships that occur in the neighborhood are being designed out in countless, seemingly insignificant ways. They're going because an economic system that is meant to be our servant has instead become our master, and it sees people too often as costly and inefficient."[415]
>
> — Andrew Simms, *Tescopoly*

A well understood outcome of the rise of the big chains has been the decimation of neighborhood and town centers. Studies from all over the Western world have tracked catastrophic declines in the number of independent grocers and specialty food shops as a result of the growth of chains. The modern supermarket has effectively replaced many town centers. The bakery, meat shop, and fruit stand are now embedded inside the grocery store. The larger-format supermarkets have also absorbed many of the services once found at independent merchants and services: banking, photo services, clothing, books, even birth registration. In her book *Shopped*, Joanna Blythman renames Britain's towns after the grocers that have colonized them: "Asdatown," "Tescotown," "Sainsburytown."[416]

In many communities home to food co-ops, the convergence of benefits to a neighborhood or town's local economy is most visible in the commercial center, where food co-ops are often located. These "main streets" benefit enormously from having any grocery store to act as an anchor. A walkable grocery store improves foot traffic for surrounding businesses and increases their sales. Whereas chains are generally reluctant to operate in these locations, food co-ops often identify them as optimal and an extension of their missions and of the Co-op Principles. Retail food stores of any kind are akin to a keystone species within an ecosystem — remove them, and the rest of the "main street" ecosystem unravels. With less human interaction happening between members of a community, we become strangers to one another, leaving us less inclined to invest time into our communities and leading us to retreat into virtual worlds of digital relationships as the only way to tend to the wounds inflicted by the loss of human interaction. As Andrew Simms describes, in these virtual worlds, "fewer social and emotional skills are needed than the full spectrum of senses we require for real life."[417] What's there to talk about when you already know what your friend, neighbor, or acquaintance is up to from their social media updates? The impact of food stores and town centers on our lives is profound.

Retention and Rearing of Community Leaders

"During the 1970s, a third of metro areas met or exceeded the national start-up rate for businesses. Today, only one in seven areas meet this threshold."[418] Starting a business in a community overrun by chains is far from promising.

Numerous studies demonstrate the impact of distant headquarters on a community's social capital — the people, relationships, and identity of a community. One study found that "local owners and managers … are more invested in the community personally and financially than 'distant' owners and managers," whereas, "branch firms are managed by 'outsiders' with no local ties who are brought in for short-term assignments, or by locals who have less ability to benefit the community because they lack sufficient autonomy or prestige."[419] This leads to "lower levels of local corporate giving, civic engagement, employment, and investment, often setting in motion further regional decline."[420]

Before it was acquired by Amazon, Whole Foods had stood out among the national chains as having a more decentralized corporate model for its 450 locations. Eleven regional offices were empowered to make product selections for their stores and run their own marketing divisions. Individual stores were given more freedom to work directly with local suppliers. Less than one year after Amazon's acquisition of the company, Whole Foods announced companywide layoffs of regional marketing positions, including in-store marketing and graphic design jobs.[421]

Enter the food co-op with no distant head office. The CEO, finance manager, marketing manager, and graphic designers — all work directly in the store or at a nearby office. Full control is headquartered in the community the co-op is serving. A Harvard Business School study found that companies headquartered locally have "the most active involvement by their leaders in prominent local civic and cultural organizations."[422] With leadership remaining 100 percent local, food co-ops are perfectly positioned to help de-colonize grocery retail and reverse the growing inequality of wealth between communities, cities, and regions.

A Different Kind of Profit

Beyond the day-to-day operational effects of food co-ops on their local economies is the very nature of their ownership structure and their relationship to "profit."

When food co-ops finance new stores and renovations with the equity of their member–owners, interest earned remains in the community — it's not sent off to distant banks. Profits from the store's operations are recirculated back into the store itself, with a portion often redistributed back to member–owners. In one year, City Market returned $656,000 of profit to 11,450 members. The average check amounted to $57. For every dollar spent in the store, this worked out to 2.4 cents returned. At the Davis Co-op, $220,000 was returned to 5,773 members. For a member spending $2,000, a $30 check was returned. A total 413 members received more than $100 at the end of the year. Member-owners were invited to redeem their returns or donate them to one of a number of community arts organizations.

Local Foodmakers – the People Behind the Products

"The co-op is an astounding incubator for food producers in the area. We used to joke that if you made a really good mud pie, the co-op would sell it."[423]

— Louisa Spencer, Poverty Lane Orchards (Lebanon, NH)

WHOLE FOODS WAS ONCE a shining example of a grocery giant that, despite its enormous size, was able to maintain supportive relationships with local foodmakers. After Amazon's takeover in 2017, everything began to change. Sal and Valerie Grays' Italian Hearts Gourmet Foods was one business that took a hit. The Grays supply retailers in Reno, Nevada, with locally made pasta sauces. Their customers include Safeway, Natural Grocers, Great Basin Community Food Co-op, and Whole Foods. For many years, Whole Foods provided shelf space for more than a hundred jars of their sauce and promoted their family business with a large-format photograph hanging in the store. In December 2017 — six months after Amazon's acquisition of Whole Foods — the photo was taken down, shelf space was reduced to 36 jars, and in-store sampling was canceled. For the Grays, being in the store to offer samples was "truly key to sales." Through sampling, customers could understand why their pasta sauce was so different from the sea of national brands, and it was a way to maintain a sense of community inside and outside of the store. Eventually, Whole Foods stopped carrying Italian Hearts, and the Grays almost lost their business.[424]

The Gray's story is identical to the stories of countless other small-scale Whole Foods' suppliers. Whereas Whole Foods once permitted direct relations between suppliers and regional offices, suppliers are

now required to work with Connecticut-based Daymon Worldwide —
a global brand consultant serving more than fifteen thousand retail
locations and sixteen thousand suppliers and manufacturers across
nineteen countries. Far from personal. Whole Foods put Daymon in
charge of inventory management, display creation, and in-store tast-
ings. With Daymon in the mix, a four-hour in-store tasting now costs
$110. The financial hit to suppliers didn't stop there. Any foodmakers
selling more than $300k of product to Whole Foods annually were
required to discount their products by 3 percent.[425]

Whole Foods' new culture hasn't only disrupted mom-and-pop
foodmakers. Larger independents are also being squeezed right out of
the market, like Ron Marks of AtlantaFresh, who laid off all 32 of his
employees after Whole Foods canceled their contract in late 2017. A
state-of-the-art, 12,000-square-foot milk-processing facility in Norcross,
Georgia, was rendered idle.

AtlantaFresh was founded in 2009. Their hand-packed mozzarella
and Greek yogurts were found on the shelves of 180 Whole Foods locations across the country. In 2015, AtlantaFresh was presented with a
hard-to-turn-down offer. Whole Foods was looking for another source
of grass-fed milk and asked AtlantaFresh if they could supply it. The
retailer was prepared to guarantee the purchase of 30,000 gallons of
milk per week. Marks agreed and was awarded a seven-year contract
worth $15 million a year. The contract would have comprised 90 percent
of AtlantaFresh' sales and would have increased revenues seven-fold.
Marks invested $2.5 million in facility upgrades. One year later, when
the milk was ready to flow, Whole Foods failed to hold up their end of
the deal. Instead of purchasing 30,000 gallons per week as promised,
they were purchasing only 10,000. By late 2017, Whole Foods canceled
the contract completely.[426] With so much invested in Whole Foods'
promises, AtlantaFresh had no option but to shutter the plant.

The stories continue. After two years supplying Whole Foods' five
stores in Vancouver, BC, with organic raw chocolate bars, Danu da
Silva of Raw Magic Chocolate was told she would need to participate
in the chain's "fair-share" program. Unbeknownst to her, Whole Foods
requires their suppliers or brokers to annually visit each of the stores

they sell into and spend a full day resetting the shelves of the entire category — in this case, *every* chocolate bar in the store. Da Silva lives an eight-hour drive from Vancouver, so she called up a friend there who had helped her out in the past. As a small business owner, Da Silva couldn't afford to pay her friend for her time, so instead offered payment in chocolate. Her friend showed up at the store and was instructed by Whole Foods staff to begin pulling all brands of chocolate bars off of the shelves, clean the shelves, and then reset the products according to a planogram provided. Da Silva received a call later that day from a shocked friend: "They basically had me cleaning shelves all day." Her friend declined to commit another four days to the other four stores. When da Silva called up her Whole Foods contact to inform him that there was no way she could ask anyone else to take on such a task, he sounded surprised. As da Silva recalls, "He explained to me that Whole Foods was doing me a great favor by providing shelf space for my products and by me giving back to the store, I was doing my 'fair share.'" [427]

These stories, and many others like them, provide ample evidence of a once-conscientious retailer having descended into the supermarket swamp. Innovative foodmakers trying to make a difference now find themselves waist-deep in it. For a foodmaker negotiating with a chain retailer, it's a "deal with the devil," says former New Hampshire Commissioner of Agriculture and dairy farmer Steve Taylor. "The chains say they want to support local food, but they just want it given to them."[428]

Food co-ops on the other hand are cultivating very different relationships with their suppliers. Prohibitive fees, discounts, or requirements to clean shelves are unheard of. As Outpost's Pam Mehnert says on the matter of slotting fees, "There's no way ethically that that makes sense to me. Especially with the local vendors ... we want them on our shelves. Our goal is to sell more local product, so why would we charge them for it? Suppliers will never control our stores' shelves."[429]

Co-ops as Small Business Incubators

Foodmakers take considerable risk starting a business. The moment they enter into a relationship with a retailer, they're making a social investment that can translate either to success or failure for their business.

It's a heavy financial investment too. Upwards of millions of dollars are invested into land, buildings, and equipment... all of it hanging on having access to eaters.

Many foodmakers are realizing that the most secure investment in a supplier-retailer relationship is a cooperative one.

Food co-ops change people's lives. Aubrey Saxton is an artisan baker of pies, cookies, and treats in southern New Hampshire. Before the Monadnock Food Co-op opened in Keene in 2013, Saxton relied on farmstands to sell her baked goods. When the co-op opened its doors, significantly more product began to flow out of her bakery. "It would be hard to find someone whose life has been more greatly impacted by the co-op than my own," says Saxton. "The opening of the co-op literally changed everything for me... they are my highest grossing customer and carry the widest range of my products. It's the place I go to shop. It's also the place I go to socialize. I spend a lot of time in the bakery with limited human contact, and I enjoy that, but once in a while I want to get out and talk to people — so I go to the co-op."[430] Today, Mondanock and the Brattleboro Food Co-op are Saxton's two biggest customers. "Many large chains are impossible to get a hold of to try to sell to ... With the co-ops, I have relationships with the people at the business ... there aren't a lot of hoops to jump through to become a supplier."[431] As a local foodmaker, Saxy Chef is bringing added benefits to the local food system. In 2015, she used 6,000 local eggs, 40 gallons of local maple syrup, 700 pounds of local blueberries, 22 pounds of spices from a local purveyor, 2,670 pounds of local apples, 1,476 pounds of regional butter, and 3,800 pounds of Vermont flour.[432]

Louisa Spencer and Steve Wood of Poverty Lane Orchards have been selling to New England food co-ops since the 1970s. Their farm has become well-known for its commitment to heirloom varieties of apples and for Farnum Hill Ciders. Of their many customers, which do include chains, their experience supplying co-ops stands out. "Ordinary grocery chains are under ruthless pressure to make a profit in a business that is incredibly difficult to make a profit in so they usually have to be hard on their suppliers," says Spencer. The most marked difference she experiences in the retailer-supplier relationship is at the point of delivery. "Co-ops are not trying to grind every cent out of the process ... not trying to cut every last penny out of every single teenage employee's every motion ... so deliveries are a lot easier at the co-ops. I can usually arrive when I need to.... I'm not held up behind some giant delivery of Diet Coke." By comparison, when Spencer used to deliver to a major supermarket in Concord, New Hampshire, she remembers showing up at 10:30 am and "everyone's on lunch." Nobody would be there to receive her product. "Co-ops pride themselves on the fact that I'm small and feeble, and often the corporate stores taking local products pride themselves on the fact that I'm small and feeble," — yet, it's an entirely different sense of pride between the two.[433]

When Poverty Lane first began supplying Hanover Co-op with apples, to her astonishment the produce manager told her that she could raise her price by two dollars a case. The chains on the other hand are often trying to drive prices down. Their relationship with Littleton Food Co-op has also been supportive. The co-op is a one-and-a-half-hour drive from her farm. To reduce the number of trips Spencer has to make, Littleton orders substantially more than they actually need. This is unheard of at most chains where storing backstock is impossible.

An important turning point for Poverty Lane came in the 1970s, when apples from thousands of miles away began arriving into their local market and in better condition than McIntosh emerging from winter storage. They realized that growing McIntosh apples was becoming "economically insane" and sustaining their farm required a new approach. They looked to fermented cider and began researching suitable varieties of apples. As Spencer recalls, the Hanover Co-op was the first to set up a staging area in their store to promote their cider. "They didn't need a story about whether or not it was going to work ... they just tried it.... They're an astounding incubator for food producers in the area ... we used to joke that if you made a really good mud pie, the co-op would sell it." Farnum Hill Ciders are now sold in five states.

Food co-ops have been incubating foodmakers for decades. Some of the biggest national brands got their start on the shelves of a food co-op. Now owned by General Mills, Annie's first major account for their Organic Mac and Cheese was Vermont's Hunger Mountain Co-op.

The product is now found on the shelves of every major chain in the United States and Canada. Siete Family Foods is another example of a small foodmaker making it big. What began as a small ziplock baggy of chips being handed to a buyer at the Wheatsville Food Co-op is now a nationally distributed line of tortillas and tortilla chips. Aqua Vitea kombucha in the small town of Middlebury, Vermont, went from the shelves of Middlebury Natural Foods Co-op to grocery store shelves across the Midwest and eastern seaboard.[434]

Landing contracts with chain retailers isn't, however, a requirement for success. Many small-scale foodmakers are happy staying small, and food co-ops allow for this possibility. Isabel Street Hot Sauces got its start at Mississippi Market and has become the Twin Cities most popular brand of local hot sauces.

By not requiring prohibitive fees, discounts, or shelf-cleaning servitude to access their shelves, food co-ops allow products to be brought to market at far less cost. With less cost to market, local entrepreneurs are encouraged to get innovative and take risks. When Lana and Brad Braun purchased a farm in the Slocan Valley of British Columbia, they constructed a commercial kitchen. The kitchen would enable them to process product from the farm into higher-value foods like tomatillo and tomato salsas. Only problem. they had zero experience. Lana walked into the Kootenay Co-op and described her vision for Hummingbird Farm. Without hesitation, the co-op said they would take whatever she could produce and see how it sold. The commitment allowed the Brauns to make investments into their farm that they might not otherwise have made, and they began to experiment with small batches of products to see what worked and what didn't. The co-op effectively became a research and development testing ground for their start-up business.

"Where else could I do a public experiment of whether or not something is actually what people want to buy," asks Braun. "I can't afford consultants." One product that's become a success was their pickled beets — a zero-waste product delivered in bulk for the co-op's self-serve tapas bar. During one of her deliveries, a co-op manager pointed out other items in the tapas bar being imported from Europe but that could easily be made locally. This led Hummingbird to begin producing sweet pickled peppers and pickled beans. The local food system was evolving right on the floor of the retail space.[435]

Spontaneous purchases of local product are also not uncommon at food co-ops — quite different than the average six to twelve months of "onboarding" it takes to bring new products to market at chain retailers. When Hummingbird had produced an oversupply of tomatoes, they transformed the surplus into sundried tomatoes. The co-op took the product without question. Even more astonishing to the Brauns was the prime shelf space the co-op provided for every item they produced. "This changed the mood of what we were doing," says Braun. "It made us realize that the only thing that could screw this up was us." There was no fear or guesswork on the commitment of the co-op, which hasn't been the case with Hummingbird's other customers. "At other retailers, you have to convince them that they should sell it … if it's not successful in two weeks… they'll drop you like a rock." At the co-op, when a product wasn't selling, co-op staff worked with her to reevaluate her approach to product quality and labeling.

Financially, the Kootenay Co-op wants their local suppliers to succeed. When the co-op puts local products on special, the price the co-op pays the supplier doesn't change. Other retailers would never do this. They would require the supplier to absorb the discount.

Salix and Sedge Farm

Starting a farm with the support of a food co-op

Cali Olleck and Brendan Parsons spent their post-secondary school years studying food, gardening, and sustainability. In 2014, they invested their personal savings into the purchase of a farm in the community of Salmo, BC. With the help of some Berkshire pigs, Olleck and Parsons converted old pasture and meadows into vegetable beds and began growing organic veggies. Rather than rely on guesswork to determine the most appropriate vegetables for the local market, they approached the Kootenay Co-op. The produce department managers laid out what the co-op needed and when. As

Parsons recalls, this gave them the "confidence" to pursue their farm plan. In that first year, they were selling head lettuce, green onions, and cilantro to the co-op.

Four years later, these young farmers have gained experience selling to many retailers, including one of Nelson's chain stores. Their relationship with the co-op has been the most rewarding. "It's just not that easy working with the other retailers," says Parsons. "The co-op's produce is 100-percent organic, so we're not required to individually sticker or twist-tie each vegetable with an 'organic' label like we have to do at other retailers."

Today, 80 percent of their family's income comes from the farm. Sales and profits are growing every year.

"The co-op is proud of what they do, and that make us proud to be a part of that. Seeing our bio and photo next to our produce makes us feel great." [436]

The People Behind the Products

Common Market Co-op in Frederick, Maryland, dedicates an entire page of their website to listing the local farmers and businesses supplying their store. The sheer diversity of foodmakers on the list offers some assurance that eating a predominantly local diet is absolutely possible.

Taking it one step further, the Kootenay Co-op's local supplier listing reads more like a local farm and food directory. Through in-depth interviews and photos, stories are told of the people behind the products. Many of the farm photos include the entire staff of the co-op's produce department, who commit to ongoing farm visits throughout the year.

Small-scale foodmakers across the United States and Canada are producing truly revolutionary products. The stories of these businesses are a testament to the power food co-ops hold to unleash the creative potential of people in the communities they operate in.

Below is a selection of just some of the Kootenay Co-op's "True Local" suppliers. The list helps capture the diversity of entrepreneurs that can emerge in any place home to a food cooperative.

Examples of the Kootenay Co-op's 145 "True Local" Suppliers

Tipiland Organic Produce — "Without the co-op, Tipiland would simply not be Tipiland," says farmer Gary Diers. Tipiland began selling produce to the co-op in 1989 and has since become one of the most productive market gardens in the West Kootenay. Perched on the side of a mountain, the certified organic farm is situated on a land co-op adjacent to the largest protected wilderness area in Southeastern British Columbia. The place is breathtakingly beautiful. Tipiland is completely off-grid and uses almost zero electricity. The only piece of machinery used on the farm is a small Italian rototiller, and their produce requires no refrigeration. Once harvested, vegetables and cut flowers are taken immediately to the co-op in a funky four-cylinder Japanese diesel. When Tipiland founder Sarah Ross first began farming the land, local produce was almost shunned. The Kootenay Co-op helped change that. The first kale on the co-op's shelves was Tipiland kale. As Tipiland and the Kootenay Co-op grew alongside each other, so did the region's organic farming community. Tipiland helped form the region's first organic certification body — KOGS. Diers and partner Inanna Judd save seeds from more than a hundred varieties of vegetables and flowers and employ six to ten farmworkers from their community of Argenta. Their workers range in age from eighteen to seventy-two years old and are paid above average for their time. In their own words, Diers and Judd are committed to providing the "purest, freshest, most nutrient-dense organic produce possible." Their produce is now sold at eight retailers in the region, all thanks to the co-op's incubating effects.[437]

Kootenay Kombucha — At only twenty-two years old, Lavinia Lidstone launched her own kombucha brewery. The co-op was her first customer. Kombucha is a naturally fermented alternative to sugary sodas and is known to support healthier digestive tracts. Lidstone uses ingredients like blue algae, reishi mushrooms, and damiana leaves. Many of her ingredients are local, and the environmental footprint of her products is staggeringly low. Kombucha is almost entirely water and most kombuchas found on grocery store shelves today are shipped thousands of miles, crisscrossing the continent. Kootenay Kombucha provides an alternative. The water flows directly off the mountains surrounding Lidstone's Slocan Valley brewery, and thanks to self-serve taps and refillable growlers, Kootenay Kombucha is a zero-waste product.

Chuckleberry Community Farm — Only ten miles from the co-op, Chuckleberry is an off-grid community of interns and volunteers who trade labor and an education in organic farming for room and board. Workers cultivate and harvest a variety of microgreens, herbs, berries, and vegetables. The farm is host to an ongoing series of sustainability and gardening workshops and retreats.

Kootenay Meadows — In 2007, Mountain Valley Farm in the town of Creston was producing high-quality organic milk from cows being fed a zero-mile diet. There was one small problem. Nobody anywhere near the farm could drink it. The sale of raw milk is illegal across Canada, and there was zero processing capacity in Southeastern British Columbia. The milk was instead being shipped to processing facilities up to seven hundred miles away, where it would be combined with conventional milk and sold as one of a handful of big-name brands. The milk would never return to the Creston Valley. Mountain Valley responded to this rather absurd state of affairs by constructing a cheese-making facility. In short order, demand for their cheese outstripped supply. As their first and largest customer, the Kootenay

Co-op was an integral part of this success. The confidence Mountain Valley received from their cheese convinced them to construct a state-of-the-art processing facility for fluid milk. Kootenay Meadows became BC's first and only fluid milk processing facility in an area the size of Indiana. The Kootenay Co-op became the first to carry their milk and cream in zero-waste, returnable glass bottles.

McIntyre Farm — Forty years ago, Vince McIntyre began growing food on an idyllic piece of land in the community of Argenta. His specialty is storage crops. Instead of relying on fossil fuels to tend to the land, Vince has only relied on horses. His low-impact, humble life has made him legendary in the Kootenay food community and has inspired new generations of farmers. After spending three years interning at McIntyre Farm, Michael Silver set up his own farm just down the road. Silver's Earth Temple Gardens has since become a supplier to the co-op's produce department.

Treasure Life Flour Mills — Ben and Claudia Herrera farm and mill certified organic heirloom grains on their farm in Creston. Their farm and mill are the first in recent memory to supply area retailers with locally grown, freshly milled flour. The co-op began carrying their products immediately — flour, hot cereal, pancake and waffle mixes. At least a few of the co-op's bread suppliers also use Treasure Life flour.

Feed Your Soul Foods — Dawna McLennan is a gifted harp player, poet, and mother, with a passion for nourishing people through food. When not playing shows or weddings, Dawna runs a business with one employee in the tiny community of Kaslo, where she prepares a diversity of vegetarian savories, sweets, and lunch items for the Kootenay Co-op's prepared foods section.

Kootenay Bakery Cafe Co-op — Once located directly in the Kootenay Co-op's retail space, the now-stand-alone bakery and café is cooperatively owned by its workers. The business is one of the only 100 percent organic cafes in Nelson and supplies the co-op with fresh breads and pizza and pie crusts.

Meadowbrook Farm & Kootenay Sprouts — Without Meadowbrook Farm, Nelson residents would have zero options for commercially available locally grown salad greens. Since 1998, their four-season greenhouse has allowed the Stavast family to deliver salad mixes and sprouts to the co-op year-round. Their greens and sprouts are also available in bulk — a perfect option for shoppers wishing to use reusable bags.

Cripple Crow Ranch — Certified organic chicken raised 100 percent on pasture by Tamara Smith. No industrial-scale barns here. The flavor is startlingly superior to any other chicken. As one of the only commercially available organic chickens in the region, the co-op has gone above and beyond to promote Tamara's products.

Spectrum Farms — Small farm producing dehydrated fruit products and soup mixes. The farm and business are a social enterprise project of the Kootenay Region Association for Community Living — a charity supporting and providing meaningful employment to low-income persons with disabilities.

Mountain Munchies — Producers of Enercheez snacks — morsels of 100 percent dehydrated BC cheese made in Nelson.

Wild Onion Nut Burgers — Linda Kassels manufactures three flavors of vegetarian burgers in the town of Rossland.

Epiphany Cakes — Artfully crafted cakes made by Melissa Owen in a residential neighborhood of Nelson. Owen employs three people.

Ariah's Edibles — Vegetarian samosas, burritos, and frozen pizzas made by Ariah Desilets in the rural community of Glade. Uses local ingredients whenever possible.

Ancestar Teas — Simone Vandersteen produces a selection of small-batch loose-leaf organic tea blends that are a staple in many Nelson homes. The names of the blends indicate their function: Laugh Tea, Dream Tea and Sensuali Tea, are three examples.

Where Does Your Food Dollar Go?

A portion of every food dollar spent at a grocery store ends up in the hands of the people who produce the food. They, in turn, go out and spend that portion in a myriad of ways — some of it for expenses incurred by the business itself, the rest for personal expenditures. Of the portion spent on the business, the more local the supplier is, the greater the chance that those expenditures will be supporting other local businesses, maybe even your own friends and neighbors. Website design, legal services, financial consultants, label printing, advertising in local community newspapers…. this is the local multiplier effect of our food dollars when we use them to purchase local foods.

The two businesses below that supply the Kootenay Co-op are just two examples of the abundant ripple effects of food dollar potential.

Uphill Bakery / Valerie's Fermented Foods (Nelson, BC) — David Beringer's bread delivery vehicle is a welcoming sight in front of the Kootenay Co-op. It looks a bit like an alien spacecraft. Beringer uses his bright orange (recumbent) electric trike to deliver freshly baked breads. The trike always sparks a conversation.

Beringer and partner Valerie Sanderson run two small businesses out of their Nelson home — each with their own dedicated spaces. While Sanderson prepares sauerkraut and soups, Beringer is baking baguettes and sourdough breads. Both rely on a diversity of customers that include restaurants, coffee shops, convenience stores, food trucks, and school lunch programs. Their combined sales of $108,000 is small, but it's a size they're comfortable operating at, and it fits the lifestyle that works for them. If it wasn't for the co-op, Sanderson doesn't believe her sauerkraut business would exist. "The co-op packaged my product for me for the first five years and even when the new store opened and I had to package it myself, they printed off the labels." Packaging and labels are an enormous challenge for small businesses; without the co-op's support, they would have likely been "an insurmountable obstacle" for Sanderson. In Beringer's case, when he wanted to update his own labels, he struggled using software at home. The co-op's marketing department stepped in and helped with the redesign.[438]

For every dollar spent on Valerie's sauerkrauts and soups, a portion ends up in the pockets of other local farmers like Janet Spicer of Spicer Farm (cabbage), the Moore family at Canyon City Farm (carrots, potatoes, beets), Angela Weir and Gord Spankie of Crooked Horn Farm (parsnips, zucchini), and Owen Broad and Nancy Gabrielse of Kettle River Farm (onions). Another portion of the food dollar ends up at Hall Printing (labels), Cowan's Office Supplies (paper, glue, tape, printer cartridges), and Phoenix Computers.

Then there are Valerie and David's personal expenditures that find their way into locally owned businesses and professionals ... once again, all thanks to people purchasing local sauerkraut and baguettes: Vince DeVito Shoes, Boomtown Sports, Secret Service Cycles, local microbrewers Nelson Brewing and Backroads Brewing, Whitewater Ski Resort, Kurama Sushi, Dr. RP Daniel's Optometry, Oso Negro Coffee, the Capitol Theatre, Dr. Scott Pentecost (dentist), and Kootenay Insurance Services.

Learning about where our food dollar goes is a fascinating and meaningful exercise. It can help us consider the power of food to support so many of our friends and neighbors and the people they employ.

Kaslo Sourdough: Bread and Pasta (Kaslo, BC) — Specializing in naturally fermented sourdough breads, Kaslo Sourdough (KS) is a family business started in 1993 in the small community of Kaslo. The Kootenay Co-op has been carrying their products almost from their beginning. In 2013, KS expanded into a line of sourdough pastas now available at retailers across Canada and online. The pasta is so unique that it's now being used at the University of Calgary in a federally funded study on the health benefits of sourdough pasta. KS mills grains on site and employs all five of the Lettrari family plus another four Kaslo residents.

When eaters purchase Kaslo Sourdough bread or pasta, they're also supporting the many businesses and organizations supported by the Lettrari family. These include local grocers Cornucopia and Sunnyside Naturals, Ace Building Supply, and local candlemaker Honey Candles. KS also sponsors and donates to local organizations like the nonprofit Kaslo Food Hub, the annual Kaslo Jazz Etc. Festival, the Kaslo Legion Ladies Auxiliary, and the Kaslo Curling Club. When KS has needed promotional materials, they turned to local artists like musician Sean Rodman, photographer Louis Bockner, graphic artist Gary Schneider, puppeteer Rose-Blanche Hudon, or graphic designer and video artist Andrew Fry. Active community service is another benefit that comes from supporting local entrepreneurs. KS founder Silvio Lettrari founded the Kaslo Trailblazer Society, a nonprofit that helps maintain the community's walking trails, while his son Stefan is the president of Kaslo Search and Rescue.[439]

Whereas chain stores tend to strip a community of the type of people willing to engage in their community, food co-ops do the opposite — they support local foodmakers, who in turn support the communities they operate in.

Planning the Co-op Shelves with Local Producers

Perhaps the clearest example of food co-ops' commitment to their suppliers are the seasonal planning meetings some co-ops host with local farmers. Whereas the dominant food system leaves one supplier pitted against another — both vying for the same shelf space — some food co-ops actively bring farmers together in a more collaborate approach.

Each winter at the North Coast Co-op, farmers meet directly with co-op staff to plan out the season. The planning process allows farmers to understand the co-op's needs for the coming year and avoid under- or over-planting crops. North Coast is also periodically asking its more-than-two-hundred local suppliers, "did we pay promptly, did we pay a fair price, did we represent your product in the best light?"

At Hanover Co-op, their crop-planning meetings date back to 1998. When General Manager Terry Appleby first arrived at the co-op in 1992, he was shocked at the glut of local pumpkins on display, and yet there wasn't one head of locally grown broccoli to be found. From the farmers' position, excess of anything in such a narrow-margin industry isn't good for business. Hanover's grower meetings enable greater on-farm efficiencies. Farmers discuss their capacities for the season and determine who's in the best position to grow what and for when. By planning out the season with each other, the grower meetings help curb the inefficiencies of a poorly coordinated local food market. "Before the growers' meetings, you'd practically be throwing seeds in the ground and hope you have a market for it in the summer," says one of Hanover's farmers. "The model of working together takes care of 90 percent of the certainty of profit — the other 10 percent is the weather." Hanover is successfully bringing stability and predictability to small-scale farming.

Threats to Food Co-ops

I N July 2018, shoppers walking into Save-On-Foods in Nelson, British Columbia, were greeted by the store's weekly flyer. Running along the top in large, bold, all-caps: "SHOP CANADIAN, SHOP LOCAL."[440]

Whereas co-ops once enjoyed a distinct advantage as a community's go-to destination for *truly* local foods, today they are confronted with an onslaught of watered-down, feel-good "local" marketing by the grocery giants. The foods advertised on the front of the Save-On-Foods flyer *do* originate from within the legal jurisdiction of what today can be called "local." Included are hothouse veggies, blueberries, lettuce, and carrots, all from British Columbia's Lower Mainland.... more than eight hours' drive away! Meanwhile, back in reality, *actual* local growers are producing all of these foods in the immediate Nelson area. By operating with such a wide geographic definition of "local," Save-On-Foods is effectively undermining the livelihoods of people in the community they conduct business in and the residents and families who benefit from the economic and social contributions of local foodmakers.

In that same month, a short walk away at another of Nelson's grocery giants, shoppers at Safeway come face-to-face with gigantic signage reading, "Look for Local ... Produced in British Columbia."[441] Below the bright red sign were eight shelves of various flavors of Santa Cruz fruit juice — a product of California.

Upon the next visit to Safeway — two months later — a handful of display bins greeted shoppers immediately upon entry.[442] One of the large-format signs read, "Eat Local — Produced in Western Canada." Safeway had taken the liberty of expanding the legal definition of "local" to the entire western portion of the country[xviii]. Sure enough, mini cucumbers grown in Medicine Hat, Alberta,[xix] were located on the "Eat Local — Produced in British Columbia" portion of the display — contravening Canadian law on two fronts.[xx] This type of behavior by the giants is relentless.

This is the new world food co-ops operate in.

Regulatory oversight of these now-ubiquitous, distorted, or outright fallacious marketing practices is nowhere to be seen, nor should consumers depend on the supermarket-advertising-dollar-dependent-media to challenge the messages they're disseminating.

So long as eaters continue to shop at dishonest grocery retailers, the future of food co-ops hangs in the balance.[xxi]

For communities already home to a food co-op, residents would be well served to ask themselves and each other, "What will we and our community lose if our co-op disappears?" The previous few chapters offer more than ample responses.

The grocery giants have become proficient at co-opting "local" marketing. Here, Safeway Canada expands the definition of "local" to the entire western portion of Canada — contravening federal origin claim laws.
Source: *Jon Steinman, Nelson, BC, September 20, 2018*

---

xviii   Western Canada includes Manitoba, Saskatchewan, Alberta, and British Columbia. Federal local labeling laws require the product be produced within the same province or 50 km across a provincial border.

xix   Medicine Hat is 435 miles (700 km) from Nelson

xx   One, falsely stating the product is from BC and is "local." Two, Medicine Hat, AB is 375 km (235 miles) from the BC border.

xxi   As does the future of local food economies.

The mini cucumbers here were grown in Medicine Hat, Alberta (not in British Columbia). The adjacent "local" sign contravenes Canadian labeling laws for this product. SOURCE: JON STEINMAN, NELSON, BC, SEPTEMBER 20, 2018

On January 8, 2019, well after Tipiland Organic Produce had put their local farm to bed for the snowy winter, Save-On-Foods in Nelson, BC, continued to display the farm's signage above organic produce from Mexico and California. Tipiland's farmers were actually away in Nepal at the time. SOURCE: JON STEINMAN, NELSON, BC, JANUARY 6, 2019

Alter Eco products on display at Save-On-Foods "Eat Local" shelving in Nelson, BC. Alter Eco is based in California. SOURCE: JON STEINMAN, NELSON, BC, DECEMBER 8, 2018

Whisps on display at Save-On-Foods "Choose Local" shelving in Nelson, BC. The brand's parent company is based in New Jersey. Adjacent is a Bioitalia pesto produced in Italy.
SOURCE: JON STEINMAN, NELSON, BC, DECEMBER 8, 2018

Fierce Competition

It's common to hear those within the food co-op community describe the movement as having fallen victim to its own success.

Before Walmart, Costco, and Kroger had become the largest retailers of organic food, there were food co-ops that only knew organic. Before the grocery giants had erected signage with the language of "local," "natural," and "farm-fresh," there were food co-ops that had embedded those words into their very mission statements. Before there were customer loyalty programs (and phony "clubs") at the chains, there had been customers whose loyalty was in *actual* ownership of their grocery store. That was "before." Today, the food co-op's competitive landscape has changed dramatically.

Along with the entry of conventional retailers into organic and local food (even if only perceptually) is the now-dominant presence of the "natural" food chain. Joining Whole Foods are the likes of Natural Grocers (140 stores in 19 states), Sprouts (300+ stores in 19 states),

New Seasons (22 stores in three states), and Earth Fare (50 stores in 10 states[xxii]). While many eaters might feel better shopping at these smaller, often more regional natural food chains, investing our food dollars in them may just be lining the pockets of their grocery giant suitors. Amazon's acquisition of Whole Foods will almost certainly *not* be the only case marking the allure of the natural foods chain. Just as natural food manufacturers are being swallowed by the likes of General Mills, Danone, and Campbell Soup, so too will natural retailers likely meet a similar fate. Some grocery giants are creating their own natural or gourmet food banners like Meijer's Fresh Thyme, H-E-B's Central Market, and Publix's GreenWise. Competition is getting fierce. Estimates are that one-third of food co-ops are experiencing declining sales. In a business with such low margins, this is a serious concern.

In Whole Foods' hometown of Austin, Texas, Wheatsville Co-op has felt the squeeze. Not only does Whole Foods, with its six Austin locations, use the city as a testing ground for new concepts, H-E-B's Central Market has blanketed the area surrounding the co-op's two stores. Natural Grocers too is only blocks away. Sales growth at Wheatsville has gone from double-down to single-digits.

When Trader Joe's and The Fresh Market moved into the area served by North Carolina's Weaver Street Market, the co-op noticed significant sales erosion in the months following. Their customer count reflected migration to those stores. Weaver Street's Carrboro store went from 10 percent sales growth to 10 percent declines, while sales growth at their Southern Village store went from 25 to 0 percent.[443]

In Portland, Oregon, the growth of New Seasons Market, Natural Grocers, Market of Choice, and Whole Foods threatens the city's three food co-ops, particularly Food Front Cooperative Grocery's two locations. At the time of writing, Food Front was in dire straits. Portland has become a mecca for conscientious eaters, and it's no longer easy for food co-ops to stake their claim among this demographic. It's particularly challenging when a chain like New Seasons Market sells itself as "your neighborhood grocer" and "locally owned and operated." The claims are only partly true. "Yes," each of New Seasons' sixteen locations in the

Portland area *are* indeed located in shoppers' neighborhoods (tongue-in-cheek). "Yes," some of New Seasons owners live in Portland; however, New Seasons' private equity owners, Endeavour Capital, is also owned by investors from Seattle, Los Angeles, and Denver. Endeavor does not seem entirely dedicated to the promise of more sustainable foods, having once held a minority interest in conventional grocery chain WinCo Foods. New Seasons has also been criticized for its role in gentrifying communities throughout Portland, and being anti-union.[444] Even less neighborly, Endeavor investor M.J. Murdock Charitable Trust is an active supporter of the right-wing advocacy group Alliance Defending Freedom[xxiii,445] ADF has been classified as a hate group.[446] For every dollar spent at New Seasons, a portion of that purchase funds anti-LGBTQ campaigns. Of course much of this goes unnoticed by shoppers.

The Co-opting of "Local"

> "What co-ops do is they show small examples of what the dominant system could capitalize on ... but then, after awhile, [the chains] have to fake it."[447]
>
> — Louisa Spencer,
> Poverty Lane Orchards (New Hampshire)

The Planet Organic story is one of many.

The full name of the Arizona-based Sprouts chain of stores is "Sprouts Farmers' Market."

One of Walmart's private labels of eggs is the brand "Farmers' Market."

Trader Joe's is "Your Neighborhood Grocery Store" — despite it being owned by Germany's Aldi Nord.

The produce sections in many of the grocery giants are littered with "Farm Fresh" signage.

When Whole Foods acquired the independent Whole Grocer in Portland, Maine, they kept the sign inside the store, "Serving Greater Portland since 1984."[448]

---

xxiii   Contributed $375,000 to ADF in 2006.

Planet Organic

[From the author] In 2008, I was speaking at the University of Alberta's International Week in Edmonton. A few blocks from my hotel was a new Alberta grocery chain, Planet Organic. Sounded right up my alley. I was in need of some snacks. After browsing the store, I opted for a bag of honey-roasted peanuts and returned to my hotel room. I began reviewing my notes for my presentation titled, "Protecting Local Food Systems from the Industrial Food System 'Box.'" The presentation cautioned those within the movement of the dominant food system's emerging interest in the movement itself, and the tactics they might be willing to engage in to extract a slice of the pie for themselves. I reached over for my bag of peanuts, and just before cracking it open, my eye caught the ingredient list. To my surprise, not one ingredient was organic. How could this be ... I purchased them at "Planet Organic"! The very top of the label even read, "Planet Organic." Turns out, the grocery store chain had merely taken on the name Planet Organic but in no way was it an organic food store. I realized in that moment that if someone like myself — a food systems' journalist investing most waking hours into investigating food — could be duped, how could everyday eaters possibly sift through the fog of grocery store deception?

Anything that has a "feel-good" factor is priceless marketing for the grocery giants. As Andrew Simms writes, it "aids in emotional bonding."[449]

The co-opting of "organic," "farm-fresh," or "natural" is also accompanied by the co-opting of "local" ... and not only in the world of food. Global mega-bank HSBC adopted the slogan "The World's Local Bank." Global mega-brewer Interbev, who had already been using the slogan "The World's Local Brewer," unsuccessfully sued HSBC in 2002 for infringing its copyright.[450] Imagine that ... "grown locally on planet earth"!

In grocery, there are certainly genuine efforts among *non*-food co-op retailers to support local producers. Even some local managers of chain stores will make an extra effort to carve out space for local products. It's not all smoke and mirrors. But what are the underlying intentions? Is it out of care, or is it simply being used as "feel-good" marketing?

Save-On-Foods capitalizes immensely on this feel-good, place-of-origin marketing. "Our Western Canadian pork is carefully raised on family farms to very high standards," reads a 2018 Save-On-Foods flyer.[451] The description feels good ... until one learns that those animals never see the light of day and the sows are kept in cage-like gestation stalls. It feels good ... until one learns that those family farms are at the mercy of one of only a few Canadian pork processors who command almost all of Canada's slaughter capacity. It feels good ... until one learns that the average number of hogs per farm in Canada is 1,720. In Manitoba, it's 4,831.[452] Meanwhile, surrounding many of Save-On's stores are family farmers raising their animals outdoors, on pasture, and they're using nearby slaughterhouses operated by people in their communities.

With most eaters having little time to consider what's happening on the other side of the messaging, mass-produced factory food is made to sound surprisingly appealing.

But what of *actual* local foods found on the shelves of chain grocers? They *do* exist. Enter the double-edged sword of chain store local food. Indeed, purchasing that product is supporting a local foodmaker. This is true. Yet, it's *also* true that embedded within that *same* food dollar is an investment into the retailer ... and thus, an investment into marketing practices that undermine that same local foodmaker. An investment into local food at a chain store is inadvertently an investment into the hollowing out of the local food system.

The "Whole Foods Effect"

From the earliest days of food co-ops, members harbored fears of their co-op getting too large and losing sight of its founding values. The threat is real. A number of co-ops described later in this chapter have met such a fate and have disappeared because of it. Other co-ops have become watered-down versions of their original selves. The Hanover Co-op went through a period in the 1980s when it seemed to have lost its cooperative spirit in its relationships with farmers. Many farmers grew to loathe the co-op and its buying practices, which had become not so dissimilar from the chain stores. Thankfully, with the arrival of General Manager Terry Appleby in 1992, the co-op turned itself around and is now a much-loved food institution.

With food co-ops facing a level of competition unlike ever before, they're having to make hard decisions that remain true to their roots and true to the changing face of retail and consumer trends. Through all of this, they risk falling victim to the "Whole Foods Effect" — growing to a scale that leaves them unable to truly serve the neighborhood as first intended. With that said, food co-ops are dramatically more insulated from the "effect." There are zero instances of food co-ops being acquired by other retailers. The only real possibility here is inter-co-op merging. This does happen. In 2016, members of The Wedge Co-op and Linden Hills Co-op voted to merge, while members of Eastside Food Co-op — who were also considering being part of the merger — voted to remain independent.

To consider the risks of a co-op getting too large, it's logical to turn our attention to the largest food co-ops to see how they've fared. Aside from the monolithic Canadian network of Federated Co-op stores and the now-defunct Co-op Atlantic (described later), PCC Community Markets of Seattle is the largest food co-op among those featured in this book. In 2018, PCC had twelve stores with another five planned. Anyone entering a PCC store will notice a distinct difference from a single-store food co-op. The vibe is a bit more subdued. One reason must certainly be the absence of the co-op's core management and administrative team right there in the store. Unlike most food co-ops, PCC houses its offices in a head office in the city's downtown — quite far from any of their retail locations. A single-store co-op on the other hand may have upwards of a few dozen people working in offices inside the store itself. Their presence in the store brings a palpable injection of energy. It's also likely that a member–owner of a *chain* of stores will feel *less* ownership than they would of a single-store co-op. Despite its relatively large size, PCC maintains considerable and positive influence on the Seattle-area food economy and is looked to by the national food co-op community as a leader. Rather than being an example of a food co-op that got too large, it's instead an example of a food co-op that is amplifying its impact through growth ... and yet, there's no question that there may be some sacrificial offerings along the way.

What sets multi-store co-ops like PCC or Outpost Natural Foods apart from any other chain is their tendency to reevaluate decisions that may have led them astray. As one example, in their efforts to streamline their supply chain, both Outpost (four stores) and PCC opted to limit their local suppliers to only those who could deliver to *all* of their locations. This was clearly going down the same road every major chain had already gone down. But for Outpost and PCC, this didn't last long. They soon realized just how many of their suppliers were unable to supply in those volumes, and so they changed course. Today, shoppers will find some products at some stores that are unavailable at other locations. It's more work for the co-ops' buyers, but their support of local suppliers is core to their missions.

Another symptom of food co-op growth is what might be called the "cornucopia effect" — a characteristic of the Whole Foods Effect. As grocery stores have expanded in size, eaters have become accustomed to a dizzying array of choice. Many food co-ops choose to compete on this front. As they vie for market share, food co-ops begin to expand their number of selections to attract more shoppers into their stores. Many co-ops also expand their in-house production of ready-to-eat foods — foods that may have traditionally been prepared by independent local suppliers. The "cornucopia effect" can do one or both of two things: it can ensure a co-op remains relevant, and/or it can cannibalize a community's local foodmakers. The "cornucopia effect" may just be an unfortunate casualty of the need to remain relevant. At the end of the day, what is certain is the future of a community's local foodmakers has more to do with eaters *choosing* locally made foods than it does a food co-op's decision on what competing products it chooses to stock or produce in-store.

The Demise of Co-op Atlantic

The risks to food co-ops of scaling up through rapid growth and of integrating into the dominant food system are best told through the demise of Eastern Canada's Co-op Atlantic. To be certain, Co-op Atlantic was a very different animal than the independent consumer food co-ops featured in this book. It was made up of independent grocery co-ops selling *conventional* foods. That said, today's food co-ops have much to learn from Co-op Atlantic's downfall.

Co-op Atlantic was also not the first of the large co-ops to fail. The Berkeley Co-op in California folded in 1988. Governance disputes and bankruptcy forced its closure after 55 years in business. At twelve stores, Berkeley was one of the largest cooperatives in the United States. In the 1970s, their size was too unwieldy, and they began selling off locations. Their 1988 demise was caused by infighting, too rapid of an expansion, and governance–employee disputes.[453] Another large co-op — Hyde Park of Chicago — opened a much larger second location in 1999, but it was downhill from there. They closed their doors in 2008, after seventy-six years in business.

After ninety years, Co-op Atlantic ended its reign in 2015 as one of Canada's largest co-ops. In its better years, it was a tremendous story of success — farmers, fishers, and consumers responding to the failures of the market to serve their best interests and communities. As a second-tier co-op of independent community-owned grocery stores, the combined stores had a 22 percent market share at their peak in the 1980s. Co-op Atlantic provided wholesaling, marketing, and business services to their independent food co-op members. Stores numbered 108 in 2000. Part of its success was its decision to compete with the giants on price. Co-op Atlantic was selling food at wholesale prices or close to it. It had officially become a discount grocer in the 1980s, and this marked the beginning of its end.[454]

When Sobeys expanded into Ontario in the 1980s (and onto Loblaw's turf), an all-out price war between the giants ensued. Co-op Atlantic was caught in the crossfire and not able to react quick enough. As it struggled to survive, it "sacrificed their co-op identity," in the words of former Co-op Atlantic Member Relations and Communications

Manager Tom Webb. To save money, Co-op Atlantic cut its member relations/education budget by a third. Suggestion boxes were removed from stores, and many once-community-oriented co-ops simply became places to buy cheap food. "In the early 1990s, almost every local co-operative had a member-relations staff person," says Webb; "a decade later, all but three of these positions had disappeared." Webb also points to a "flawed management system" to support their member locations. Management both at the organizational level and within the stores themselves was weak. Managers didn't understand co-ops. Webb recalls meeting a disgruntled store manager of several years who had just finished meeting with two of the co-op's board members. "As we walked to his office, he shook his head and said, 'Those guys think they own the place.'"[455]

Governance was also a contributing factor to the demise. Food co-ops, which have long relied on boards of directors elected by their members, have historically elected volunteer directors without the expertise one might expect is needed to govern a business — particularly a business as cutthroat and nuanced as grocery retail. For many food co-op members, lack of experience was a symbol of their co-op's community-driven DNA — a countercultural "middle-finger" that said, "We can do this on our own!" Most food co-ops today continue to rely on this model, but it didn't work for Co-op Atlantic. "Board members were not required to qualify to run for the board nor take board training," recounts Webb. "In general, board members were fine and decent people with whom you could entrust your children but not, alas, your co-operative." Even today, co-ops with five hundred members use the same governance approach as co-ops of fifteen thousand members. In this culture, many general managers of Co-op Atlantic locations learned to control their boards, not the more appropriate other way around. This too exists among food co-ops today. I personally recall meeting a GM in 2015 at the annual conference of food co-ops who remarked that most of her board was in attendance and that she thought it was important for her to be there so the directors "wouldn't get any funny ideas." There are both benefits and risks of inexperienced volunteer boards.

Co-op Atlantic sold off its assets in 2015 to Sobeys. This left most independent food co-ops in Eastern Canada reliant on their competitor for their wholesaling needs.

Since the demise of Co-op Atlantic, many local food co-ops have shuttered their doors. River Hebert (Nova Scotia), a community of one thousand, no longer has any grocer. In Tabusintac (New Brunswick), no grocery store is left after their co-op of seventy-five years closed. Musquodoboit (Nova Scotia) — closed after seventy-eight years. St. Anthony's (Newfoundland) — closed after 105 years.

Closed

Most co-ops are weathering the new climate of grocery retail…

… most.

Between January 2017 and June 2018, at least seven co-ops closed.

In 2017, Amazing Grains Food Co-op in Grand Forks, North Dakota, closed its doors after forty-four years. The board cited increased competition leading to decreased sales. Natural Grocers arrival to town is said to have contributed. The co-op experienced a 30 percent loss in sales following their arrival.

In Columbus, Ohio, Clintonville Community Market closed after seventeen years. Competition was also said to be a factor. Eat Local Sudbury in Ontario made a good run of it for eleven years but dropped from $1 million in sales to half that. The co-op closed in 2018. East Lansing Food Co-op closed in 2017 after forty-one years. Fresh Thyme and Whole Foods had opened nearby. Good Earth Market of Billings, Montana, closed in 2017 after twenty-three years. New competition contributed to its closure

Competition isn't the only contributor to co-op closures. Montana's Missoula Community Food Co-op closed in 2017 following financial difficulties. It was a rare case of a co-op requiring member labor in order to shop at the store. It didn't work. By the time the co-op removed this requirement, it was too late. Glens Falls Food Co-op (NY) suffered a similar fate, having also relied on volunteer member labor.

Cost of real estate was a big factor leading to the closure of Toronto's West End Food Co-op in 2018. When the store's lease came up on its existing space, no other affordable real estate could be found in Toronto's pricey real estate market.

The Baltimore Food Co-op closed after one year in 2012. River City Food Co-Op in Evansville, Indiana, closed in 2017 after twelve years. Dubuque Food Co-op of Iowa closed in 2017 after three years. Company Shops Market of Burlington, North Carolina, closed in 2018 after seven years.

Relevance

> "You can't be an economic alternative if you're not around."[456]
>
> — Karen Zimbelman, quoted in
> "Food Co-ops in a Struggle," *The New York Times*, 1984

In an age of grocery chains mimicking food co-ops' almost-every product offering, how do food co-ops remain relevant? Relevance today is either a co-op's greatest challenge or its most exciting opportunity. All depends on the response.

Beyond the more tangible generators of relevance such as products and services, at the core of the relevance question is "co-op comprehension" — "what is a co-op anyway and what makes them so important?"

A thorough read of this book should help you understand what truly sets cooperatives apart ... that's the whole point of it in the first place! Realistically, however, this book *won't* make it into the hands of every eater, and co-op comprehension is far from embedded within the dominant culture, nor is it adequately understood among a substantial portion of existing food co-op member–owners, managers, and board directors. Surveys show that more than 74 percent of Americans — three in four — don't have a clue what a co-op is. Another 14 percent have a partial idea. The remaining 12 percent were limited to understanding co-ops as they exist in whatever sector that person was involved in.[457] As Stuart Reid of the Food Co-op Initiative asks, "Can we base our relevance on a concept that less than 12 percent of the public understands?"[458] Reid calls this a "conundrum," particularly when new co-ops are most relevant to people in areas where co-ops are rare or nonexistent. In the absence of strong co-op comprehension, the relevance of food co-ops is left to the winds of perception. For many eaters, co-ops are just simply another grocery store option, period.

Relevance can begin with a name. Some co-ops intentionally omit the word "co-op" from their name altogether. Some die-hard cooperators may be quick to judge such a move as an abandonment of cooperative solidarity, but it may just be what enables these co-ops to remain relevant within the communities they operate in. In some places where cooperatives of many types have failed, the word "co-op" conjures up strong adversarial responses. As Phil Ricord of North Coast Co-op said in 1991, "The word 'co-op' raises the hair on the arms of a large segment of our community."[459] Outpost Natural Foods, Bloomingfoods, and Three Rivers Market are three examples of co-ops that *don't* incorporate "co-op" into their name. City Market was once known as Onion River Co-op before changing its name, and Central Co-op flip-flopped from Central Market to Madison Market and back to Central Co-op. PCC sees the "co-op" term as communicating exclusivity and chooses to not include it in their name.[460] In an effort to differentiate themselves from the tide of "natural" chains, PCC also updated their name in 2018 from PCC Natural Markets to PCC Community Markets. Whatever choice a co-op makes, using the language of food cooperation and "natural foods" requires a delicate balancing act of community comprehension, perception, and relevance.

Remaining relevant involves taking a long hard look at a co-op's governance model, buying guidelines, workplace culture and engagement with members. It involves making hard decisions on the use of plastic packaging in the increasingly popular category of ready-to-eat meals, or choosing whether or not to mingle conventional foods among the more natural of selections.

For some co-ops — particularly those in markets already served by many grocery retail options — broadening the co-op's base of customers may be entirely unnecessary and maybe even damaging. The Viroqua Food Co-op, despite having only 15 to 17 percent of members shopping exclusively at the store, has comfortably chosen to uphold a

100 percent organic produce section.[461] They're not budging. Remaining relevant looks different for every food co-op.

Remaining relevant can be most challenged through growth. Multi-store co-ops with central offices run the risk of losing relevance in the neighborhoods they operate in. To counteract this, these co-ops make considerable effort to maintain the uniqueness of each individual location. At Weavers Way's Ambler store, a twenty-person advisory committee ensures the co-op meets that community's needs. The Ambler store has more conventional products than their other locations. At Outpost Natural Foods, each location has its own vision statement. Outpost's original store has noticeably more vegetarian and vegan options, while their Bayview store has a made-to-order café because of lack of restaurants in the area. Unlike chains, multi-store co-ops adapt to their surroundings.

Ideology

> "How can co-ops unstick themselves from their own personal perspectives of what their co-op should be and feel really comfortable to receive from the community what they actually want."[462]
>
> — Melissa Cohen, General Manager,
> Isla Vista Food Co-op (2018)

First and foremost, co-ops serve their members. For consumer co-ops with membership open to anyone, this also makes them in service to their communities. Everything else a co-op does is entirely up to the co-op. Enter the threat of ideologies and their risk to a co-op's relevance. As Brett Fairburn writes, "One generation's imagining may not work for those who come after."[463] This is certainly true among food co-ops, where the greatest internal conflicts often occur when existing ideologies are challenged.

With the exception of the Park Slope Food Co-op, most of the large food co-ops would likely have *not* celebrated many more birthdays had they continued to reside in the ideology of member–labor. Food co-ops learned that service is best delivered through well-trained paid staff. They remained relevant because of it.

Many of the co-ops of 1970s Minneapolis–St. Paul were established in low-income neighborhoods, yet their strong countercultural ideologies kept some of them from truly serving the people living nearby.

Had many food co-ops remained in their vegetarian ideologies, they too would have likely failed to remain relevant to their communities. Same goes for all of a co-op's product buying guidelines. Food ideologies are of little use if they threaten the co-op's existence. A co-op packaging bulk foods in individual plastic-wrapped servings may seem completely antithetical to its waste reduction ideology, but if shoppers aren't purchasing bulk foods using their own reusable containers, it may just be the only way to retain customers.

Governance is another area of considerable ideological constraint. As existing food co-ops exploded in popularity in the 1990s, many continued using the same governance model entrenched at their inception. As Pam Mehnert says of today's co-ops, "Many are just catching up to what their governance model even is." Mehnert, who has worked extensively through the food co-op community, thinks it's time to reevaluate co-ops' reliance on *volunteer* boards of directors.[464]

"Small is beautiful" is another ideology that characterizes food cooperatives. You'd be hard-pressed to find anyone in the movement who disagrees, but food co-ops are increasingly discovering that small may also erode a co-op's relevance. Fear of growth can be traced back to as early as 1971, when anti-growth members of PCC spun off to form their own co-op — Capitol Hill Co-op[xxiv].[465] Food co-ops have definitely proven that small can indeed be beautiful and sustainable, and they're also demonstrating larger is beautiful too. The Wheatsville Co-op unabashedly celebrates itself as a business looking to make a profit. "We try very hard to make people understand that through their shops, we make money, which then generates all of the good things we get to do," says Wheatsville's Raquel Dadomo. "More stores equals more impact ... it's what we do with our profit that makes us different."[466]

---

xxiv   Capitol Hill Co-op closed in 1976 and was replaced by Central Co-op.

Institutional Isomorphism

Brett Fairburn writes of the risk of "institutional isomorphism" — the "tendency of human creations, however different or unique they were at the time of their creation, to conform over time to one model or a few models that are conventional and widely known." Co-ops have long been a victim of this. Whether a necessity for survival and relevance or an organizational shortcoming, the tendency to conform to the status quo is real. "People may know at the outset that a co-operative is different because of the circumstances surrounding its creation. Over time, however, the initial understanding may fade in memory. The business itself, under competitive pressures in the market, may look and behave much like its competitors. People may forget that it is different (or that is supposed to be different), and in the end they may perceive it to be (or it may actually be) just like a conventional business," writes Fairburn.[467]

Food co-ops are constantly in need of reminding themselves and others of *who* they are and *why* they are.

Member Engagement

The participation of member–owners in laying out the future of their grocery store is one of the unique characteristics that set co-op stores apart from any other. Having member–owners as board directors is the most obvious expression of this. But what of the thousands of other members who almost certainly have important perspectives on their co-op's future? Many co-ops are highly proficient at engaging members through surveys, comment cards, focus groups, or casual conversations in the store. This level of engagement ensures co-ops remain relevant.[xxv] There are, however, many co-ops who *don't* adequately engage their members. This represents a threat to their future. Without consistently listening and responding to the owners of the store, co-ops may fail to remain relevant and members may easily view them as no different from non-cooperative stores. The responsibility of maintaining this relationship falls on the board, management, and member–owners themselves.

---

xxv   As Tom Webb of Saint Mary's University says, "If 281,000 volunteers are actively editing Wikipedia each month, why can't 5,000 co-op member contribute to planning at their co-op?"

The latter responsibility is the most interesting. Co-op members are often quick to judge or criticize their co-op, and yet many have never filled out a survey, participated in a focus group, or even attended an annual meeting. Members have obligations.

It's also not enough to simply feel good about your food co-op, and yet shop somewhere else. Shortly after a start-up co-op in Minnesota opened its doors, sales were surprisingly below expectations. It turned out only half of the co-op's new members were regularly using the co-op. More stunning, only three-quarters of the one thousand members who loaned $1 million to the development of their co-op were shopping there.[468]

The future of co-ops is completely dependent on an engaged community of members who participate and shop at their store.

Growing Food Co-ops,
Growing the Movement

S HOPPING AT THE KOOTENAY Co-op's previous location (pre-2017) was an exercise in patience. With $14 million in sales coming out of only 4,800 square feet of retail space, the co-op's over 9,300 active members became well-versed at avoiding head-on shopping-cart collisions. Turning any corner in the store was often accompanied with an "excuse me" or a "sorry." The store was convivial. It was crowded. So crowded, it kept many in the community from shopping its shelves — particularly as it couldn't accommodate full-size shopping carts. Nor did it have a parking lot. It wasn't uncommon to be enjoying a beverage on the street-front patio only to watch the same car go by once, twice, maybe even three times in search of street parking near the store. The conditions were stifling the co-op's potential. In the ten years between 2006 and 2016, the co-op's membership and sales both doubled. Staff were making more frequent trips from the backroom warehouse to restock shelves, and the cramped workplace was becoming a safety hazard. The building itself was never designed as a grocery store. The co-op was operating at the scale of a 20,000-square-foot grocery store in a space a quarter of that size. The need for a larger store became obvious in 2006.

At the time, two grocery stores were operating in Nelson's downtown: the co-op and Extra Foods (a Loblaw banner). The Extra Foods location was the only workable downtown location for the co-op. The co-op waited patiently ... six years, to be exact. When Extra Foods' lease came up in 2012, instead of renewing with Loblaw, the local owners of the building sold the property to the Kootenay Co-op.

Rather than just construct a stand-alone modern grocery store, the co-op saw an opportunity to maximize the benefit of the rather large downtown footprint. Downtowns are vital to the economic and social well-being of communities, and the co-op chose to develop the land into a hub of community activity that could bring life to an end of the downtown that had become neglected. The proposed development became known as Nelson Commons and included fifty-four residential units in a four-story building with commercial units spread throughout the ground floor. The co-op would take up 21,000 square feet of commercial space. When assessing the options to hire a developer, it became clear that the greatest economic benefit to the co-op and to the community would be to keep the development local. The co-op chose to become the developer.

Before any financial lenders would take the project seriously, two things needed to happen: the co-op would need to demonstrate that its member–owners were behind the project with their own financial risk, and it would need to secure a hefty portion of residential unit pre-sales. The first of the two requirements (known as member loan campaigns) is standard procedure in the world of food co-op expansions. The second requirement … would become a first in food co-op history.

While the co-op constructed its condominium sales office and show suite at a location across from the construction site, board directors and management began putting together a strategy to raise $1.5 million in unsecured loans from its member–owners. Over a five-week campaign, the co-op raised $1.78 million from 179 members. It took a lot

Kootenay Co-op Member Loan Campaign (2013) (Figures in CAD)

Campaign Budget	$32,000
Campaign Duration	5 weeks
Total Lenders	179
$1,000–$9,999	113
$10,000–$24,999	35
>$25,000	31
Largest Loan	$250,000
Total Raised	$1,777,200

Source: Kootenay Co-op

longer to gather adequate pre-sales of the condos, but once that goal was reached, institutional lenders were ready to commit.

The institutional investors were unique. Conventional banks would never have taken a project like this seriously. This is a common challenge among food co-ops. A number of Canadian credit unions on the other hand are deeply committed to supporting the growth of the co-op movement — particularly Vancity. Without Vancity's investment, the project almost certainly would have never gotten out of the ground. A handful of regional credit unions also chipped in.

In 2015, the first construction crane to ever grace Nelson's skyline was erected. As the tallest structure in Nelson at the time, it became a temporary monument to the Kootenay Co-op having grown up. It was also a symbol of the promise of food co-ops to community economic development and the power of local food to transform communities. The crane became front-page news on Nelson's weekly newspaper — particularly when people were caught climbing it after-hours![469]

The construction injected over four million dollars into the more than thirty-five local businesses involved in site excavation, engineering and architecture, the manufacturing of cabinets, shelving, checkout counters, signage, and bike shelters, and the installation of electrical and metal work.

In December 2016, Nelson Commons was complete, and the doors opened to the co-op's new 21,000-square-foot space. Full-size shopping carts were waiting at the door... as was parking for forty-seven vehicles (including Nelson's first electric vehicle charging stations).

The new store required sixty new jobs. At 170+ employees, the co-op became Nelson's largest nongovernmental employer. A full-service meat department meant local farmers would have easier access to eaters. A fifty-four-seat cafe would amplify the store's role as a place of community connection, and a 1,900-square-foot kitchen would permit the store to meet the rising demand for ready-to-eat and grab-and-go items.

For its 2018 fiscal, sales skyrocketed at the co-op post-expansion, with 29.7 percent sales growth over 2017 and 55.1 percent over 2016. It's estimated the co-op now maintains a 15 percent share of Nelson's grocery market. It successfully secured its relevance among the shifting sands of consumer trends and a tightening competitive climate.

Sales at the Kootenay Co-op Pre- and Post-expansion

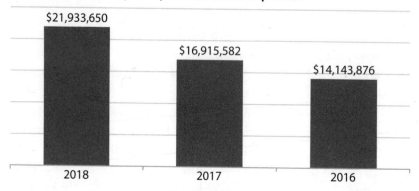

Sales skyrocketed at the Kootenay Co-op following its expansion in 2017. Fiscal 2017 represents 6 months in the previous location and 6 months in the new location.
SOURCE: KOOTENAY CO-OP

Wages & Benefits at the Kootenay Co-op Pre- and Post-expansion

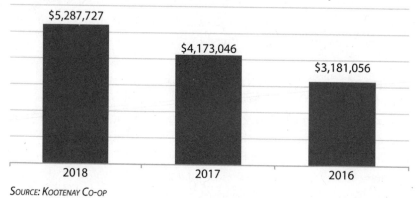

SOURCE: KOOTENAY CO-OP

Expansions mean co-ops can grow their local impact and become more attractive places for people to shop. "The point isn't to open a store, it's to grow community," says Outpost's Pam Mehnert.[470] It's clear that the more people choose to shop at food co-ops, the more resilient and connected our communities, local economies, and local food systems become.

While the grocery giants parasitically feed off each other and the food system through price wars, dominance over the supply chain, and

Purchases by the Kootenay Co-op of True Local Meat
(following the introduction of an in-store butcher and
meat department)

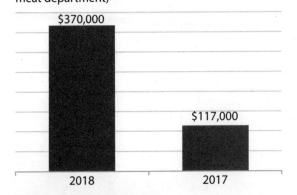

$370,000

$117,000

2018   2017

Source: Kootenay Co-op

*Kootenay Co-op's
previous location
1991–2016.*
Source: Jon Steinman

a trail of destructive practices, more and more eaters are waking up to this more cooperative reality.

Before their recent expansion, the Viroqua Food Co-op was passing $7 million in sales through only three checkouts. Their kitchen — only built for $1,000 of volume — was churning out $5,000 of product a day.

While Natural Grocers and Sprouts were expanding into their backyard, Great Basin Community Food Co-op signed up 1,487 new members in 2017 and posted 13.7 percent sales growth.

The Portland Food Co-op (Maine) projected $2.5 million of sales in its first year (2008) and achieved $3.25M in year one, $3.75M in year two, and $4.3M by year three.

Kootenay Co-op at Nelson Commons, 2017. SOURCE: JON STEINMAN

One of the more notable challenges researching this book was gaining access to food co-op managers, many of whom were waist-deep in member loan campaigns, expansions, and new store development. The future of food co-ops is looking promising.

Start-Ups

> "When co-ops like Outpost started in the '70s we were totally focused on product lines — 'we're about natural,' 'we're about organic,' 'there has to be no pesticides,' 'we have to be restrictive and that's what's going to make us different.' The start-ups today are about serving their communities."[471]
>
> — Pam Mehnert, GM, Outpost Natural Foods (2018)

Of the 134 co-ops that opened between 2008 and 2018, 74 percent of them have been successful. They represent an injection of 160,000 eaters into the food co-op movement. More than one hundred co-ops are in the works.[472]

What makes many of these start-ups so exciting is they're small. They're demonstrating that size doesn't matter. Growth may indeed amplify a co-op's impact, but competing in a market of mega-stores does not necessarily require matching their scale. Myles Robertson of the 2,800-square-foot Purple Porch Co-op in South Bend, Indiana, believes their smaller-format store gives them an advantage over the larger more established co-ops. "Because we're small, we're scrappy — we're able to pivot faster than a large store that's been around for thirty years." Having only been around since 2009, Purple Porch is far from being out of the weeds. Business is tight and growth likely necessary. But starting small has helped them figure themselves out.[473]

With so many start-ups having now tasted success or failure, the formula for making it work has been coming together. Since 2005, the Food Co-op Initiative has been the most important organization supporting start-ups. FCI publishes a "Cookbook" of best practices for developing food co-ops and helps organize the annual Up and Coming Conference that attracts three hundred aspiring food cooperators. FCI is funded by the most influential institutions shaping the sector, including more than thirty-five existing food co-ops. Their website includes resources on launching capital campaigns, legal primers, real estate, and store design, tips on designing lawn signs and websites, and answers to questions like, "Why does opening a co-op take so long?"

Why (Some) New Co-ops Fail:

- Very small retail spaces (500–1,500 square feet)
- Start-up budgets significantly below co-op averages
- Unusually short or truncated development timelines
- Over-reliance on member labor
- Premature site selection
- Converting or saving the local grocery store

Source: Stuart Reid, Food Co-op Initiative, 2012[474]

Without question, the success of a start-up food co-op is entirely dependent on passion, integrity, and commitment. Before River Valley became one of the most successful start-ups of the Newest Wave, residents committed years of their life to recruiting new members. Supporters of the Ambler Food Co-op went door to door telling people about their proposed community-owned grocery store.

It takes three to five years to take a food co-op from conception to reality, making commitment among many dedicated people a require-ment for success. Also important is adopting a relevant vision. The success of any start-up hinges on a vision that serves the community, not just any one person or small group.

Among new food co-ops, almost none stock more than 75 percent organic products. Many are taking a 50/50 approach to "clean conven-tional" and organic product selections.[475]

Beginning in 2016, the phone calls to FCI began to change. The calls were coming from more rural locations than ever before and from low-income urban communities. Both were telling the same story: "We've lost our grocery store." These food desert communities are being steered into cooperation. FCI estimates upwards of ten calls a month from people in one of these two categories. If these particular start-ups can prove to be successful, it will mark an exciting turning point for the movement — an opening of its arms to embrace a much wider demographic than co-ops have traditionally served. These are exciting times. They might even make CLUSA's James Warbasse a bit of a prophet. Almost one hundred years ago in 1925, he wrote, "There may come a time, when the American people will be forced into coop-eration, as they are in Europe. In this sense, the middle class, in order for the cooperative movement to succeed, must sink in to the ranks of the working class to propel the development of a consuming class con-sciousness, which would unite the poor, working and middle classes."[476]

Financing Food Co-ops

In 2011, Maine philanthropist S. Donald Sussman gave the start-up Portland Food Co-op a five-year, rent-free lease to a building. He included $44,000 to renovate it. The co-op buying club began using the space to take deliveries of products, organize member pickups, and host meetings. It was a generous yet unconventional way to get a food co-op off the ground.

Conventional banks don't tend to take co-ops seriously. Of all start-ups in the United States, about 20 percent of them secured a conventional lender.[xxvi] When the Co-op Market in Fairbanks, Alaska, embarked on their start-up journey, no commercial lender in the area was willing to take the risk. Instead, the co-op was able to rely on loans from the USDA, University of Alaska Fairbanks, Golden Valley Electric Association, LEAF (Local Enterprise Assistance Fund), and National Cooperative Bank (NCB). Even American credit unions aren't reliable sources of lending because of lending limits placed on them.[xxvii] Some American lenders like Shared Capital Cooperative are specifically focused on lending to co-ops, with 25 percent of their investments going into food co-ops.

Grants are another source of financing co-ops can access. FCI awards $10,000 grants to the start-ups they work with.

Member loan campaigns are also standard funding sources. Green Top Grocery in Bloomington, Illinois, set a record for a start-up member capital campaign of $1.4M. Member loans for start-ups can amount to 25 to 50 percent of a new co-op's financing. This is true economic democracy. Where better for people to invest their money than into their own community.

Local government funding may also be available for start-up co-ops. Hub City Co-op in Spartanburg, South Carolina, received $350k from the city ($200k as a low-interest loan, $150k as a grant). Sugar Beet Co-op in Oak Park, Illinois, received $500k in tax increment financing from the municipality. While not a start-up, Three Rivers Market in Knoxville, Tennessee, received $450k in gap financing to help them relocate and expand. Municipalities are wise to invest in food co-op development. Food co-ops are incubators and hubs for local economies.

---

xxvi   Rough estimate from FCI.
xxvii   Limits at Canadian credit unions are far less burdensome.

Co-ops Supporting Co-ops

Operating in the shadows of the highly coordinated efficiencies of the big chains, food co-ops that pride themselves on their independence are at a severe disadvantage. National Co-op Grocers (NCG) is the pinnacle example of food co-ops combining resources to compete. At a more regional level, the Neighboring Food Co-op Association (NFCA) in the Northeast pools the resources of its 35 member co-ops to analyze and grow their collective impact and to support the emergence of new food co-ops through a formal partnership with the Food Co-op Initiative (FCI). This cooperation among cooperatives is central to the cooperative identity.

The solidarity among food co-ops is touching. A food co-op on the West Coast understands that their success is also dependent on the success of food co-ops on the other side of the country.

Whether it's hosting a session at the annual conference of food co-ops and sharing their stories, or helping fund nonprofit food co-op development agencies, food co-ops are constantly supporting one another.

Without food co-ops across the country coming to its rescue, North Carolina's Weaver Street Market may not be here today. From its founding in 1998, the co-op grew quickly, expanding its first location several times, opening a full-service restaurant in 2000, then opening a second store in 2002. In 2008, they opened a third store along with a 25,000-square-foot central kitchen and warehouse. At the same time, Trader Joe's and The Fresh Market arrived into the local market. Customer counts plummeted. Between that and a weak economy, the co-op's cash eroded, and they were unable to service their debt. The co-op desperately needed to raise $1.35 million in cash. The response from the movement was overwhelming. National Co-op Grocers stepped in and was able to offer a direct loan to Weaver Street and rallied other member co-ops to join in. A total $650k was raised from eight food co-ops and two cooperative distributors. Among them was Ever'man Cooperative Grocery in Pensacola, Flordia, who provided $200k. "To allow Weaver Street to fail would allow non-cooperative competitors to achieve such dominance in that prime market area that success by another future cooperative would be very unlikely," said Ever'man's GM John Russo. "We couldn't stand by and watch that happen, not only to them and their community, but to all of us [cooperatives]." The local Self-Help Credit Union offered to process the loans. An additional $500k was raised from member–owners and several suppliers converted over $200k in past-due payables to term debt.[477]

Weaver Street returned to cash-positive in 2009. In 2018, they opened their fourth location — the first food co-op in the city of Raleigh.

"In the 1970s, when our co-op started, we lived in a world that was polarized by war, political differences, inequality, injustices, and social unrest. These social conditions strongly influenced our early days of creating a cooperative store, owned by the community and quite different from the capitalistic endeavors of the time. While some may draw similarities from that time in our co-op's history to the world we live in today, there are many differences in how both our co-op and the market for natural and organic foods developed over forty-seven years of time. We didn't have an organic industry in the 1970s, so the co-ops (not the private sector) were there to create one. We didn't have the knowledge of how to run a business, so we experimented with different options that aligned with our social values. We ran our grocery store much differently than the chains or independent grocers of the time, never charging "slotting fees" or allowing vendors to control our store shelves. We used volunteer labor until we could create a workforce that offered careers and fair wages to folks in our community. We created a market for local farmers and vendors, while others ignored them as insignificant, difficult to work with, or not fitting with company standards.

And over forty-seven years, we've grown from a single store with a few hundred co-op member–owners, to our multi-location, multi-function co-op owned by over 22,000 community members. We've kept millions upon millions of dollars recirculating right here in this local market. Something about our co-op today makes it feel as though we've come full circle. Grocery stores and organic specialty stores have become so big that we are not only smaller by comparison, we intentionally operate in a smaller, more meaningful way. All of the mergers today are about cutting out the middle person and eliminating the inefficiencies of working directly with smaller vendors. Of course we not only work directly with small vendors, we spend the time helping local entrepreneurs start their own business by offering their products first at the co-op.

Today the future seems to be directed toward the "faceless transaction" online, while our intent is to create an experience in our stores where the community can come together and know the names and faces of their neighbors, and support the union jobs in our workforce. We had a good year last year — we made a little money. But I'd rather define the "good" by other measures. Good is employing more people full-time (64 percent), with fair wages and competitive benefits. Good is doing business with our local/regional vendors — 80 percent who come from 100 miles or less to Outpost. Good is reducing our carbon footprint by 89 percent of what it was five short years ago. Good is selling a greater percent of organic products (45 percent) than other regular grocers (5 percent). Good is donating less than perfect or short-dated products to area food sources that can use them, then composting the things we can't. We exist to do something good in our community. Good is about making an impact — not just selling good food." [478]

— Pam Mehnert, General Manager, Outpost Natural Foods

Epilogue: Where Do We Go from Here?

"Let yourself be silently drawn by the strange pull of what you really love. It will not lead you astray."

— Rumi

WHEN U.K. GROUP ANTI-APATHY INVITED ten people to try and live without supermarkets for one month, one participant broke down and bought small amounts of food at supermarkets. She spent much of her time without milk and bread and ate out a lot. "The difficulties I faced have spoken volumes about what the large supermarkets have done to local accessibility."[479]

At one time, it was certainly possible to envision a capitalist economy that would have equitably served the food needs of entire nations … that is so long as strong government oversight was on hand to ensure power in the marketplace would never be at the expense of consumers. A cooperative capitalist economy may have indeed emerged. Instead, *Grocery Story* has made it abundantly clear that this reality never did materialize. It would be foolish to believe that it ever will, and there's not much left to salvage. Public spaces, including the shelves of our grocery stores, have been privatized into fewer and fewer hands. Even publicly owned buildings and institutions sign multiyear contracts with multinational food and beverage providers that effectively shut out the possibility of local businesses feeding people. The commons have by and large been privatized.

The cooperative model has proven itself as the most readily accessible way out — a means through which our most cherished public spaces can be returned to the hands of the people they were meant to benefit.

Much of what this book boils down to is *trust* in the marketplace, *trust* in our communities — being able to enter into our grocery stores without feeling that we're somehow entering into battle. It shouldn't be all that much to ask for — *trusting* that the people providing our families with food have our highest interests and values at heart. With the option of consumer-owned grocery stores, each of us has a wonderful opportunity to abandon the need to "demand" and "fight" for what we want, and to instead *create* a space that feels genuine, honest, and right. Food co-ops offer us this opportunity — to abandon the stresses of fight-or-flight that accompany so many of our relationships to food ... to shift our concentration from prices, shrinking package sizes, harmful ingredients, and social injustice and into the barn-raising efforts of constructing and strengthening food co-ops and our communities. Food co-ops empower us unlike any other space to nurture long-term healthy relationships to our food, communities, and the Earth. They make it possible to "be the change" and not the sheep. They make it possible to invest our food dollars into the next seven generations. They make it possible to sanctify our supermarkets.

Residing in the culture of Separation means our food can only ever be fed to us — through stories that are being told *to* us, not *by* us. In Separation, the grocery giants are granted free rein to tell us whatever stories they want us to hear — stories that have the power to literally shape our reality.

Assisting us into a blossoming age of food cooperativism, I hope you will join me in some long-overdue deep-cleaning of our windows of perception...

> From Expense into Investment: No longer shall my food purchases be expenses, they will be investments into my health, my family, my neighbors, and my community. They will be investments into the next generations.
>
> From Scarcity into Abundance: No longer shall I reside in the energy of scarcity. I will instead see the abundance that surrounds me and that is waiting to burst forth.

From Victims and Perpetrators into Collectivism: No longer shall I carry the burden of victimhood nor see others as victims or perpetrators. I will instead see myself as one part of the whole — an active contributor to the well-being of *all* people, not just myself.

From Disempowerment into Empowerment: No longer shall I believe myself to be powerless. I am immensely powerful and when joined cooperatively with others, infinitely powerful.

From Reaction into Intention: No longer will I over-expend my energy by *reacting* to the injustices around me but will instead place most of my energy into *intention* — into creating the more beautiful world my heart knows is possible.

My hope is that, upon finishing this book, you will be inspired to do one of three things:

- Convene your community's first meeting of its first cooperative grocery store, or join up with a group already meeting.
- Become a member–owner of an already-established food co-op near you.
- Love, more deeply than ever before, the food co-op you already shop at ... and ... feel absolutely confident to describe to your family, friends, and neighbors, why your community-owned grocery store is so important.

When you put this book down, go to your kitchen, open your refrigerator, look inside, and ask yourself, how are you about to change the world?

Where to Now?

Directory of Consumer Food Co-ops
A complete directory of existing independent consumer food co-ops in the United States and Canada. Includes a directory of start-ups.

Who Owns Your Grocery Store?
A comprehensive list online of the major grocery chains in Canada and the United States and the banners they operate.

Starting a Food Co-op Resources
A list of resources online to help you begin your journey for starting a food co-op.

Why Food Co-ops? (Talking Points to Use in Your Community)
Having successfully finished reading *Grocery Story*, you are now a well-equipped ambassador of the food co-op movement — a voice for good food, community development, and the Age of Reunion. Give yourself a well-deserved pat on the back. Now the work begins of informing your friends, colleagues, and neighbors… but where to begin? A resource of talking points to use in your community can be found online.

www.grocerystory.coop

Acknowledgments

WITHOUT FLAVOR, I would have never known of the more beautiful world my heart knows is possible. Thank you flavor. Thank you to the Kootenay Co-op and the many hands and hearts that have held it for so many years. It was the Kootenay Co-op that first introduced me to what every grocery store hopes to become when they grow up. Thank you Zoë Creighton for first nominating me to join the Co-op's board of directors. Thank you to the people in and around Nelson, British Columbia. What a special place to draw inspiration from. Thank you to my wonderful, deeply loving wife, Mary Ann, for being by my side and supporting the wild ride it is to make a book. And to my parents for their relentless, unwavering support. Thank you to everyone who has chosen to document the often-undocumented history of the co-operative movement. Thank you Marc Levinson, Joanna Blythman, Andrew Simms, and Barry Lynn for your inspiring writing that eased me into my research. Thank you to the thorough reviewers who critiqued my manuscript: Tom Webb, Ken Meter, Richard Sexton, Ari Derfel, Russell Precious, and Linda Steinman. Thank you to New Society Publishers. The work you do and the gifts you offer to the world are of a magnitude deserving of infinite praise for generations to come. It's an honor to join your family.

Thank you to the food co-ops who participated in the research phase:

Apple Street Market
Brattleboro Food Co-op
Hanover Co-op Food Stores
New Pioneer Food Co-op
North Coast Co-op
Outpost Natural Foods

Chequamegon Food Co-op
Community Food Co-op (MT)
Great Basin Community Food
  Co-op
Harmony Food Co-op
Hunger Mountain Co-op

Isla Vista Food Co-op
Kootenay Co-op
Middlebury Natural Foods
  Co-op
Mississippi Market
Monadnock Food Co-op
People's Food Co-op (MN/WI)
People's Food Co-op (OR)

Portland Food Co-op
Purple Porch Co-op
Renaissance Community Co-op
River Valley Co-op
Viroqua Food Co-op
Weavers Way Co-op
Wheatsville Food Co-op

Grocery Story's Supporters

G ROCERY STORY and the 2019 book tour would not have been possible without the financial support of co-ops, cooperatively minded businesses, and many patient individuals who invested early on through the book's crowdfunding campaign.

Sponsors

Horizon Distributors
Established in 1976 as a worker-owned co-operative, Horizon Distributors is Western Canada's leading distributor of organic and natural grocery products. In 1998, Horizon transitioned to private ownership and continues to flourish from its deep roots in co-op culture and policy. (horizondistributors.com)

Vancity
Vancity is a values-based financial cooperative with more than 525,000 member-owners. With a vision to redefine wealth, Vancity uses its assets to help improve the financial well-being of its members and support the development of socially, economically, and environmentally sustainable communities. (vancity.com)

Nelson Kootenay Lake Tourism
Nestled in the southeastern corner of British Columbia, along Kootenay Lake, are six vibrant communities: Nelson, Balfour, Kaslo, Ainsworth Hot Springs, Lardeau, and Meadow Creek. This region is a four-season destination quietly famous for its mix of culture, adventure, and history. (nelsonkootenaylake.com)

Rochdale Farms (rochdalefarms.coop)
seven roots (sevenrootsgroup.com)
Organically Grown Company (organicgrown.com)
Kaslo Sourdough (pastafermentata.com)

BC Co-op Association (bcca.coop)
Nelson & District Credit Union
East Kootenay Credit Union
Kootenay Savings Credit Union
Grand Forks Credit Union
Heritage Credit Union
People's Food Co-op (MN/WI)
Viroqua Food Co-op
Middlebury Natural Foods Co-op
Weavers Way Co-op
Oryana Community Co-op
Monadnock Food Co-op
River Valley Co-op
BriarPatch Food Co-op
Outpost Natural Foods
Open Harvest Co-op Grocery

Crowdfunders

From the 2017 Kickstarter campaign

Aaron Marks
Alexis Steinman
Alon Gelcer
Alyssa Nebel
Amy Garvey
Ancestar Teas
Andrea Langlois
Andrew Earnshaw
Andrew Jarrett
Angela Harrington
Anna Topf
Anne Grube
Anne Wilson
Ari Derfel
Arran Stephens
Arzeena Hamir

Bahni Turpin
Barbara Wells
Becky Livingston
Becky Young
Bill Lander
Bob Olsen
Brante Farrell
Brenda Pfahnl
Brian Saunderson
British Columbia Meatworks
Bronwyn Murray
C. Smith
Carly Steinman
Charles Levkoe
Cheralynne Kennedy
Chris Lowe
Chris McLeod

Chris Yli-Luoma
Claire Stannard
Clare and Paul Kelly
Daily Groceries Co-op
Damon Lawrence
Dan Miller
Dana Grossman
Dancing Rooster Sriracha
Daniel Tourigny
Darcy Kopas
David Reid
David Walsh
David Cater
Debbie LaChapelle
Debbie MacGregor
Della McLeod
Delphi Psmith
Diana Luepke
Dianne Matenko
Donald D. DeVeau
Donna Macdonald
Donovan Kitt
Doug Close
Dragana
Dustin Hiles
Elaine Moore
Emma Cubitt
Erica Konrad
Erin Brown
Freya Shaw
Giulio Delle Nuvole Piccioli
Glenn Mehalek
Gregoire Lamoureux
Guy Dauncey
Hillary Wong

James Baxter
Jeff Wren
Jen Ito
Jen Kluger
Jesse Watts
Jesse Farrell
Jillian Gould
JoAnn Lowell
Jocelyn Carver
Joe Karthein
John Kingsmill
John Bryant
Jonathan Gould
Joy McCallum
Judy Wapp
Kaj Gyr
Kate Safin
Kathryn Spears
Kathy Dumont
Larry Diener
Laura Sacks
Laurie Langille
Learner Limbach
Lee Herman
Lelainya Harvey
Leona Keraiff
Lesley Clint
Lesley Payne
Linda Jones
Linda Steinman
Lisa Maslove
Lisa Willott
Liz Babcock
LJ Bartle
Lucas

Marilyn Takefman
Mark Huddleston
Mark Steinman
Mark Tinholt
Mary Nagelhout
Matt Kleinmann
Melissa Hemphill
Melissa Garrity
Michael Davis
Mike Cole
Miriam Needoba
Naasko Suffiad
Nancy McConachie
Ness Benamran
Nettie Takefman
Nichole Felix
Nicole Melanson
Nicole Chaland
Norman Hill
Olivier Asselin
Ophelia Kwong
Paul and Karuna Erickson
Paula Sobie
Paula Rogers
Paula Schnese
Peter Donkers
Rae
Richard Larochelle

Robyn Irwin
Rochelle Prunty
Ronald Heber
Roy van Norstrand
Russell Precious
Saanich Organics Farmer
Schuyler Hoffer
Shauna Loves Kootenay Food
Sheila Pratt
Soups in Season Uphill Bakery
Staci Stevens
Stephanie Lorencz
Stuart McKinnon
Sue Hegedus
Sylvia Davidson
Tanin Shunter
Tannis Mathers
Terence Buie
Terisa Stanley
Till Krüss
Tina Cradock-Henry
Todd Kettner
Tom Wilde
Tony Reische
Tyler Masse
Vicky Morrison
Wendy & Barry Nelson
Zoë Creighton

Endnotes

1 University of Minnesota Extension, "The Future of Rural Grocery Stores | UMN Extension," accessed December 30, 2018, extension.umn.edu/vital-connections/future-rural-grocery-stores.

2 "Trends in U.S. Local and Regional Food Systems — Report to Congress" (USDA Economic Research Service, January 2015).

3 "USDA ERS — Food Expenditures," (2014 figures), ers.usda.gov/data-products/food-expenditures/.

4 Marc Levinson, *The Great A&P and the Struggle for Small Business in America* (New York: Farrar, Straus and Giroux, 2013).

5 Ibid.

6 Philip B. Kurland, *The Supreme Court and Patents and Monopolies* (University of Chicago Press, 1975).

7 Lincoln Frederick Schaub and Nathan Isaacs, *The Law in Business Problems; Cases and Other Materials for the Study of Legal Aspects of Business* (New York, Macmillan, 1921), archive.org/details/lawinbusinesspro00scharich.

8 Levinson, *The Great A&P and the Struggle for Small Business in America.*

9 "The Bread War," *Hamilton Evening Democrat*, October 12, 1901.

10 Zachary Garrison, "Bernard Heinrich Kroger," *Immigrant Entrepreneurship: German-American Business Biographies, 1720 to the Present* (German Historical Institute, August 28, 2014), immigrantentrepreneurship.org/entry.php?rec=49.

11 "About Us | Piggly Wiggly," accessed September 17, 2018, pigglywiggly.com/about-us.

12 "The Kroger Co.: Corporate News & Info: Historic Timeline," accessed September 17, 2018, thekrogerco.com/corpnews/corpnewsinfo_timeline.htm.

13 "Biography: Loblaw, Theodore Pringle, Volume XVI (1931-1940), Dictionary of Canadian Biography," accessed September 17, 2018, biographi.ca/en/bio/loblaw_theodore_pringle_16E.html.

14 Levinson, *The Great A&P and the Struggle for Small Business in America.*

15 Garrison, "Bernard Heinrich Kroger."

16 Levinson, *The Great A&P and the Struggle for Small Business in America.*

17 "Denies Kroger-Safeway Merger," *Wall Street Journal*, October 1, 1929.

18 "Safeway History," *Groceteria.Com* (blog), January 13, 2009, groceteriacom/store/national-chains/safeway/safeway-history/.

19 Garrison, "Bernard Heinrich Kroger."

20 Ibid.

21 "Biography: Loblaw, Theodore Pringle."

22 "Dominion, A&P Brands Kaput," *The Hamilton Spectator*, August 7, 2008,sec. News, thespec.com/news-story/2105119-dominion-a-p-brands-kaput/.

23 "Safeway Canada History," accessed September 17, 2018, safeway.ca/about-us/history.

24 Levinson, *The Great A&P and the Struggle for Small Business in America*.

25 Leo S. Carameli Jr, "The Anti-Competitive Effects and Antitrust Implications of Category Management and Category Captains of Consumer Products," *Chi.-Kent L. Rev.* 79 (2004): 1313.

26 Woodrow Wilson, *A Crossroads of Freedom: The 1912 Speeches of Woodrow Wilson* (Yale University Press, 1956), http://archive.org/details/crossroadsoffree007728mbp.

27 Henry J. Friendly, ed. Alfred Lief, *University of Pennsylvania Law Review and American Law Register* 85, no. 3 (1937): 330–32, doi.org/10.2307/3309092.

28 "Let's Look at the Facts: A Biography of Louis Brandeis," accessed September 17, 2018, economist.com/books-and-arts/2009/09/24/lets-look-at-the-facts.

29 Laura D. Phillips, "The Economics and Ideology of American Fair Trade: Louis Brandeis and Open Price Associations, 1911–1919," n.d., 10.

30 Woodrow Wilson, *A Crossroads of Freedom*.

31 "Nomination of Louis D. Brandeis. Hearings before the Subcommittee of the Committee on the Judiciary, United States Senate, on the Nomination of Louis D. Brandeis to Be an Associate Justice of the Supreme Court of the United States," accessed September 17, 2018, archive.org/details/cu31924018175715.

32 "The Regulation of Competition Versus the Regulation of Monopoly by Louis D. Brandeis, Louis D. Brandeis School of Law Library," accessed May 10, 2018, http://louisville.edu/law/library/special-collections/the-louis-d.-brandeis-collection/the-regulation-of-competition-versus-the-regulation-of-monopoly-by-louis-d.-brandeis.

33 Louis Brandeis, "Cut-Throat Prices: Competition That Kills," *Harper's Weekly*, November 15, 1913.

34 Gerald Berk, *Louis D. Brandeis and the Making of Regulated Competition, 1900-1932* (Cambridge, New York: Cambridge University Press, 2009).

35 "The Antitrust Laws," Federal Trade Commission, June 11, 2013, ftc.gov/tips-advice/competition-guidance/guide-antitrust-laws/antitrust-laws.

36 Ibid.

37 Berk, *Louis D. Brandeis and the Making of Regulated Competition, 1900–1932*.

38 Ibid.

39 Levinson, *The Great A&P and the Struggle for Small Business in America*.

40 Ibid.

41 *The Chain Store Industry under the National Industrial Recovery Act: The Proceedings of the Chain Store Meeting Held in Washington, D. C., on June 22, 23, 24, 1933, to Consider Industry Action under the Industrial Recovery Act — and the Agricultural Adjustment Act.* (New York: National Chain Store Association, 1933).

42 Levinson, *The Great A&P and the Struggle for Small Business in America*.

43 Ibid.

44 Ibid.
45 Paul Ellickson, "The Evolution of the Supermarket Industry: From A&P to Wal-Mart," in *Handbook on the Economics of Retail and Distribution* (Edward Elgar Publishing, 2011), 368–91, doi.org/10.2139/ssrn.1814166.
46 "The Kroger Company | Encyclopedia.Com," accessed September 17, 2018, encyclopedia.com/social-sciences-and-law/economics-business-and-labor/businesses-and-occupations/kroger-company.
47 Ellickson, "The Evolution of the Supermarket Industry."
48 Ibid.
49 Ibid.
50 "What a Difference a Decade Makes: Tesco's Boss Terry Leahy 10 Years Ago," September 24, 2014, managementtoday.co.uk/difference-decade-makes-tescos-boss-terry-leahy-10-years-ago/article/421098.
51 Joanna Blythman, *Shopped: The Shocking Power of British Supermarkets* (London: Harper Perennial, 2007).
52 "Global Food Industry" (USDA Economic Research Service, 2017), ers.usda.gov/topics/international-markets-trade/global-food-markets/global-food-industry.aspx.
53 "2018 Directory of Supermarket, Grocery & Convenience Store Chains" (Chain Store Guides, LLC, March 2018).
54 "USDA ERS: Retail Trends," accessed May 14, 2018, ers.usda.gov/topics/food-markets-prices/retailing-wholesaling/retail-trends/.
55 Evan Mangino and Maria Arbulu, "Canada: Retail Foods, Retail Sector Overview, 2018," GAIN Report (USDA Foreign Agricultural Service, June 26, 2018).
56 Tom Karst, "H-E-B Controls South Texas Market Share," *The Packer,* January 22, 2018, thepacker.com/article/h-e-b-controls-south-texas-market-share.
57 "Kroger Market Share across the Country: Chain Store Guide," *Newsroom: Chain Store Guide* (blog), April 25, 2016, http://newsroom.chainstoreguide.com/2016/04/kroger-market-share-across-the-country/.
58 "Kroger Discloses Cincinnati Market Share: 'We Use It as a Benchmark,'" *Cincinnati Business Courier,* accessed May 14, 2018, bizjournals.com/cincinnati/news/2015/10/29/kroger-discloses-cincinnati-market-share-we-use-it.html.
59 "Market Share: Publix," Strategic Sales Insights (F&D Reports [using Nielsen TDLinx data], April 2017).
60 Andrew Simms, *Tescopoly: How One Shop Came out on Top and Why It Matters* (London: Constable, 2007).
61 "Market Share: Publix."
62 "Grocery Wars Intensify in Texas | Jeff Green Partners," accessed May 14, 2018, jeffgreenpartners.com/grocery-wars-intensify-in-texas/.
63 Barry C. Lynn, "Killing the Competition," *Harper's Magazine,* February 2012, harpers.org/archive/2012/02/killing-the-competition/4/.
64 Wright Patman, "H. R. 8442, A Bill to Amend Section 2 of the Clayton Act," Pub. L. No. H.R. No. 8442, 74th Cong., 1st Sess., 79 Cong. Rec. 9077 (1935).

65 Phillip Longman, "Why the Economic Fates of America's Cities Diverged," *The Atlantic*, November 28, 2015, theatlantic.com/business/archive/2015/11/cities-economic-fates-diverge/417372/.

66 "Franklin D. Roosevelt: Message to Congress on Curbing Monopolies," The American Presidency Project, April 29, 1938, presidency.ucsb.edu/ws/?pid=15637.

67 Ibid.

68 Thomas W. Ross, "Winners and Losers under the Robinson-Patman Act," *The Journal of Law & Economics* 27, no. 2 (1984): 243–71.

69 Thurman W. Arnold, *The Bottlenecks of Business* (Washington, DC: BeardBooks, 1940).

70 "Great Atlantic & Pacific Tea Co., Inc. v. FTC, 440 U.S. 69 (1979)," Justia Law, n.d., supreme.justia.com/cases/federal/us/440/69/.

71 Marc Levinson, *The Great A&P and the Struggle for Small Business in America*.

72 United States v. New York Great Atlantic & Pacific Tea Co. (United States Court of Appeals Seventh Circuit — United States v. New York Great Atlantic & Pacific Tea Co., 173 F.2d 79 [7th Cir. 1949] February 24, 1949).

73 Ellickson, "The Evolution of the Supermarket Industry."

74 A. K. McKelvey, "Loblaw Companies Ltd.: An Investment I Like," *The Globe and Mail* (1936–Current); Toronto, ON, December 10, 1956.

75 Thomas W. Ross, "Introduction: The Evolution of Competition Law in Canada," *Review of Industrial Organization* 13, no. 1/2 (1998): 1–23.

76 Levinson, *The Great A&P and the Struggle for Small Business in America*.

77 "Enforcement of Fair-Trade Laws in Non-Fair-Trade Jurisdictions," *The University of Chicago Law Review* 22, no. 2 (1955): 525, doi.org/10.2307/1598434.

78 Bruce W. Marion, *The Organization and Performance of the U.S. Food System* (Lexington, MA: Lexington Books, 1986).

79 "The Evolution of U.S. Merger Law," Federal Trade Commission, July 18, 2013, ftc.gov/public-statements/1996/08/evolution-us-merger-law.

80 Lynn, "Killing the Competition."

81 Marion, *The Organization and Performance of the U.S. Food System*.

82 Longman, "Why the Economic Fates of America's Cities Diverged."

83 Barry C. Lynn and Center for Catholic Studies, Seton Hall University, "The Antitrust Case against Wal-Mart," *The Chesterton Review* 32, no. 3 (2006): 538–42, doi.org/10.5840/chesterton2006323/443.

84 Longman, "Why the Economic Fates of America's Cities Diverged."

85 Bobby J Martens, Frank Dooley, and Sounghun Kim, "The Effect of Entry by Wal-Mart Supercenters on Retail Grocery Concentration," n.d., 23.

86 Ibid.

87 Paul Ellickson, "The Evolution of the Supermarket Industry."

88 Noel Basker, "The Evolving Food Chain," n.d., 32.

89 Peter Behr, "Wave of Mergers, Takeovers Is a Part of Reagan Legacy," *Washington Post*, October 30, 1988, washingtonpost.com/archive/business/

1988/10/30/wave-of-mergers-takeovers-is-a-part-of-reagan-legacy/e90598
c2-628d-40fe-b9c6-a621e298671d/.

90 Phil R. Kaufman, *Structural Change in the U.S. Food Industry*, n.d.

91 Ibid.

92 Leo S. Carameli Jr., "The Anti-Competitive Effects and Antitrust Implications of Category Management and Category Captains of Consumer Products," *Chi.-Kent L. Rev.* 79 (2004): 1313.

93 S. Wood, "Revisiting the US Food Retail Consolidation Wave: Regulation, Market Power and Spatial Outcomes," *Journal of Economic Geography* 13, no. 2 (March 1, 2013): 299–326, doi.org/10.1093/jeg/lbs047.

94 "Report: Amazon and Alternative Formats Will Bring 'Carnage' to Supermarkets," *Food Dive*, accessed May 16, 2018, fooddive.com/news/grocery--report-amazon-and-alternative-formats-will-bring-carnage-to-supermarkets/507117/.

95 "History of Our Firm | McKinsey & Company," accessed September 17, 2018, mckinsey.com/about-us/overview/history-of-our-firm.

96 Paul B. Ellickson, "Does Sutton Apply to Supermarkets?" *RAND Journal of Economics* 38, no. 1 (March 2007): 43–59, doi.org/10.1111/j.1756-2171.2007.tb00043.x.

97 Paul R. Messinger and Chakravarthi Narasimhan, "Has Power Shifted in the Grocery Channel?" *Marketing Science* 14, no. 2 (May 1, 1995): 189–223, doi.org/10.1287/mksc.14.2.189.

98 Richard Kochersperger, *Food Industry Distribution Center Benchmark Report*, 1997.

99 Food & Water Watch, "In Re: Proposed Albertsons-Safeway Supermarket Merger," April 7, 2014.

100 Pierre Kobel, Pranvera Këllezi, and Bruce Kilpatrick, *Antitrust in the Groceries Sector & Liability Issues in Relation to Corporate Social Responsibility* (Berlin, Heidelberg: Springer, 2015).

101 Ángel González, "Haggen Sues Albertsons for $1 Billion over Big Grocery Deal," *The Seattle Times*, September 1, 2015.

102 Lynn, "Killing the Competition."

103 Alexis de Tocqueville, Eduardo Nolla, and James T. Schleifer, *Democracy in America*, English ed. (Indianapolis: Liberty Fund, 2012).

104 Richard Volpe, "The Relationship between National Brand and Private Label Food Products: Prices, Promotions, Recessions, and Recoveries," *Economic Research Report*, December 2011.

105 Ibid.

106 "Why Are America's Farmers Killing Themselves in Record Numbers?" *The Guardian*, December 6, 2017, sec. US news.

107 "The Farm Crisis: Its Causes and Solutions, The National Farmers Union's Submission to the Ministers of Agriculture Meeting" (National Farmers Union [CA], July 5, 2005).

108 "USDA ERS: Farm Household Income Forecast," accessed May 20, 2018,

ers.usda.gov/topics/farm-economy/farm-household-well-being/farm-household-income-forecast/.

109 Ibid.

110 "The Farm Crisis: Its Causes and Solutions."

111 Randy Schnepf, "Farm-to-Food Price Dynamics," CRS Report for Congress (Congressional Research Service, September 27, 2013).

112 "USDA ERS: Quick Facts," accessed May 20, 2018, ers.usda.gov/data-products/food-dollar-series/quick-facts/.

113 Schnepf, "Farm-to-Food Price Dynamics."

114 Ibid.

115 "USDA ERS: Food Dollar Series," accessed May 20, 2018, ers.usda.gov/data-products/food-dollar-series/.

116 Ibid.

117 "The Farmer's Share" (National Farmers Union [US], March 28, 2018), nfu.org.

118 Reyes Tirado, "Ecological Farming: The Seven Principles of a Food System That Has People at Its Heart" (Greenpeace International, May 2015).

119 Richard J. Sexton, "Grocery Retailers' Dominant Role in Evolving World Food Markets," *Choices* 25, no. 2 (2010).

120 "Agrium: 2001 Annual Report" (Agrium, 2001).

121 Gill Hyslop, "Cold Cereals USA: The Top 10 Brands in the First Half of 2017," *Bakeryandsnacks.Com*, August 2, 2017.

122 Caroline E. Mayer, "There's a Price War inside the Box! Kellogg Stuns Industry with Cuts on Most of Its Cereals," *Washington Post*, June 11, 1996.

123 "Grocery Goliaths: How Food Monopolies Impact Consumers" (Food & Water Watch, December 2013).

124 Clint Peck, "The Price Spread Debate," *Beef Magazine*, January 1, 2003.

125 Ibid.

126 "USDA ERS: Price Spreads from Farm to Consumer," accessed May 21, 2018, ers.usda.gov/data-products/price-spreads-from-farm-to-consumer/.

127 "The Farm Crisis: Its Causes and Solutions."

128 PricewaterhouseCoopers, "The Economic Contribution of Small to Medium-Sized Grocery Retailers to the Australian Economy, with a Particular Focus on Western Australia" (National Association of Retail Grocers of Australia, June 2007).

129 Daniel S. Hosken, Luke M. Olson, and Loren K. Smith, "Do Retail Mergers Affect Competition? Evidence from Grocery Retailing," *Journal of Economics & Management Strategy* 27, no. 1 (March 2018): 3–22, doi.org/10.1111/jems.12218.

130 Volpe, "The Relationship between National Brand and Private Label Food Products."

131 Benaissa Chidmi and Olga Murova, "Measuring Market Power in the Supermarket Industry: The Case of the Seattle-Tacoma Fluid Milk Market," *Agribusiness* 27, no. 4 (September 2011): 435–49, doi.org/10.1002/agr.20276.

132 Food & Water Watch, "In Re: Proposed Albertsons-Safeway Supermarket Merger."

133 Ibid.

134 Joanna Blythman, *Shopped: The Shocking Power of British Supermarkets* (London: Harper Perennial, 2007).

135 "Market Concentration Can Benefit Consumers, but Needs Scrutiny," *The Economist*, August 31, 2017.

136 "Supermarkets Admit Milk Price Fix," *BBC News,* December 7, 2007, http://news.bbc.co.uk/2/hi/business/7132108.stm.

137 Sexton, "Grocery Retailers' Dominant Role in Evolving World Food Markets."

138 Richard J. Sexton and Mingxia Zhang, "Can Retailers Depress Lettuce Prices at Farm Level?," *California Agriculture* 49, no. 3 (May 1995): 14–18, doi.org/10.3733/ca.v049n03p14.

139 R. J. Sexton, "Market Power, Misconceptions, and Modern Agricultural Markets," *American Journal of Agricultural Economics* 95, no. 2 (January 1, 2013): 209–19, doi.org/10.1093/ajae/aas102.

140 Blythman, *Shopped*.

141 Marina Strauss, "With Safeway Deal Complete, Sobeys Demands PriceCuts from Suppliers," *The Globe and Mail,* January 8, 2014.

142 Gastronomica, "A Tale of Two Dairies | Barry Estabrook," *Gastronomica* (blog), November 17, 2010, gastronomica.org/2010/11/17/tale-two-dairies/.

143 Mike Rosmann, "All Should Be Aware of Indicators of Farmer Suicide," *Illinois Farmer Today,* July 7, 2017, agupdate.com/illinoisfarmertoday.

144 "Farmers Need, Want Mental Health Help: Survey," *U of G News* (blog), June 28, 2016, news.uoguelph.ca/2016/06/farmers-need-want-mental-health-help-survey/.

145 Owen Roberts, "Mental Health Advocate Gets the Picture," *RealAgriculture.Com*, November 2017, https://www.realagriculture.com/2017/11/mental-health-advocate-gets-the-picture/.

146 Charles Fishman, "The Wal-Mart You Don't Know," Fast Company, December 1, 2003.

147 Daniel Lashof and Dennis Tirpak, "An Overview of Fruit and Vegetable Standards Relating to Cosmetic Appearance and Pesticide Use," Policy, Planning, and Evaluation (United States Environmental Protection Agency, 1992).

148 Ibid.

149 Ann Powell, Interivew for *Deconstructing Dinner* television series, 2012.

150 A.L.T. Powell et al., "Uniform Ripening Encodes a Golden 2-like Transcription Factor Regulating Tomato Fruit Chloroplast Development," *Science* 336, no. 6089 (June 29, 2012): 1711–15, doi.org/10.1126/science.1222218.

151 Ibid.

152 "Study Suggests Nutrient Decline in Garden Crops over Past 50 Years," UT News | The University of Texas at Austin, December 1, 2004, news.utexas.edu/2004/12/01/nr_chemistry.

153 Joanna Blythman, *Shopped*.

154 C.W. McCoy et al., "Management of Arthopod Pests and Plant Diseases in Citrus Agroecosystems," *Proc. Tall Timbers Conf. Ecol. Anim. Control Habitat Manage.*, 1976, 1–18.

155 W.A. Simanton, "Losses and Production Costs Attributable to Insects and Related Anthropods Attacking Citrus in Flordia in 1961." (USDA Coop. Econ. Insect. Rep., 1962).

156 David Steinman, *Diet for a Poisoned Planet: How to Choose Safe Foods for You and Your Family* (New York: Ballantine Books, 1992).

157 Malcolm Knox, "Supermarket Monsters: Coles, Woolworths and the Price We Pay for Their Domination | The Monthly," *The Monthly*, August 2014.

158 "Safe Quality Food Institute," accessed June 7, 2018, sqfi.com.

159 G.A. Feenstra, "Who Chooses Your Food: A Study of the Effects of Cosmetic Standards on the Quality of Produce" (Los Angeles, CA: Calprig, 1988).

160 Knox, "Supermarket Monsters."

161 Blythman, *Shopped.*

162 Suzanne Goldenberg, "Half of All US Food Produce Is Thrown Away, New Research Suggests," *The Guardian*, July 13, 2016.

163 "Most Food Waste from Households Not Supermarkets Say Retail Body," *Environment Times*, January 20, 2015.

164 John Hayes, "UK House of Commons Hansard Debates | Column 536" (2002).

165 John Plender, Martin Simons, and Henry Tricks, "Cash Benefit: How Big Supermarkets Fund Expansion," *Financial Times*, December 6, 2005.

166 Sarah Butler, "Tesco Delayed Payments to Suppliers to Boost Profits, Watchdog Finds," *The Guardian,* January 26, 2016, sec. Business.

167 Government of Canada, "Competition Bureau Statement Regarding Its Inquiry into Alleged Anti-Competitive Conduct by Loblaw Companies Limited," November 21, 2017.

168 Ibid.

169 Ibid.

170 Sarah Butler, "Supermarkets Watchdog Gets Ready to 'Sort out the Bullies,'" *The Observer*, March 31, 2013, sec. Business.

171 John Plender, Martin Simons, and Henry Tricks, "Cash Benefit."

172 Gary Rivlin, "Rigged: Supermarket Shelves for Sale" (Center for Science in the Public Interest, September 2016).

173 "Category Management: An Interview with FTC Commissioner Thomas B. Leary" (Federal Trade Commission, Spring 2005).

174 Leo S. Carameli Jr., "The Anti-Competitive Effects and Antitrust Implications."

175 "Packaged Seafood Executive Agrees to Plead Guilty to Price-Fixing Conspiracy" (U.S. Department of Justice, Office of Public Affairs, December 21, 2016).

176 "Progressive Grocer Honors 2016 Category Captains," *Progressive Grocer*, November 7, 2016.

177 Jim Milliot and Steven Zeitchik, "Group Protests Borders's Category Management Policy," *Publishers Weekly*, July 1, 2002.

178 Rivlin, "Rigged: Supermarket Shelves for Sale."

179 Blythman, *Shopped*.

180 Rivlin, "Rigged: Supermarket Shelves for Sale."

181 "SEC FILING | Safeway Inc. Form 10-K for Fiscal Year Ended January 3, 2015" (United States Securities and Exchange Commission, March 4, 2015).

182 "US Consumer Packaged Goods and Retail Trade Budgets at a Tipping Point," Equity Research (Goldman Sachs, November 3, 2015).

183 Albert A. Foer and American Antitrust Institute, *The Next Antitrust Agenda: The American Antitrust Institute's Transition Report on Competition Policy to the 44th President of the United States* (Lake Mary, FL: Vandeplas Pub., 2008).

184 Rivlin, "Rigged: Supermarket Shelves for Sale."

185 "'Payola' at the Supermarket," *CBS News*, February 3, 2000, cbsnews.com/news/payola-at-the-supermarket/.

186 Robert Pitofsky et al., "Report on the Federal Trade Commission Workshop on Slotting Allowances and Other Marketing Practices in the Grocery Industry" (Federal Trade Commission, February 2001).

187 Rivlin, "Rigged: Supermarket Shelves for Sale."

188 "Payola Rules," Federal Communications Commission, May 24, 2011, fcc.gov/consumers/guides/fccs-payola-rules.

189 "Slotting Allowances and Payola: Do They Deserve Different Regulatory Treatment? | ATR | Department of Justice," November 16, 2006, justice.gov/atr/slotting-allowances-and-payola-do-they-deserve-different-regulatory-treatment.

190 Marianne Jennings, "The Economics, Ethics and Legalities of Slotting Fees and Other Allowances in Retail Markets," *Journal of Law and Commerce* 21, no. 1 (Fall 2001).

191 Ralph Nader, "Slotting Allowances in Supermarkets," November 6, 1994, nader.org/1994/11/06/slotting-allowances-in-supermarkets/.

192 "2017 Kroger Fact Book" (Kroger, 2017).

193 Nirmalya Kumar and Jan-Benedict E. M. Steenkamp, *Private Label Strategy: How to Meet the Store Brand Challenge* (Boston: Harvard Business School Press, 2007).

194 Paul W. Dobson and Li Zhou, "The Competition Effects of Lookalike Private Label Products," in *National Brands and Private Labels in Retailing*, (Cham: Springer International Publishing, 2014), 17–26, doi.org/10.1007/978-3-319-07194-7_2.

195 Ibid.

196 Ibid.

197 Ibid.

198 Ibid.

199 Ibid.

200 Ibid.

201 John M. Connor, Richard T. Rogers, and Vijay Bhagavan, "Concentration Change and Countervailing Power in the U.S. Food Manufacturing

Industries," *Review of Industrial Organization* 11, no. 4 (August 1996): 473–92, doi.org/10.1007/BF00157774.

202 Marc Levinson, *The Great A&P and the Struggle for Small Business in America.*

203 "The State of Private Label Around the World" (Nielsen, April 2014).

204 Ibid.

205 Nathaniel Meyersohn, "Trouble in Big Food: America's Cereal, Soda and Soup Companies Are in Turmoil," *CNNMoney*, May 21, 2018.

206 Chase Purdy, "The Death of the 'Big Food' Era Is Imminent after the Industry's Biggest Lobbying Group Crumbles," *Quartz*, March 5, 2018.

207 John L. Stanton and Kenneth C. Herbst, "Slotting Allowances: Short-term Gains and Long-term Negative Effects on Retailers and Consumers," *International Journal of Retail & Distribution Management* 34, no. 3 (March 2006): 187–97, doi.org/10.1108/09590550610654357.

208 "The Use of Slotting Allowances in the Retail Grocery Industry" (U.S. Federal Trade Commission, November 2003).

209 Carameli. "The Anti-Competitive Effects and Antitrust Implications."

210 Sexton, "Grocery Retailers' Dominant Role in Evolving World Food Markets."

211 "Delta Blames H-E-B in Bankruptcy Case," *The Packer*, January 6, 2012.

212 Ama Sarfo, "Grocery Chain Beats Antitrust Suit Over Produce Restrictions," *Law 360*, January 17, 2013.

213 Sexton, "Grocery Retailers' Dominant Role in Evolving World Food Markets."

214 Rivlin, "Rigged — Supermarket Shelves For Sale."

215 Barry C. Lynn, "The Case for Breaking Up Wal-Mart," *AlterNet*, July 23, 2006, alternet.org/story/39251/the_case_for_breaking_up_wal-mart.

216 "Standards | Safe Quality Food Institute," accessed September 18, 2018, sqfi.com/standards/, sqfi.com/standards/.

217 Abdelhakim Hammoudi, ed., *Food Safety, Market Organization, Trade and Development* (Cham: Springer, 2015).

218 Paul Verbruggen and Tetty Havinga, "The Rise of Transnational Private Meta-Regulators," *SSRN Electronic Journal*, 2014, doi.org/10.2139/ssrn.2512843.

219 "Chairman Roberts Announces Committee Staff Hire | The United States Senate Committee On Agriculture, Nutrition & Forestry," December 20, 2017, agriculture.senate.gov/newsroom/rep/press/release/chairman-roberts-announces-committee-staff-hire.

220 Earl W. Kintner, ed., *The Legislative History of the Federal Antitrust Laws and Related Statutes* (New York: Chelsea House Publishers, 1978).

221 Blythman, *Shopped.*

222 Ibid.

223 Liz Harrison, "Slogans," *The Grocer*, March 25, 2006.

224 Blythman, *Shopped.*

225 Sheena Goodyear, "Loblaws' French's Ketchup Snub Sparks Patriotic Backlash," *CBC News*, March 16, 2016.

226 "This Peeled Avocado Is Causing Viral Internet Outrage," *TODAY.Com*, March 17, 2016.

227 Blythman, *Shopped.*

228 Brian Andreas, *Story People: Selected Stories & Drawings of Brian Andreas.* (Decorah, IA: StoryPeople, 1997).

229 Charles Eisenstein, *Sacred Economics: Money, Gift, & Society in the Age of Transition* (Berkeley, CA: Evolver Editions, 2011).

230 Ibid.

231 Kathleen Rodgers, *Welcome to Resisterville: American Dissidents in British Columbia* (Vancouver: UBC Press, 2014).

232 Kathleen Rodgers and Darcy Ingram, "Ideological Migration and War Resistance in British Columbia's West Kootenays: An Analysis of Counter-culture Politics and Community Networks among Doukhobor, Quaker, and American Migrants during the Vietnam War Era," *American Review of Canadian Studies* 44, no. 1 (January 2, 2014): 96–117, doi.org/10.1080/02722 011.2014.887128.

233 Fred A. Bernstein, "Greetings from Resisterville," *New York Times*, November 21, 2004, sec. Fashion & Style.

234 Rodgers, *Welcome to Resisterville.*

235 Evan Mangino and Maria Arbulu, "Canada: Retail Foods, Retail Sector Overview 2018," GAIN Report (USDA Foreign Agricultural Service, June 26, 2018).

236 "Top 5 Richest People in B.C.," *Canadian Business,* November 21, 2013.

237 "Canada's Richest People: The Complete Top 100 Ranking," *Canadian Business,* November 9, 2017.

238 "Five Canadians Are as Rich as 30% of the Population, Not Two," *Canadian Business,* January 16, 2017.

239 From a personal interaction with the author, n.d.

240 Ibid.

241 "Driftless Region | Viroqua Food Co-op," accessed June 12, 2018, viroquafood. coop/about-us/driftless-region.

242 Author interview with Ken Meter, Crossroads Resource Center, September 2018.

243 Danielle Renwick, "Twenty-Five Years Later, 'the Town That Beat Walmart' Is Back on the Map," *The New Food Economy*, July 11, 2017.

244 Ibid.

245 Author interview with Jan Rasikas, Viroqua Food Co-op, April 2018.

246 *The Canadian Co-operator*, August 1911.

247 Karl Polanyi, *The Great Transformation: The Political and Economic Origins of Our Time*, 2nd Beacon Paperback ed (Boston: Beacon Press, 2001).

248 John Restakis, *Humanizing the Economy: Co-operatives in the Age of Capital* (Gabriola, BC: New Society Publishers, 2010).

249 Brett Fairbairn and Nora Russell, eds., *Co-operative Canada: Empowering Communities and Sustainable Businesses* (Vancouver, BC: UBC Press, 2014).

250 "Cooperative Identity, Values & Principles | ICA," accessed June 14, 2018, ica. coop/en/whats-co-op/co-operative-identity-values-principles.

251 Author interview with Tom Webb, Saint Mary's University, September 2018.

252 "Facts and Figures | ICA," accessed September 18, 2018, ica.coop/en/facts-and-figures.

253 Fairbairn and Russell, *Co-operative Canada*.

254 "About the Co-op," Seward Community Co-op, accessed September 18, 2018, seward.coop/coop/about.

255 "Business Review," Twin Cities Co-op Partners, accessed September 18, 2018, tccp.coop/article/business-review/.

256 Fairbairn and Russell, *Co-operative Canada*.

257 "Cooperatives Can Build Resilience during Crises | UN DESA | United Nations Department of Economic and Social Affairs," July 8, 2013, un.org/en/development/desa/news/social/cooperatives.html.

258 Ibid.

259 Daniel McCabe, "Economics Shrugged," *University Affairs*, March 9, 2009.

260 Leon C. Megginson, "Lessons from Europe for American Business," *Southwestern Social Science Quarterly* 44, no. 1 (1963): 3–13.

261 Restakis, *Humanizing the Economy*.

262 Andrew Simms, *Tescopoly: How One Shop Came out on Top and Why It Matters* (London: Constable, 2007).

263 Polanyi, *The Great Transformation*.

264 "Fenwick Weavers' Society Charter: Scottish Labour History, Learning Zone, National Library of Scotland," accessed September 18, 2018, nls.uk/learning-zone/politics-and-society/labour-history/fenwick-weavers.

265 "BBC: History, British History in Depth: The Rural Exodus," accessed September 18, 2018, bbc.co.uk/history/british/victorians/exodus_01.shtml.

266 "BBC: GCSE Bitesize: The Poor Law," accessed June 19, 2018, bbc.co.uk/schools/gcsebitesize/history/shp/britishsociety/thepoorrev1.shtml.

267 Restakis, *Humanizing the Economy*.

268 Joshua L Carreiro, "Consumers' Cooperation in the Early Twentieth Century: An Analysis of Race, Class and Consumption," n.d., 222.

269 Restakis, *Humanizing the Economy*.

270 Emil Sekerak and Art Danforth, *Consumer Cooperation : The Heritage and the Dream* (Santa Clara, CA: Consumer Cooperative Pub. Association, 1980), archive.org/details/consumercooperat00seke.

271 "Cooperative Identity, Values & Principles | ICA."

272 Restakis, *Humanizing the Economy*.

273 Greg Patmore and Nikola Balnave, *A Global History of Co-operative Business*, 2018.

274 Ian Macpherson, "Co-operative Movement," *Canadian Encyclopedia*, accessed June 14, 2018, thecanadianencyclopedia.ca/en/article/co-operative-movement/.

275 Fairbairn and Russell, *Co-operative Canada*.

276 Ian MacPherson and Canadian Co-operative Association, *A Century of Co-operation* (Ottawa, ON.: Canadian Co-operative Association, 2009).

277 Carreiro, "Consumers' Cooperation in the Early Twentieth Century."

278 Kimberly Zeuli and Robert Cropp, "Cooperatives: Principles and Practices in the 21st Century," 2004.

279 Steven Bernard Leikin, *The Practical Utopians: American Workers and the Cooperative Movement in the Gilded Age* (Detroit: Wayne State University Press, 2005).

280 "Cooperatives in the U.S.," Center for Cooperatives | University of Wisconsin-Madison, accessed June 19, 2018, uwcc.wisc.edu/whatisacoop/history/.

281 Jessica Gordon Nembhard, "Black Cooperatives in the United States: An Excerpted History from Research by Jessica Gordon Nembhard," *Federation of Southern Cooperatives*, n.d.

282 Jessica Gordon Nembhard, "Cooperative Ownership in the Struggle for African American Economic Empowerment," *Humanity & Society* 28, no. 3 (August 2004): 298–321, doi.org/10.1177/016059760402800307.

283 Lawrence B Glickman, *Buying Power: A History of Consumer Activism in America* (Chicago, London: University of Chicago Press, 2012).

284 Carreiro, "Consumers' Cooperation in the Early Twentieth Century."

285 Ibid.

286 Ibid.

287 Ibid.

288 Bryant Simon, "Not Going to Starbucks: Boycotts and the Out-Sourcing of Politics in the Branded World," ed. Craig Thompson, *Journal of Consumer Culture* 11, no. 2 (July 2011): 145–67, doi.org/10.1177/1469540511402448.

289 Carreiro, "Consumers' Cooperation in the Early Twentieth Century."

290 Lizabeth Cohen, *A Consumer's Republic: The Politics of Mass Consumption in Postwar America* (New York: Vintage Books, 2004), site.ebrary.com/id/10048 850.

291 Carreiro, "Consumers' Cooperation in the Early Twentieth Century."

292 William E. B. Du Bois, *Black Reconstruction in America: 1860–1880,* 1. ed (New York: The Free Press, 1998).

293 Anne Meis Knupfer, *Food Co-ops in America: Communities, Consumption, and Economic Democracy* (Ithaca, NY: Cornell University Press, 2013).

294 Ibid.

295 Carreiro, "Consumers' Cooperation in the Early Twentieth Century."

296 Author interview with Allan Reetz, Hanover Co-op, April 2018.

297 Ibid.

298 Knupfer, *Food Co-ops in America.*

299 Carreiro, "Consumers' Cooperation in the Early Twentieth Century."

300 George Melnyk, *The Search for Community: From Utopia to a Co-operative Society* (Montréal, Buffalo: Black Rose Books, 1985).

301 Knupfer, *Food Co-ops in America.*

302 Ibid.

303 Ibid.

304 William C. Ronco, *Food Co-ops: An Alternative to Shopping in Supermarkets* (Boston: Beacon Press, 1974).

305 Restakis, *Humanizing the Economy.*
306 Maria McGrath, "*That's Capitalism, Not a Co-op*": *Countercultural Idealism and Business Realism in 1970s U.S. Food Co-ops*, vol. 2 (Business and Economic History On-Line, 2004).
307 Author interview with Dave Gutknecht, Cooperative Grocer Magazine, May 2018.
308 Ronald W. Cotterill, "Declining Competition in Food Retailing: An Opportunity for Consumer Food Cooperatives?" *The Journal of Consumer Affairs* 12, no. 2 (1978): 250–65.
309 McGrath, *"That's Capitalism, Not A Co-op."*
310 Carolyn Kott Washburne, "A Natural Order," *Milwaukee Magazine*, October 7, 2014.
311 Ben Hewitt, *The Town That Food Saved: How One Community Found Vitality in Local Food* (Emmaus, PA: Rodale, 2011).
312 McGrath, *"That's Capitalism, Not A Co-op."*
313 Robert Sommer, "Consumer Co-ops: Alternative Economic and Social Units," *Alternative Lifestyles* 5, no. 2 (1982): 109–17, doi.org/10.1007/BF0108 3248.
314 Ibid.
315 Robert Sommer et al., "Customer Characteristics and Attitudes at Participatory and Supermarket Cooperatives," *Journal of Consumer Affairs* 17, no. 1 (1983): 134–48.
316 Ronco, *Food Co-ops.*
317 Charles Klotzer, "Revolution in the Making," FOCUS Midwest, April 1981.
318 Craig Cox, *Storefront Revolution: Food Co-ops and the Counterculture,* Perspectives on the Sixties (New Brunswick, Rutgers University Press, 1994).
319 "History | Ontario Natural Food Company," accessed September 18, 2018, onfc. ca/history.
320 Hongzhi Gao, "CRS Workers' Cooperative: A Case Study in Cooperative Evolution and Survival" (Simon Fraser University, 1993).
321 Laura Bieger, ed., *Revisiting the Sixties: Interdisciplinary Perspectives on America's Longest Decade,* North American Studies 32 (Frankfurt am Main: Campus-Verl, 2013).
322 Rodgers, *Welcome to Resisterville.*
323 Ibid.
324 Ibid.
325 Ibid.
326 "East End Food Co-operative | The Co-operative Learning Centre," accessed June 20, 2018, learningcentre.coop/resource/east-end-food-co-operative.
327 Gao, "CRS Workers' Cooperative."
328 Sommer, "Consumer Co-ops."
329 Lisa Belkin and Special to the New York Times, "The Consumer Co-op Enters a New Age," *The New York Times,* August 18, 1984, sec. Style.
330 McGrath, "'That's Capitalism, Not a Co-op.'"

331 Andrew Pollack, "Food Co-ops in a Struggle," *The New York Times*, February 23, 1985, sec. Business Day.
332 McGrath, "'That's Capitalism, Not a Co-op.'"
333 Ibid.
334 Cotterill, "Declining Competition in Food Retailing."
335 Ibid.
336 Sommer, "Consumer Co-ops."
337 McGrath, "'That's Capitalism, Not a Co-op.'"
338 Knupfer, *Food Co-ops in America*.
339 Joan Stockinger and Dave Gutknecht, "The Twin Cities Cooperative Local Food System: A Case Study and Commentary" (Cooperative Development Services, 2014).
340 Author interview with Rochelle Prunty, River Valley Co-op, August 2018.
341 Author interview with Jacqueline Hannah, Food Co-op Initiative, April 2018.
342 Avery Yale Kamila, "Natural Foodie: Portland Food Co-op Plans to Open Grocery Store Downtown," *Press Herald*, September 4, 2013.
343 Author interview with John Crane, Portland Food Co-op, January 2018.
344 "A History of the Menomonie Market Food Co-op, 1973-2015," 2015.
345 Author interview with Jon Megas-Russell, Brattleboro Food Co-op, December 2017.
346 Durham Co-op Market, "Building a Broader Base" (June 1, 2018).
347 Robert Sommer, "Consumer Co-ops: Alternative Economic and Social Units."
348 "Healthy Foods Healthy Communities: Measuring the Social and Economic Impact of Food Co-ops" (National Co-op Grocers, 2012).
349 Durham Co-op Market, "Building a Broader Base," June 1, 2018.
350 Author interview with Pam Mehnert, Outpost Natural Foods, April 2018.
351 Thomas Boothe, *Food Coop* (Lardux Films, 2016).
352 Ibid.
353 Ronald W. Cotterill, "Declining Competition in Food Retailing."
354 Dave Gutknecht, "Sales and Labor in 20 Retail Food Co-ops," *Cooperative Grocer*, November 1985.
355 "Healthy Foods Healthy Communities."
356 "Cooking Nightmares | Porch," accessed July 5, 2018, porch.com/resource/cooking-nightmares.
357 Author interview with Melissa Cohen, Isla Vista Food Co-op, March 2018.
358 Ibid.
359 Susan Pagani, "This Cooperative Grocery Store Wants to Break the Diversity Mold," *Civil Eats*, September 20, 2016.
360 Michelle Bruch, "Seward's Friendship Store Opens on 38th Street," *Southwest Journal*, 2016.
361 Ana Sofia Joanes, *Fresh* (Ripple Effect Films, 2009).
362 "Prices Beat Haggen, Whole Foods, & Fred Meyer | The Community Food Co-op," *Community Food Co-op* (blog), February 7, 2018, communityfood.coop/co-op-prices-beat-the-competition/.

363 Leo Horrigan and Michael Milli, *Food Frontiers* (Johns Hopkins Center for a Livable Future, 2016).

364 Pierre Kobel, Pranvera Këllezi, and Bruce Kilpatrick, *Antitrust in the Groceries Sector & Liability Issues in Relation to Corporate Social Responsibility* (Berlin, Heidelberg: Springer, 2015).

365 *The Problem We Face* (Renaissance Co-op, 2015).

366 Alana Rhone et al., "Low-Income and Low-Supermarket-Access Census Tracts, 2010–2015," Economic Information Bulletin (USDA Economic Research Service, January 2017).

367 Sarah Ellis, "After Piggly Wiggly Exit, Hungry Columbia Community Could Build Own Grocery Store," *The State*, April 23, 2017.

368 Author interview with Marnie Thompson, Fund for Democratic Communities, August 2018.

369 Author interview with Sohnie Black, Renaissance Co-op, May 2018.

370 Lauren Fiechtner et al., "Effects of Proximity to Supermarkets on a Randomized Trial Studying Interventions for Obesity," *American Journal of Public Health* 106, no. 3 (March 2016): 557–62, doi.org/10.2105/AJPH.2015.302986.

371 Eliza Ronalds-Hannon, "Private Equity Can Still Get Rich From a Struggling Supermarket," *Bloomberg.Com*, November 10, 2017.

372 Ibid.

373 Jeff Wells, "Private Equity Loves Supermarkets, but Do Retailers Benefit?," *Food Dive*, September 7, 2017.

374 Ibid.

375 Steve Watkins, "Kroger Discloses Cincinnati Market Share: 'We Use It as a Benchmark,'" *Cincinnati Business Courier*, October 29, 2015.

376 Andria Carter and Dan Yount, "Jesse Jackson Calls for Kroger Boycott, Supports Black, West End Residents," *Cincinnati Herald*, April 12, 2018.

377 Author interview with Melissa Cohen.

378 Katina Boyce and David Treering, "A Report to City Council: Cincinnati Fresh Food Retail Financing Fund: Proposed Elements" (The Food Trust, September 10, 2012).

379 "Our Harvest Cooperative 2016-2017 Annual Report," n.d.

380 Greg Olsen and Tanner Segbers, *Putting the Grocery Back in the Grocery Store: The Story of the Clifton Market*, 2017.

381 Author interview with Christopher DeAngelis, Apple Street Market, April 2018.

382 Steve Tarter, "Can a Grocery Co-op Solve Peoria's Food Desert Problem?" *Journal Star*, February 28, 2018.

383 Hannah Alani Halani, "North Charleston City Council Discusses Possibility of Food Co-op for Shipwatch Square," *Post and Courier*, November 20, 2017.

384 Melinda Clynes, "A Co-op for the People: The Rocky Process of Developing the Detroit People's Food Co-op," *Model D*, January 15, 2018.

385 Blythman, *Shopped*.

386 Levinson, *The Great A&P and the Struggle for Small Business in America*.

387 Author interview with Bonnie Hudspeth, Neighboring Food Co-op Association, April 2018.

388 Stockinger and Gutknecht, "The Twin Cities Cooperative Local Food System."

389 Walter Goldschmidt et al., *Small Business and the Community : A Study in Central Valley of California on Effects of Scale of Farm Operations : Report of the Special Committee to Study Problems of American Small Business, United States Senate, Seventy-Ninth Congress, Second Session, Pursuant to S. Res. 28 (Extending S. Res. 298-76th Congress), a Resolution to Appoint a Special Committee to Study and Survey Problems of American Small Business Enterprises, December 23, 1946.* (Washington: U.S. G.P.O., 1946).

390 John W. Bennett, ed. Walter R. Goldschmidt, *American Anthropologist* 51, no. 1 (1949): 118–23.

391 Stockinger and Gutknecht, "The Twin Cities Cooperative Local Food System."

392 "Based on Author Surveys of over 40 Food Co-ops.," n.d.

393 Stockinger and Gutknecht, "The Twin Cities Cooperative Local Food System."

394 Hellman's (Unilever), *Eat Real Eat Local* (Film), 2010.

395 "2009 New Hampshire Statutes: Title XL, Agriculture, Horticulture and Animal Husbandry (Includes Chapters 425–439): Chapter 426, Standards for Farm Products: Section 426:5 Use of Words," Justia Law, accessed September 19, 2018, law.justia.com/codes/new-hampshire/2009/TITLEXL/CHAPTER426/426-5.html.

396 Canadian Food Inspection Agency, Government of Canada, "Origin Claims," March 22, 2014, inspection.gc.ca/food/labelling/food-labelling-for-industry/origin/eng/1393622222140/1393622515592?chap=4.

397 Restakis, *Humanizing the Economy.*

398 "Detailed Food Spending, Canada, Regions and Provinces" (Table: 11-10-0125-01: Statistics Canada, Government of Canada, n.d.), accessed September 19, 2018.

399 "USDA ERS — Food Expenditures," n.d., accessed July 16, 2018.

400 "Detailed Food Spending, Canada, Regions and Provinces."

401 "USDA ERS — Food Expenditures," accessed July 16, 2018.

402 Statistics Canada, Government of Canada, "Number of Households, Median Income and Median Income Rank, Canada, Provinces and Territories," September 13, 2017, www150.statcan.gc.ca/n1/daily-quotidien/170913/t001a-eng.htm.

403 Statistics Canada, "Detailed Food Spending, Canada, Regions and Provinces."

404 Statistics Canada, "2016 Census Topic: Population and Dwelling Counts," February 8, 2017.

405 "5% Is Generally Used by Those Involved in Local Food Advocacy Work. Actual Estimates of Local Food Sales of the $774-Billion US Grocery Retail Market Are between 1.5%–2% but Many Local Food Sales Outside of Formal Channels Are Not Recorded. Hence the 5% Figure.," n.d.

406 "Weaver Street Market Annual Report 2018," n.d.

407 The Lord Peston, Ennew CT, "Neighbourhood Shopping in the Millennium" (Nottingham: University of Nottingham Business School, 1998).

408 Civic Economics, "Central Co-op: Feeding the Washington Economy," Fall 2017.

409 Civic Economics, "Central Co-op: Feeding the Washington Economy."

410 Ibid.

411 "National Food Hub Directory, Data.Gov," accessed September 19, 2018, catalog.data.gov/dataset/national-food-hub-directory.

412 Author interview with Nicole Sallaberry, Great Basin Community Food Co-op, April 2018.

413 "USDA ERS: Food Expenditures," n.d., accessed July 16, 2018.

414 Sylvain Charlebois, "Canada's Food Price Report 2018" (Dalhousie University, University of Guelph, 2018).

415 Simms, *Tescopoly*.

416 Blythman, *Shopped*.

417 Simms, *Tescopoly*.

418 Open Markets Institute, "Regional Inequality & Monopoly," *Monopoly Basics* (blog), accessed July 17, 2018, openmarketsinstitute.org/explainer/regional-inequality-and-monopoly/.

419 Richard Brunell, "The Social Costs of Mergers: Restoring Local Control as a Factor in Merger Policy," SSRN Scholarly Paper (Rochester, NY: Social Science Research Network, July 24, 2007), papers.ssrn.com/abstract=992272.

420 Phillip Longman, "Why the Economic Fates of America's Cities Diverged," *The Atlantic*, November 28, 2015.

421 Hayley Peterson, "Whole Foods Is Slashing Marketing Jobs in Its Latest Post-Amazon Push to Cut Costs," *Business Insider*, March 23, 2018.

422 Rosabeth Moss Kanter, *World Class: Thriving Locally in the Global Economy* (Touchstone, 1997).

423 Author interview with Louisa Spencer, Poverty Lane Orchards, May 2018.

424 Correspondence with Valerie Gray, Italian Hearts Gourmet Foods, July 2018.

425 Abha Bhattarai, "Whole Foods Places New Limits on Suppliers, Upsetting Some Small Vendors," *The Washington Post*, January 5, 2018.

426 Joe Fassler, "This Creamery Took on Millions in Debt for a Contract with Whole Foods. Then Whole Foods Bailed," *The New Food Economy*, March 8, 2018.

427 Author interview with Danu da Silva, Raw Magic Chocolate, August 2018.

428 Author interview with Steve Taylor, Taylor Farm; New Hampshire Commissioner of Agriculture (1982–2007), May 2018.

429 Author interview with Pam Mehnert, Outpost Natural Foods, April 2018.

430 Aubrey Saxton, "Speech at 2016 Annual General Meeting, Monadnock Food Co-op," 2016.

431 Author interview with Aubrey Saxton, Saxy Chef, April 2018.

432 Brianna Shipley, "The Saxy Chef," *Edible New Hampshire*, December 30, 2016.

433 Author interview with Louisa Spencer, Poverty Lane Orchards.

434 Food co-op interviews, 2018.

435 Author interview with Lana Braun, Hummingbird Farm, July 2018.

436 Author interview with Brendan Parsons, Salix and Sedge Farm, July 2018.

437 Author interview with Inanna Judd, Tipiland Organic Produce, May 2018.

438 Author interview with Valerie Sanderson & David Beringer, Valerie's Fermented Foods & Uphill Bakery, June 2018.

439 Author interview with Heidi Lettrari, Kaslo Sourdough, April 2018.

440 "Save-on-Foods Weekly Flyer," July 2018.

441 "Author's Direct Experience at Safeway's Nelson, BC Location," July 2018.

442 "Author's Direct Experience at Safeway's Nelson, BC Location," September 2018.

443 Mari Roseman, "Co-ops Support Weaver Street Market," *Cooperative Grocer*, April 2010.

444 Benjamin Romano, "New Seasons Greeted by Curious Shoppers and Protesters as It Opens Ballard Store," *The Seattle Times*, May 9, 2018.

445 "Grants Archive," M.J. Murdock Charitable Trust, accessed September 19, 2018, murdocktrust.org/grant-opportunities/grants/.

446 "List of Organizations Designated by the Southern Poverty Law Center as Anti-LGBT Hate Groups," *Wikipedia*, September 17, 2018.

447 Author interview with Louisa Spencer, Poverty Lane Orchards, May 2018.

448 Stacy Mitchell, "The Local Face of a Mega-Retailer," *The Bollard*, Fall 2007.

449 Andrew Simms, *Tescopoly*.

450 Susie Mesure, "Interbrew Launches Legal Battle against HSBC's 'Local' Slogan | The Independent," *Independent*, December 27, 2002.

451 "Save-on-Foods Weekly Flyer."

452 Statistics Canada, "The Changing Face of the Canadian Hog Industry," July 29, 2014.

453 Michael Fullerton, *What Happened to the Berkeley Co-op? A Collection of Opinions* (The Center for Cooperatives, 1992).

454 Author interview with Tom Webb, Saint Mary's University; and former Member Relations Manager, Board Director, Co-op Atlantic, August 2018.

455 Tom Webb, "Failure of Co-op Atlantic | Co-op Grocer Network," *Cooperative Grocer*, April 2016.

456 Andrew Pollack, "Food Co-ops in a Struggle."

457 Howard Brodsky, "Building a Better World Now: Cooperatives for a Better World" (2016).

458 Stuart Reid, "Are Food Co-ops Still Relevant? | Co-op Grocer Network," *Cooperative Grocer*, October 2017.

459 Dave Gutknecht, "Co-op Distributors Close: Mountain Warehouse and Whole-Food Express | Co-op Grocer Network," *Cooperative Grocer*, December 1991.

460 Elizabeth Pontefract, "Strategic Differentiation at PCC Community Markets" (June 1, 2018).

461 Author interview with Jan Rasikas, Viroqua Food Co-op, April 2018.

462 Author interview with Melissa Cohen, Isla Vista Food Co-op, March 2018.

463 Fairbairn and Russell, *Co-operative Canada*.

464 Author interview with Pam Mehnert, Outpost Natural Foods, April 2018.

465 "About PCC," PCC Community Markets, accessed September 20, 2018, pccmarkets.com/about/.

466 Author interview with Raquel Dadomo, Wheatsville Co-op, April 2018.

467 Fairbairn and Russell, *Co-operative Canada*.

468 *Why Does Participation Matter? — CE Pugh* (CDS — Cooperative Board Leadership Development Library, 2014).

469 "Mischief-Makers Climb Nelson Commons Crane," *Nelson Star,* June 8, 2015.

470 Author interview with Pam Mehnert.

471 Ibid.

472 Author interview with Jacqueline Hannah.

473 Author interview with Myles Robertson, Purple Porch Co-op, April 2018.

474 Stuart Reid, "Why (Some) New Co-ops Fail," *Cooperative Grocer,* December 2012.

475 Author interview with Jacqueline Hannah, Food Co-op Initiative.

476 Carreiro, "Consumers' Cooperation in the Early Twentieth Century."

477 Mari Roseman, "Co-ops Support Weaver Street Market."

478 "Outpost Natural Foods, Annual Report 2017." n.d..

479 Simms, *Tescopoly*.

Index